women TEACHING women LEARNING
HISTORICAL PERSPECTIVES

Copyright © 2006 Inanna Publications and Education Inc.

First edition, 2006.
Individual copyright to their work is retained by the authors. All rights reserved. Except for the use of short passages for review purposes, no part of this book may be reproduced or transmitted in any form or by any means, electronically or mechanically, including photocopying, recording, or any information or storage retrieval system, without prior permission in writing from the publisher. All correspondence should be addressed to Inanna Publications and Education Inc.

Inanna Publications and Education Inc.
212 Founders College
York University
4700 Keele Street,
Toronto, Ontario M3J 1P3
Telephone: 416.736.5356
Fax: 416.736.5765
Email: inanna@yorku.ca
Web site: www.yorku.ca/inanna

Interior Design: Luciana Ricciutelli
Cover Design: Val Fullard
Front cover: (detail) Student teachers practice teaching kindergarten at the Toronto Normal School [ca. 1898]. Archives of Ontario RG 2-257 Acc. 13522 Ontario teachers' colleges historical files.

We acknowledge the support of the Canada Council for the Arts for our publishing program.

Printed and Bound in Canada.

Library and Archives Canada Cataloguing in Publication:

Women teaching, women learning : historical perspectives / Elizabeth M. Smyth and Paula Bourne, editors.

ISBN 0-9736709-3-2

1. Women in education–History–19th century. 2. Women teachers–History–19th century. 3. Women–Education–History–19th century.
I. Smyth, Elizabeth M. (Elizabeth Marian), 1954- II. Bourne, Paula, 1941-

LC1481.W65 2005   370.82   C2005-906605-9

women TEACHING women LEARNING
HISTORICAL PERSPECTIVES

ELIZABETH M. SMYTH AND PAULA BOURNE, EDITORS

INANNA Publications & Education Inc.
Toronto, Canada

*For Alison Smith Prentice –
scholar, mentor and friend*

Contents

Acknowledgements	9
Introduction *Elizabeth M. Smyth and Paula Bourne*	11

I. The Lives of Women Teachers

Getting Things Done: Donalda J. Dickie and Leadership Through Practice *Rebecca Priegert Coulter*	23
Sustaining the Fire of "Scholarly Passion": Mary G. Hamilton (1883-1972) and Irene Poelzer (1926-) *Dianne M. Hallman and Anna H. Lathrop*	45
And Gladly Teach? The Making of a Woman's Profession *Marjorie Theobald*	65
Cecilia Fryxell: The Life of a Swedish Educator *Inga Elgqvist-Saltzman*	85

II. Regulating Women: Social Work, Teaching and Medicine

A Passion for Service: Edith Elwood and the Social Character
of Reform
    Cathy James   105

Gender and Class: State Formation and Schooling Reform
in 1880s Toronto
    Harry Smaller   131

"All Matter Peculiar to Woman and Womanhood": The Medical
Context for Women's Education in Canada in the First Half of the
Twentieth Centuiry
    Wendy Mitchinson   158

III. Women's Public and Private Lives

Travel Lessons: Canadian Women "Across the Pond" 1865-1905
    Susan Mann   177

"'Giving Myself a Toni, Write Thesis Tonight":
Negotiating Higher Education in the 1950s
    Alison Mackinnon   195

The Ideology of Domesticity: Re-constructions Across Three
Generations in Ontario
    Cecilia Reynolds   213

Contributor Notes   232

List of Illustrations   235

Acknowledgements

Bringing this volume to publication has been the result of the dedicated efforts of many people. We wish to thank the contributors for their ongoing support; the anonymous reviewers whose insightful comments helped us to strengthen the collections contents and, Luciana Ricciutelli, Editor-in-Chief of Inanna Publications and Education Inc. for her work in bringing the collection to its final form.

We owe a special thank you to Patricia Doherty and the Centre for Women's Studies in Education at the Ontario Institute for Studies in Education of the University of Toronto for their ongoing support of this project.

Introduction

ELIZABETH M. SMYTH AND PAULA BOURNE

Women Teaching, Women Learning: Historical Perspectives is a collection of leading edge scholarship building on the work of Canadian feminist historian Alison Prentice who, for more than 40 years, has actively contributed to the field of social history in general and the history of education specifically. Contributors to the collection, drawn from Canada, Australia, and Sweden, are representative of an array of researchers whose work has been influenced by that of Alison Prentice. Their contributions are also generational—some written by professional contemporaries of Prentice, others by current and past collaborators, still others by her students. As well, the contributors are representative of the scholarly transitions currently occurring within the academy. Some are at the beginning of their careers; others in the middle and still others have recently retired from their university appointments.

Together, the essays reflect a variety of methodologies and frameworks used in contemporary social history, especially the history of education and women's history. They all focus on the complex interplay of women and education—with education broadly conceptualized as occurring at home, at school, and in the community.

It was with her first book *The School Promoters: Education and Social Class in Mid-Nineteenth Century Upper Canada*[1] that Alison Prentice burst onto the historical scene. In it, she argued that the ideology of public education put forth by Egerton Ryerson, the first Chief Superintendent of Education in Upper Canada, was rooted in his experience with economic and social change. Ryerson, she explained, viewed schools as agents of social change that could raise the intellectual and moral levels of the lower classes, thus bridging the gap between the elite and the poor. This book established Prentice's life-long reputation as a leading scholar in the field of Canadian social history. Her personal and professional interest in women teachers crystallized in 1974 when she, Harvey Graff, and Wendy Bryans organized a session on that topic at the Canadian Association for American Studies. As she explained in a 1999 essay, "my quest over the years has increasingly been to record and analyze the feelings, motivations and actions of the rank and file in educational history, especially the women who taught in Canadian classrooms."[2] Not only did she write about teachers, but she also taught the history of education to both women and men in her courses at York University and the Ontario Institute for Studies in Education (OISE).

Several of this book's authors wrote theses supervised by Prentice at OISE (there are 45 such masters and doctoral theses). Dianne Hallman, Cathy James, Anna Lathrop, Cecilia Reynolds, and Harry Smaller were encouraged by her to examine the intersection of gender and social history, and to explore the roots of the institutions in which they taught, thereby making history real, personal, and relevant. Their work, like that of Prentice's other students, resulted in pioneering studies of race, religion, and power relationships in schools and other institutions of learning in nineteenth- and twentieth-century Canada.

Prentice's scholarship on women teachers led her to be a sought-after examiner and collaborator by both her national and international colleagues. Rebecca Coulter, whose doctoral thesis was examined by Prentice, has shaped her research on contemporary Ontario teachers' work from the historical work on women teachers in the nineteenth century that Alison Prentice conducted with Marta Danylewycz.[3] Prentice's extensive publications and participation in many national and international meetings, including the Berkshire Conference on Women's History and the International Standing Conference for the History of Education, enabled links to be forged among an international community of researchers. Australian scholars Alison Mackinnon and Marjorie Theobald and Swedish scholar Inga Elgqvist-Saltzman are representative of those researchers who have drawn upon her analytical frameworks to examine the complexities of teachers' professional and personal lives, explored in the 1998 edited collection *Education into the 21st Century: Dangerous Terrain for Women*.[4]

Prentice's influence extended beyond the field of the history of education into the larger field of Canadian social history. With Susan Mann, then of the University of Ottawa, she assembled one of the first collections of essays on women in Canadian history, aptly titled *The Neglected Majority*,[5] which, along with her thirteen monographs and 50-plus book chapters, articles, book reviews, and resource collections can be found on university syllabi for Canadian social history. With fellow feminist scholars Gail Cuthbert Brandt, Paula Bourne, Naomi Black, Beth Light, and Wendy Mitchinson, Prentice coauthored the pioneering text *Canadian Women: A History*.[6] This scholarly collaboration was drawn together and sustained by Prentice's scholarly passion to promote a more inclusive and interdisciplinary view of history, one that extends beyond the university classrooms into elementary and secondary schools, community-based settings (such as museums and galleries), and informal networks of learning among community-groups. Prentice herself founded one such group—the Ontario Women's History Network (OWHN).

This Collection

The ten essays in this book reflect the scholarship generated by researchers influenced by Alison Prentice, and explore aspects of women's formal and informal education in the nineteenth and twentieth centuries. Thus we meet subjects in such traditional institutional-based settings as schools and universities as well as in informal learning networks that arose from travel and involvement in social activism. Written in a variety of styles and utilizing a variety of methodologies, the essays indicate the directions in which researchers have moved, using Prentice's own work, or their collaborations with her, as a springboard for further studies.

Methodologically, both public and private sources to situate women's educational experience are used. As Rebecca Coulter explains in her essay, there are numerous challenges involved in "reconstructing women's lives from ... published writings, from the scant records left in various archives and from the recollections of others." Meeting these challenges, as the authors in this collection do, enriches our knowledge of women, teaching, and learning. Susan Mann, Alison Mackinnon, and Inga Elgqvist-Saltzman draw upon personal papers and diaries to construct how some women carved out opportunities unavailable to many others of their sex. Marjorie Theobald and Harry Smaller utilize state records to reconstruct elements of teachers' personal and professional work. Cecilia Reynolds, Dianne Hallman and Anna Lathrop use the tools of oral history. Text and document analysis are employed by many authors, most notably by Rebecca Coulter, Wendy Mitchinson, and Cathy James. Several of the authors utilize their own voice in the essays—a technique drawn from current feminist scholarship that questions the nature of objectivity, and is in line with the historiographical tradition arguing that history and autobiography are sometimes interwoven.[7]

The essays are presented in three thematically-linked sections: the lives of women teachers, regulating women and women's public and private lives.

The Lives of Women Teachers

The study of teachers' lives, alone and in groups, characterized much of Prentice's own research and professional interest. This theme is explored by the authors in the first section. The essays of Rebecca Coulter, Dianne Hallman and Anna Lathrop, Marjorie Theobald, and Inga Elgqvist-Saltzman, examine nineteenth- and twentieth-century teachers' lives and work in Canada, Australia and Sweden.

Rebecca Coulter's subject, Donalda Dickie, was a western Canadian teacher-educator, whose textbooks influenced generations of teachers and students not only in Alberta but also across Canada. A life-long learner herself, Dickie interspersed her time as a teacher educator with her own further education, studying at Oxford University and the University of Toronto, from where she graduated with a Ph.D. in History in 1929. Coulter demonstrates that through her life, her teaching and her writing, Dickie provided "leadership and inspiration to teachers" even though in the context of her times, neither Dickie nor her colleagues would have characterized her as such. Coulter argues for the inclusion of textbook writing as a means of exerting educational leadership—an argument as timely for today's faculties of education as it was for Dickie's Normal School times. This essay makes an important contribution to our understanding of how women educators have historically exercised leadership—and begins to address a lacunae in the history of education.

Dianne Hallman and Anna Lathrop's co-written essay analyzes the lives and careers of Mary Hamilton and Irene Poelzer, two women whom the authors argue consciously articulated an education aimed at empowering women. Mary Hamilton was the principal of the Margaret Eaton School, the first school of higher education for women entering the field of physical education. Irene Poelzer, a retired university professor and a woman religious, developed the first feminist course in the College of Education at the University of Saskatchewan. Like Coulter's subject, Hallman and Lathrop's subjects influenced generations of students and scholars and demonstrate different ways of building a scholarly community. By reflecting on the experience of Hamilton and Poelzer, Lathrop and Hallman question the impact of increased institutional pressures (especially the commodification of the intellectual enterprises surrounding tenure and promotion) on contemporary academics' abilities to encourage the development of "scholarly passions" within today's students.

Marjorie Theobald's essay examines the historical roots of a contemporary problem. She points out that the woes of the teaching profession, most notably a crisis in morale that perhaps can be associated with the perceived low status of the profession, reported to a 1998 Australian Senate inquiry are not new, and, in fact, are echoed in many archival sources. Theobald argues that in almost every generation, historians can find strong evidence of teachers' woes. To understand present concerns, Theobald suggests that we look to the past and examine the centrality of gender in the history of the teaching profession, concluding that professionalism, status and merit must be viewed through the lens of gender. While Theobald examines teaching in an Australian context, her findings concerning the experience of women in the profession of teaching is resonant not only in an international context but also across other feminized fields, such as nursing. She concludes that one cannot clearly understand the nature of the profession without a deep appreciation of women's lives.

Inga Elgqvist-Saltzman's essay analyzes the life and work of Cecilia Fryxell, a nineteenth-century Swedish teacher educator. Fryxell's papers, preserved in the archives of Kalmar Teachers' College, were used by Elgqvist-Saltzman with her own teacher education students to explore persistent issues in teacher education. Through their reflections on Fryxell's writings, students came to see

Introduction

that "old fogeys" had a lot to teach them. In this essay, Elqvist-Saltzman shares with contemporary readers some of Fryxell's thoughts on discipline, pedagogy and the character of an effective teacher. Reading Elgqvist-Saltzman's translation from the original nineteenth-century Swedish, readers get a sense of the influence of religious metaphors, which, at times, may seem a bit jarring to contemporary English-oriented ears, but which very much reflect the environment in which Fryxell lived and worked. As is the case with British historian Pam Hirsh's analysis of the life and works of Elizabeth Hughes, (who she argues is the "founding mother of teacher education at Cambridge"),[8] Elgqvist-Saltzman calls for a re-examination of such pioneering women of teacher education, whose strategies for exercising leadership and power were undertaken within both formal and informal structures. Thus, Elqvist-Saltzman illustrates in a Swedish context what Coulter illuminates in a Canadian one, that working in times and places where women educational leaders were neither dominant in numbers nor in influence, historians need to utilize different tools to uncover how these women perceived and exercised the roles in which they were engaged.

Another theme that is examined throughout some of the essays in this section is the interaction of religion and social norms in shaping women's opportunities and activities. The lives of the Canadian Poelzer and Swedish Fryxell point out the ways in which women educators served as social activists and advocates for women, and demonstrate the tensions which arose as they moved toward larger social issues. Poelzer began her life as a woman religious within the Institute of the Blessed Virgin Mary (the Loretto Sisters) and later moved to join the Sisters for Christian Community (SFCC), where she saw greater flexibility and support for spiritual, social, and professional development. For Fryxell, her personal religious journey through a number of movements within the Swedish Lutheran Church, including the Non-Conformist Church Movement and the Swedish Missionary Society, significantly influenced her personal and pedagogical thought as she rejected elements of coercive religious practices (especially that of arranged marriage) and led her to construct an alternative life path for herself.

Regulating Women: Social Work, Teaching and Medicine

The next three essays examine how state institutions attempted to influence women's lives. By regularizing the emerging professional fields of medicine, social work and teaching, with rigid class definitions, gendered and race structures and patriarchal control, the state influenced the paths of women's education and participation. Cathy James and Harry Smaller analyze the impact of the professionalization of social work and teaching on women. Wendy Mitchinson's essay considers the role of medicine through the interaction between medical literature and education.

Cathy James's subject, Edith Elwood, a key figure in the emergence of Canadian social work, played a leading role in the Canadian settlement movement, and worked to improve the lives of women and children through education in informal settings. While marriage and motherhood took her from her ten-year career as a paid employee of the Evangelia Settlement House, Elwood continued her settlement work in the volunteer sector, thus again blurring the distinctions between public and private philanthropy. Like many women before her whose enterprises were subsumed into a male-dominated bureaucracy, her legacy (and indeed her name) has been forgotten by subsequent generations and historians of the profession. Yet, as James argues, her career has much to teach us about the sources of women's power and leadership, the role of women in state formation and the social character of social reform.

Harry Smaller focuses on the formal setting of schools and the work of women teachers at a time of increased state control over education. He uses as the lens of analysis women's resistance to control. The issues he raises—class size, teachers' power over daily activities, and concerns over teachers' responsibilities for more than the academic development of their pupils—have a contemporary ring. Smaller explores how the Toronto Teachers' Association gave women the experience of leadership and the opportunity to exercise power in a public sphere. Thus, he argues, women were able to effect change in policy initiatives. Finally, by drawing parallels between historical and contemporary issues, he points out the extent to which the state formation process must be viewed through the lens of time. Students, families and communities, divided by relations of gender and class, continue to have restructuring and change imposed upon them—often with less than positive results.

Wendy Mitchinson's essay examines medical beliefs in the first half of the twentieth century. She explores how patriarchal structures within the field of medicine sought to restrict women's access to education. Her analysis of medical texts—medical journals published in Canada, textbooks read by medical students, popular and health literature and medical advice books—clearly demonstrates how patriarchy delineated and narrowed educational opportunities for women. Mitchinson begins by examining the medical perceptions of the female body through childhood and puberty that argued that the body controlled when and if education should occur. She explores how experts viewed the ideal education for women, based to a large extent upon the belief that it should be different and in line with their bodies and their roles as future wives and mothers, and how those theories were implemented in classroom and extra curricular settings. The advice of the medical experts and their questions about the influence of both personnel (female teachers) and curricular structures harken to contemporary debates on the achievements of boys, feminist educators' continuing concerns about male-centered school curriculum, and gender demographics within the teaching profession.

Together these three essays raise new questions concerning how women, both individually and collectively, reacted against structures which shaped their lives. James, Smaller and Mitchinson challenge notions of women as passive receptors of male-generated action. They point out how, in some instances,

Introduction

women sought opportunities to become agents of change, as they contributed to and advanced the lives of girls and women. Chords struck by all three authors resonate across the centuries as historical roots of contemporary issues are clearly identified.

Women's Public and Private Lives

While the interplay between women's public and private roles underpin all essays, the final three by Susan Mann, Alison Mackinnon and Cecilia Reynolds examine most explicitly how women in different generations sought to bridge this gap by creating new paths. In two of the essays, international perspectives are utilized as both transborder and transnational patterns impacting on domesticity are woven while in the third, the locus is stationary as the subjects spent the majority of their lives in communities near to their birthplace.

Susan Mann's subjects, nineteenth-century women travellers, both literally and figuratively, push boundaries. Her thirteen subjects are Canadian middle-class women—eleven English and two French Canadian. Her sources are their travel diaries and letters, written in the latter half of the nineteenth and first decade of the twentieth centuries. Her subjects reveal how patterns of travel challenge the current theories postulated by literary scholars who set up home and travel destination as opposites.[9] Mann argues that home is both their domestic dwelling place in Canada and the spaces encompassed by their travels. Further, domesticity and empire enabled these women to develop frameworks and strategies for personal and intellectual safety. She concludes that these women traveled without trespassing, using strategies they had learned at home to protect them abroad—in some instances "they held their noses and averted their eyes."

Alison Mackinnon draws her subjects from samples of Australian and American women graduates of the 1950s. Utilizing data drawn from questionnaires, alumnae records, diaries and journals, she documents the experience of the "swing bridge generation," exploring how higher education made a difference in their lives. She queries the accuracy of both American and Australian popular culture's categorization of the 1950s as "conservative and backward" and points out that few graduates found marriage and motherhood a full-time pursuit for more than a few years. Paid employment and unpaid work in the voluntary sector were pursued by many—with some having active careers in both. Mackinnon calls for more research to expand and revise the traditional historical interpretation of this decade to include accounts of the conflicting personal and professional demands it posed for educated women. She challenges historians to explore the 1950s to find the roots for both the theory and the leadership of 1960s feminism.

Cecilia Reynolds's study focuses on the ideology of domesticity. She compares women's educational and work experience over three generations in the twentieth century. She explores the interplay among gender, individual, and societal norms through the lenses of women from "small town" Ontario, across generations who lived and worked close to their birthplaces. Dividing her subjects into the grandmothers, mothers and daughters, she presents conclusions that feature commonalties and differences across these three generations, once again illuminating the persistent tensions which women experience in their personal and public lives.

In each essay, the authors explore and challenge historical and contemporary understanding of domesticity as a fixed or static ideology by illustrating the extent to which their subjects made individual choices and/or resisted the chance to do so. For Mann's subjects, travel provided educational and social opportunities for self and family. For some subjects of Mackinnon and Reynolds, education created both opportunities and challenges as the pull of unpaid and paid work, and childrearing and career aspirations created tensions within both their domestic and professional domains.

New Directions

The essays collected in this book illustrate how Alison Prentice's research and writings have helped reshape the historical discipline. She began writing when history as a field and history within the academy were changing from monolithic accounts of white men's activities, experience, and achievements to encompass more inclusive accounts that took into consideration issues of gender, race, class, and sexual orientation. Prentice played an important role in that process. The contributors to this collection expand on her scholarship and raise further questions concerning women's historical experience while identifying the need both for new initiatives and linkages between historical and contemporary events.

Several authors implicitly ponder if women's fight for equal access to education in coeducational settings has benefited women. The all-female models of education, represented in the essays by Hallman and Lathrop and Mackinnon, make us reflect whether such institutions may have been more conducive to the full development of women's intellectual and social needs. Has coeducation advanced or limited opportunities for women? This question continues to be a focus for modern debates about the pros and cons of single versus mixed gender schooling from the earliest grades.

The changing role of women within organizational structures is shown in many essays. In some cases, institutions changed as they began to include women in all professional and service ranks; in others, women created new ways of living their lives more in tune with their values and beliefs. Donalda Dickie, Coulter's subject, redefined power as leadership and inspiration. Theobald's women teacher activists, typified by Florence Johnson, created networks through political activity that enabled them to be insulated from the cultural stigma of being a single woman. Was the same true for the Women Teachers' Association of the Smaller study and their contemporaries across Canada? What impact did the changes in structures have on the personal and professional identities of women and men? From another perspective, did the original

Introduction

structures change women, or did women change the structures?

Future research needs to focus on the roles played by individual women, with strong religious orientations, in cultural change. For example, Elgqvist-Saltzman's Fryxell has been overlooked by generations of Swedish scholars. Hallman and Lathrop's Poelzer also held strong religious beliefs. For several other subjects in this collection, religion played an important part in their lives (though it may have been personal rather than public). Is a woman's strong religious affiliation viewed by scholars as suspect, thus diminishing her worth as a subject for academic investigation?

The assumptions that have been made about domesticity are both challenged and reinforced by the subjects of Mann, Reynolds, and Mackinnon. Mann's women travellers were empowered by domesticity and empire, a finding that calls for the extension of current theoretical work. The same argument for further theoretical work can be made from the work of Reynolds and Mackinnon. Can the current generation of women scholars recognize the potential for collecting valuable oral history from the 1950s generation of women?

In 2002, Alison Prentice reflected:

> What our children need to learn from history is that the standard versions need to be questioned and the standard views queried, along with the myths. All history can do is raise a series of very difficult questions, as life does.[10]

Women Teaching, Women Learning complements Alison's scholarly objectives by documenting many of the complexities inherent in the lives of women thus contributing to a more nuanced historical record.

Notes

[1] A. Prentice, *The School Promoters: Education and Social Class in Mid-Nineteenth Century Upper Canada* (Toronto: McClelland and Stewart, 1977).

[2] A. Prentice, "Workers, professionals, pilgrims: tracing Canadian women's teachers' histories" in K. Weiler and S. Middleton, (eds.), *Telling Women's Lives: Narrative Inquiries in the History of Women's Education* (Buckingham: Open University Press, 1999), 25-42.

[3] The articles by A. Prentice and M. Danylewycz, "Teachers, Gender and Bureaucratizing School Systems in Nineteenth Century Montreal and Toronto," *History of Education Quarterly* (Spring 1984): 75-100; "Revising the History of Teachers: A Canadian Perspective," *Interchange* 17, 2 (1986): 135-46; "Teachers' Work: Changing Patterns and Perceptions in the Emerging School Systems of 19th and Early 20th Century Central Canada," *Labour/le travail* (Spring 1986): 59-80; and A. Prentice, M. Danylewycz, and B. Light, "The Evolution of the Sexual Division of Labour in Teaching: A Nineteenth Century Ontario and Quebec Case Study," *Social History/histoire sociale* 16, 3 (May 1983) 81-109, have

all informed the conceptual framework and methodology for Rebecca Coulter's (Principal Investigator) Social Science and Humanities Research Council of Canada funded study "The History of Ontario Women Teachers in the 20th Century" that examines the efforts of women teachers to promote social reform, equity, and social justice for themselves and others.

[4] A. Prentice, I. Elgqvist-Saltzman and A. Mackinnon, (eds.), *Education into the 21st Century: Dangerous Terrain for Women?* (London: Falmer Press, 1998).

[5] S. Mann Trofimenkoff and A. Prentice, (eds.), *The Neglected Majority: Essays in Canadian Women's History* (Toronto: McClelland and Stewart, 1977).

[6] A. Prentice, P. Bourne, G. Cuthbert Brandt, B. Light, W. Mitchinson and N. Black, *Canadian Women: A History* (2nd edition) (Toronto: Harcourt Brace Canada, 1996).

[7] See, for example, the work of S. Reinharz, *Feminist Methods in Social Research* (New York: Oxford University Press, 1992); Marjorie L. DeVault, *Liberating Method: Feminism and Social Research* (Philadelphia: Temple University Press, 1999); T. Zeldin, *An Intimate History of Humanity* (London: Vintage, 1997).

[8] P. Hirsch and M. McBeth, *Teacher Training at Cambridge: The Initiatives of Oscar Browning and Elizabeth Hughes* (London: Woburn, 2004).

[9] See, for example, S. Bunkers and C. Huff, (eds.), *Inscribing the Daily: Critical Essays on Women's Diaries* (Amherst: University of Massachusetts Press, 1996); L. Hoffman and M. Culley, (eds.), *Women's Personal Narratives: Essays in Criticism and Pedagogy* (New York: Modern Language Society of America, 1985).

[10] Unpublished Address delivered by A. Prentice to "The Future of the Past" Conference, University of Western Ontario, London, Ontario. March 16, 2002 Program available: http://www.ssc.uwo.ca/history/happenings/futureofthepast/Home.htm.

I.
The Lives of Women Teachers

Getting Things Done

Donalda J. Dickie and Leadership Through Practice

REBECCA PRIEGERT COULTER

Donalda James Dickie (1883-1972) was a progressive educator whose career offers a clear example of the ways in which women provide leadership in education even as they are excluded from positions of formal authority. A normal school instructor for most of her paid working life, Dickie educated teachers, wrote textbooks for students and teachers, developed programs of study and curriculum materials, and actively participated in the wider educational and women's communities. She exercised what can be called the power of practice to provide direction to the learning experiences of children and teachers in schools across Canada. Indeed, Dickie marshalled a capacity for intellectual work, a deep understanding of the actual nature of classroom teaching, and an ability to sustain a lifelong commitment to the heavy demands of instructional labour, research and writing to become one of Canada's most influential educational leaders during the first half of the twentieth-century.

While democratic, populist and feminist impulses have extended the meaning of leadership to include roles well beyond formal positions of authority held by appointment within a hierarchical structure, we know remarkably little about the ways in which female educators exercised leadership historically. Dickie's story opens up questions about the nature and form of women's leadership in state systems of schooling and forces us to consider how women in the past "did leadership" while being denied recognition as leaders. Indeed, so strong was the discursive exclusion of women from notions of public leadership that Dickie probably did not even recognize herself as a leader; rather, like so many women, she would have described herself as a person who "just got things done."[1] Certainly this is how she was described by her contemporaries who saw her as a "doer" or, as a younger male contemporary put

Rebecca Priegert Coulter

1.1. *Portrait of Donalda Dickie, date unknown, courtesy of Alberta Archives.*

it, "the little red hen" of Alberta education,[2] a reference simultaneously laudatory and derisive and reminding us of the ambivalence which confronts women of ambition. Dickie, herself, claimed to be "just a teacher."[3] It is precisely as a "doer" and a teacher, however, that she was able to provide leadership within an increasingly self-conscious teaching profession and why she was so widely recognized in her time as a central player in the progressive education movement.

Dickie was successful because the instructional leadership she offered was based on two important principles. First, Dickie situated herself within the largely female teaching force and respected those with whom she worked. She was continuously involved with a network of teachers who collaborated with her on new textbooks, tested materials she developed, and provided feedback about new programs or curriculum. Her links to the field also provided her with the passion and the power to negotiate from a position of strength within the wider national network of normal school instructors, university professors, officials in provincial departments of education, and school trustees. Put another way, she could work "down" with the mostly female teaching force or "up" with the almost wholly male administrative structure. A second hallmark of her leadership was found in her ability to combine an understanding of a

Getting Things Done

better, more just and peaceful world with usable curriculum content and practical teaching ideas. That is, Dickie had a conscious political philosophy that leaned towards humanism and social reform, and an educational philosophy that valued both subject matter knowledge and child-centred pedagogy. Dickie devoted a great deal of time and effort to sharing this perspective with teachers both during initial preparation and through in-service programs. She spoke directly to teachers in professional journal articles, teacher education textbooks and various instructional manuals. She embedded her own curriculum design and personal pedagogical approaches within the textbooks she wrote. She developed concrete, child-friendly learning materials along with specific pedagogical strategies over several decades, thereby offering classroom teachers practical methods for carrying through on more abstract principles. Thus Dickie engaged many commonly recognized leadership strategies including collaboration, networking, and mentoring.

Yet even as she modelled an active agency, she was caught in the contradictions facing women carving out professional careers within the institutions of the state. As a teacher, she was expected to educate the young for citizenship while, by virtue of her sex, she was denied even the right to vote.[4] As a graduate student, she entered Oxford University at a time when she could not supplicate for a degree because she was a woman.[5] She toiled for nearly 35 years as a Normal School instructor but never held an administrative post or a position with formal authority with her employer, Alberta's Department of Education. And despite playing a central role in the development of progressive education and writing the recognized teacher education text in the field, her contributions have been rendered almost invisible in Canadian educational history.[6] Dickie, then, is one of those female educators who stood

> hip-deep in cultures saturated with phallocentric knowledges, in institutional structures ruled epistemologically and procedurally by men and masculinist signifiers, and in a discipline which, despite its historical terrain as "women's work" ... remains [in] the theoretical and administrative custody of men.[7]

How she negotiated these circumstances not of her own choosing to actively create a realm of influence and some power, and how she used specific strategies to survive and even flourish in a world she could only partially understand because of her location within it, is the subject of this chapter.

Early Influences

Apart from a short autobiographical note written for her family, Dickie left no personal papers. Her life must be reconstructed from her published writing, from the scant records left in various archives, and from the recollections of others. In this regard, the difficulties of reclaiming Dickie's life are not unusual for as Carolyn Heilbrun points out, women's biographers have too often been forced "to reinvent the lives their subjects led" from "what evidence they could find."[8] It remains true that while I was able to find many of the "facts" of Dickie's existence, her thoughts and feelings about that experience are elusive. Of course, we cannot even fully grasp how our own lives were shaped and, if we are the least bit self-reflective, we constantly interpret and reinterpret our personal histories as we pass through them, so it should not be surprising, though it is frustrating, that the life of another seems constantly to slip into the shadows. Or perhaps, slipping in and out of the shadows is an appropriate metaphor for Dickie who evaded the normative script, and lived the ambiguous life of a professional woman claiming a small enclave in the foreign territory of male hegemony.

In common with the rest of us, the circumstances of Dickie's early years proved crucial to her identity. Her origins in a Scottish Presbyterian family and community with a high regard for reading and learning almost certainly shaped her views about the importance of education in one's life[9] and her own life modelled the continuous pursuit of knowledge. Born in Hespeler, Ontario, on 5 October 1883, the eldest child of Hannah (Ann) Shepherd Hall Dickie and William Stewart Dickie, a school teacher,[10] Dickie was orphaned at four years of age.[11] She and her two younger brothers fell under the care of their paternal grandmother, Mrs. James Dickie, a widow who likely offered a model of female independence and courage. While Dickie described her grandmother as "a clever, interesting and very entertaining woman" and her childhood as "happy and stimulating," it also appears true that as the eldest of the three orphaned siblings, Dickie came to feel a special responsibility for the care of her brothers and a close attachment to them.[12] She also spent time working in various families in the community, assisting with childcare and other household tasks. This, along with the care of her brothers, may have been part of the practical experience that encouraged the rapport with children and understanding of childhood so often commented on by others reviewing her later work and accomplishments.[13]

Dickie's sense of Canadian nationalism and connection to place which so shaped her writing on citizenship and country also went back to her early life in southwestern Ontario. She had strong ties to the farm where she had spent her first years, claiming that "under those grey roofs people of my blood have lived for generations, out of that earth I sprang."[14] She went on to observe,

> My feeling for that bit of earth is more than love. It has in it something of the sacredness of love for a mother, something of the passion that flares between man and woman, something that is deeper than either. Here are my roots. This is my land.[15]

As an adult she was an anglophile, but she was also a descendant of the Dickies who had come to Canada from Scotland to escape poverty after the Napoleonic Wars and the Land Clearances.[16] The cultural memory of hardship and immigration that passes from one generation to the next must at least partially account for Dickie's positive rendering of Canada's multicultural heritage and her support for the development of a social safety net to counter the worst effects of poverty and unemployment.

Becoming a Teacher

Like many Canadians of the day, Dickie also had the experience of migrating from one region to another. While still in elementary school she moved to Souris, Manitoba with her grandmother and then to Moose Jaw, in what is now Saskatchewan, to enter high school.[17] In 1901, taking up one of the few occupational choices open to women, she attended the Regina Normal School. In its souvenir magazine which she co-edited, Dickie is described as "one of our cleverest junior members both in spheres of literature and teaching."[18] This evidence provides the earliest indication we have that people were beginning to take note of Dickie's intelligence, her abilities to master both content and pedagogy, and her willingness to roll up her sleeves and get things done. While at normal school, Dickie made important contacts and at least one of her classmates, H. C. Newland, would go on to join her in playing a leading role in progressive education in Alberta.[19]

When she completed her Normal School training, Dickie was eighteen years old and an independent young woman with a Second Class Interim Certificate. She began to teach in a small school at Westview, just outside Moose Jaw for a salary of $45 per month, gaining her permanent professional certificate on 30 December 1903.[20] But further education was never far from her mind. When she had saved enough money, she returned to Ontario to take her senior matriculation at Galt Collegiate,[21] and then registered at Queen's University in 1906. For three academic years (1906-1909) she completed her course work extramurally, but for the 1909-1910 term she was in-residence to meet the degree requirements set by Queen's University.[22] To fund her academic studies she engaged in a common practice for Ontario university students and went west in the summer to teach.[23] Her school teaching experiences were important for they provided Dickie with an understanding of the difficulties of rural education, a reality she was to keep in mind for the rest of her career. Her identification with the women working alone in one-room schools scattered across the Canadian landscape shaped her approach to pedagogy and made her a strong, though not uncritical, advocate for women teachers when she served on curriculum committees or confronted male academics. Her teaching in southern Saskatchewan may also have been key to the special sensitivity she developed to the situation of Canada's First Nations, a sensitivity that would later make its way into many of the textbooks that she wrote.

While a student at Queen's, Dickie excelled academically. In 1909 she won the University Medal for English and in 1910 the University Medal for History.[24] Arthur G. Dorland, who became a respected Canadian historian, knew Dickie at Queen's and recalled:

> I did not get the gold medal [in history]. This was awarded instead to a brilliant woman student, Donalda Dickie, who having won the medal in English extramurally the previous year (the first time—and so far as I am aware the last time—it was ever won by an extramural student) entered Queen's for her final year, and also captured the history medal. This was a very proper recognition of unusual merit. Miss Dickie was not only more mature in her thinking, but she surpassed the rest of the class also in the quality of her writing and in her powers of expression.[25]

In fact, because of her exceptional academic achievements, Dickie was awarded the M. A. degree in humanities in 1910, rather than the baccalaureate.[26]

Queen's was a post-secondary setting that provided "the kind of comfortable and intimate environment that appealed to academically bright students from 'homes of moderate means'."[27] More importantly it was an institution that encouraged its students to take up lives of public service.[28] Many leading progressive educators of the twentieth-century were Queen's graduates, among them John Harold Putnam.[29] William Aberhart, a fellow teacher who graduated the same year as Dickie, went on to become Premier and Minister of Education in Alberta's first Social Credit government in 1935, precisely at the time when the province was introducing a new curriculum co-authored by Dickie.[30] For Dickie, the Queen's connection offered a shared background and contacts with many like-minded educators and others in public service, thus according her a place in what we now call a network of influence.

The Education of a Normal School Instructor

Although she probably did not know it, Dickie was poised to exercise leadership in the educational community. Someone in Alberta had recognized her gifts, for immediately upon graduation from Queen's, Dickie was offered a position on the staff of the Practice School affiliated with the Calgary Normal School, and then, in 1912, she was appointed to teach at the new Provincial Normal School in Camrose, Alberta. Her memories of this period were typically upbeat: "For the first year Dr. James Miller, the principal and I were the only members of staff and each taught half the subjects. It was hectic, but great fun."[31] In that year she also published her first article, "Dramatization as a Method in Composition," in a professional journal, followed shortly after by two articles on the teaching of Canadian history.[32] The pattern of her professional career was established. She was to teach at all of Alberta's three Normal Schools, being transferred from one to another as enrolments and provincial finances dictated, until her retirement in 1944[33] while also producing journal articles, school textbooks, workbooks and teacher manuals in several subject areas.

Although she now held a job of high status for a woman, Dickie's desire for academic achievement persisted. Having completed her M. A., she almost immediately began post-graduate work by taking summer classes in history and

Getting Things Done

English at Columbia University.[34] Then, in April, 1916, she entered a B.Litt. program at Somerville College at Oxford University.[35] She wrote about this experience revealing the wonder and joy she felt at being in England and, especially, at Oxford. It is as though she could not believe her good luck and her enthusiasm for the rituals of student and college life was unbounded. She spoke of the libraries with awe, calling them "an inspiration" and proclaiming her mornings in the Bodleian "unforgettable." And she was completely taken with the history and beauty of the university and its surroundings. She was not oblivious to the war raging in Europe, had experienced fear during the crossing of the Atlantic and, while at Oxford, helped with the care of the wounded who were housed in some of the colleges. But despite the material shortages and harsh realities of war, Dickie remained enthralled with the possibilities of the intellectual life she found at Oxford.[36]

While there, she met and became fast friends with Eglantyne Jebb, who went on to become principal of the Froebel Institute at Roehampton, and whose cousin of the same name founded the Save the Children Fund.[37] This lifelong friendship undoubtedly provided an entrée to a rich world of educational debate in England, including the New Education Movement, and positioned Dickie in the wider international discourses of progressive education.[38] It also is reported that Dickie was acquainted with Vera Brittain, Winifred Holtby, Dorothy Sayers and other prominent women who were students at Somerville College in the same period[39] and hence we might conclude that Dickie was exposed to what Brittain called "a universal tide flowing so strongly toward feminism."[40]

On 9 April 1917, Dickie's youngest brother, Thomas, was killed at Vimy Ridge[41] and in June she left Oxford, 42 days short of completing her residency.[42] Whether this was because she was required to return to her post at the Camrose Normal School or because she wished to join her fiancé who had been gassed at the front and was in hospital in Winnipeg, Manitoba, where he ultimately died, is unclear.[43] In any event, she only returned to Somerville College in 1921 to complete her residency and continue work on her thesis. Before she had completed her thesis, her supervisor died and she decided to transfer to the doctoral program at the University of Toronto in 1926 and complete her graduate work there.[44]

During the 1926-27 academic year, Dickie took a leave of absence to complete her residency at the University of Toronto although it was described inaccurately and a bit dismissively by the (male) principal of the Calgary Normal School as a year "partly of rest and partly of further research work abroad."[45] It would not have been surprising if Dickie had required some rest at this point for she had just completed a text on teaching composition, compiled a book of poetry for student use, developed an elementary school language arts series called *Learning to Speak and Write*, and prepared a series of eight Canadian history readers.[46] She also was working full-time as a teacher educator, doing research for and writing a dissertation, continuing to supervise extra-curricular activities at the normal school, and speaking at teachers' conventions. In this context, "just getting things done" was a mind-boggling feat! In 1929 she successfully defended her dissertation, "John Foxe's *Acts and Monuments of the Church*," and convocated in the spring of 1930, making her one of only six women to earn a University of Toronto Ph.D. in history prior to 1960.[47] She also became a member of a very small and select group of educators who held doctorates in Canada. With the Ph.D., Dickie now had an additional credential to enhance her intellectual authority and her academic credibility, an increasingly important consideration in the field of education.[48]

Earning a Ph.D. was a remarkable accomplishment, not only because Dickie did so while maintaining a commitment to her teaching and to her publishers, but because, as Mary Kinnear points out, at that time doctorates were rare and university teaching, let alone normal school teaching, did not require an advanced degree.[49] Despite her stellar academic record, nowhere is there a hint that Dickie was ever considered for a post in a history department, a result, no doubt, of the fact that at the time the hiring of new faculty was done informally with department chairs seeking "good men" and senior male professors recommending their male graduate students.[50] As Beverley Boutilier and Alison Prentice argue, the professionalization of history by the first half of the twentieth-century meant that the discipline became, by definition, one that "privileged male experience and preserved most permanent academic jobs for university-trained men."[51] Donald Wright is even more blunt: "Sexism not only protected the status of history as a masculine discipline but protected the academic labour market for men."[52] It is, of course, possible that Dickie, herself, did not wish to teach in a university and that she did not actively seek work there. But why then did she complete a doctorate in history rather than education? Surely the paucity of female professors in history departments, in general, suggests that more than personal preference was at work here.[53]

In a world of systemic and overt sexism, academic achievement can signify both a woman's recognition that she must be exceptional and her hope that merit will trump gender. In Dickie's case, achievement pulled her towards the centre of power but gender pushed her to the margins, leaving her to lead from the middle as it were, through the strategy of "practical action."[54] However, this leadership strategy was a two-edged sword. A woman's work could be exploited but without the need to provide either monetary recognition or appointment to administrative positions. On the other hand, there was power in practice for it was through action or work, often done collectively, that women could make change and assert control over their world. Put another way, practical action did not necessarily offer a big reward at the individual level, but it could pay large social dividends.

Instructional Leadership Through Textbook Writing

In her mid-30s, Dickie was ready to embark on what would become one of her major leadership projects. When she returned to Canada from Oxford in 1917 and took up her position at the Camrose Normal School, she was asked to teach history but "found the history text books in use by the children in the Practice School not only uninteresting but literally incomprehensible to most of their young readers." She concluded "that I probably could not do worse and determined to try my hand."[55] As a result of this decision, Dickie began a writing and publishing effort that extended into the 1960s. If she were to be denied opportunities to lead from a formal position of authority, she would shape education in another way and promulgate a progressive and meliorist reading of the world along with a child-centred pedagogy through teaching materials.

Textbooks were, and are, the ubiquitous tools of state education. In the first half of the twentieth-century, when teachers had few other resources to rely on, especially in the isolated rural schools, textbooks regularly determined what would be taught and became particularly significant instruments for developing a national identity and Canadian citizenship.[56] Textbooks, and the guides for teachers which came with them, could also shape teaching methods. Furthermore, because the majority of Canadians did not complete high school in the early decades of the twentieth-century, what they learned in elementary school can be seen as especially important in shaping political consciousness and notions of citizenship. In this context, Dickie's textbooks take on particular significance for through them she was able to structure what teachers taught and children learned about their nation and their social responsibilities. Her purpose was clear. "[W]e in Canada have our own traditions, our own ideals and our own history. This is what we want our children to know."[57] Of course, Dickie was not alone in seeking this goal. School textbooks, in general, promoted a distinct kind of Anglo-Canadian nationalism that provided some distance from, but did not wholly reject, the British connection, while also carefully mediating the links between Canada and the United States.[58] The Canadian state also turned to schools to assimilate an immigrant population, extinguish "foreign" languages, erase ethnic identities and teach the young how "Canadians" lived. As a result, textbooks often contained racist content, downplayed social conflict, and reinforced traditional patterns of gender relations[59] and Dickie's work was not completely free of these flaws. In general, however, her books were more open to diversity and difference, subtly challenging hegemonic beliefs and leading readers towards tolerance and understanding.

Although she spoke out against hyphenated Canadianism,[60] Dickie also pointed out the advantages of a multicultural population and encouraged teachers to help children appreciate the richness immigrants brought to their new country. She emphasized the hard work and harsh conditions immigrants faced in their desire for a better life. In her portrayal of the peoples of Canada's First Nations, Dickie made a commendable effort to provide accurate and fair information. Her textbooks included native stories as well as information about traditional and contemporary life in First Nations communities. Aboriginal children were shown living in loving families with home routines comparable to those of other children. Dickie was very open-minded about the role of medicine men, natural healing processes and native spirituality. And in a sly turn of the table, through which we can appreciate Dickie's humour, the Chicken Dance Society was compared to other men's service clubs, the Masons and Elks.[61]

Positive comments about Aboriginals were scattered throughout Dickie's books. In a language arts text, for example, she noted that "Indians were fine speakers" and exhorted students to emulate their model.[62] In her introduction to a story about an Aboriginal man she asked, "Do you admire clever people? You will find a hero in this tale if you do."[63] Thus she troubled racist stereotypes by naming the man both clever and heroic. In her history texts, Dickie was critical of the treatment of native peoples in Canada. In contrast to her usually pro-government renderings of events, she recognized that Canada's "actions were not always fair or wise"[64] and that the treaties "did create many difficulties and problems for the Indians, problems which have not yet been met successfully."[65] Indeed, she calls the Canadian government "negligent" in its treatment of the Indians and Métis.[66] Dickie's most unique contribution in textbook writing was the preparation of two readers, a pre-primer and a primer, featuring Aboriginal children as protagonists.[67] These two readers are likely the first Canadian examples of what we would now call inclusive curriculum material. Both readers offer a very positive, albeit somewhat sentimental and anglicized, view of Aboriginal children and their families.

Dickie also challenged the dominant gender discourse of the day, not by hammering home the political history of women's struggle for the right to vote, but by making apparent women's efforts to secure the future of Canada. For example, students learned that mothers and fathers worked equally hard to clear the land and build farms. Youngsters were informed about the important work of the nuns in schools, hospitals and social services and were reminded that "housekeepers spent their lives in crushing toil."[68] Sixth graders read about Madame La Tour who, in the absence of her husband, took command over a group of men to defend an Acadian fort. They also learned about the possibility of male anger when a woman was successful. They could not have missed Dickie's admiration as they read about Marie Maisonat who went from the pranks and fun of girlhood to politics when she "discovered that she loved power, knew how to win it, knew how to use it."[69] Similar woman-positive material can be found in the readers Dickie compiled and there are clear examples of what we might now call a critical anti-sexist pedagogy. For example, after students read Longfellow's poem, "Stay at Home, My Heart," with its claim that for women "To stay at home is best," they find this question: "Nowadays girls are nurses and teachers and stenographers and doctors. Do the girls of to-day think that staying at home is the best?"[70]

This is not a claim that Dickie's texts were overtly feminist or even consistent in their portrayal of girls and women for there is much material that is more

Getting Things Done

conservative and traditional. But it is clear that girls using Dickie's texts would find affirming material and all students would be required to think about gender relations. It is also true that because of Dickie's interests in the lives of ordinary people, past and present, young people using her texts were exposed to stories about workers and farmers, about the technologies of work, and the various elements of daily living. Housework was recognized as work and as part of the economy, a rather forward idea for the time. More than other textbook writers of the period, Dickie appeared sensitive to class issues and much in sympathy with hard-working people trying to make ends meet. She compared possessive individualism unfavourably with co-operative community values and even pointed out to school children the way in which competitive practices in education created adults who cared only for personal success. She explained the systemic nature of poverty and unemployment and warned young people not to blame the victims. And, by 1950, she was very supportive of the growing welfare state, speaking positively of the country's family allowance program, unemployment insurance, old age pensions and other health and welfare initiatives. She retained her cheery optimism about Canada, always emphasizing that while mistakes were made, governments tried to do their best for the people. In this regard, she revealed a progressive conviction about the benevolent state and fostered the Canadian commitment to peace, order and good government.

It is difficult to assess the influence of Dickie's textbooks on young Canadians for we cannot know with certainty how teachers used the material, nor what students learned from it. Nonetheless, we do know that Dickie's textbooks were commended to use by leading educators. For example, Thornton Mustard of the Toronto Normal School, wrote a glowing introduction to Dickie's series, *Junior Language*, which ended with the exuberant claim, "A new day, my masters, in the teaching of English Composition!"[71] Textbooks authored or compiled by Dickie were authorized or approved for use in many provinces and often over several decades. Selections from Dickie's Canadian history readers, chosen and compiled by Helen Palk, a Manitoba teacher and Normal School instructor, appeared under the title, *Pages from Canada's Story*. This textbook was used in Alberta, Saskatchewan, Manitoba, Ontario, Prince Edward Island and Quebec and may have been used in other provinces. It first appeared in 1928, was reprinted at least 25 times by 1961, with revisions in 1936, 1949 and 1951.[72] The title page of *The Great Adventure* indicates it was authorized for use in Alberta and Newfoundland and approved for use in Ontario and likely was used elsewhere, as well, since it was favourably reviewed in the popular media and in academic journals and won the Governor-General's Award for Juvenile Literature. This book also went through many printings after its first appearance in 1950 and as late as 1977, five years after Dickie's death, appeared as a sound recording in Alberta.[73] Similarly, the Canadian Parade reading series compiled by Dickie and three teachers, went through many reprintings after first appearing in 1947. Authorized for use in Alberta and British Columbia and approved for permissive use in Ontario, this series was supported by teacher manuals and workbooks, additions that further ensured that the textbooks would become the curriculum. And Sutherland observes that these readers were used in three provinces for a twenty-year period.[74] Thus the evidence points to a very influential role for Dickie's textbooks for a large part of the twentieth-century. It was probably no accident that the federal government called on her to write the remedial reading program for soldiers during World War II.[75]

Despite Dickie's advanced degrees and obvious competence, taken-for-granted gender norms and masculinist organizational practices denied her opportunities to hold formal leadership positions in the education system. Like other women excluded from the hierarchy of educational administration, she was forced to look for alternative arenas in which to play out her capacities and skills and introduce the reforms she thought necessary. From among her limited options, she chose textbook writing as an important means to provide instructional leadership. Here was a form of power open to her and she fully exercised it even after she retired as a normal school instructor in 1944. Revealing her lively sense of humour she wrote, "Now that I have retired and can write all the time, the only hope I can see for Canada is reforestation."[76] In the 1960s, she was working on a history of the Commonwealth nations when old age caught up with her and robbed her of the mental acuity needed to complete that task.[77]

Exercising Leadership Through Curriculum Development

By the time she was 50, Donalda Dickie had gained enough credibility to move closer to the centre of power and become an educational insider. She was highly educated and widely recognized for her textbook writing and her progressive pedagogical approaches that she had championed for many years as part of a larger transnational movement. She worked quietly and persistently for change from within the educational system but was not seen as a threat to the existing relations of power or established modes of operation. She got along well with men and was among the few women who were admitted to membership in the Education Society of Edmonton, a group of senior stakeholders in education who met on a regular basis to study new developments and discuss future directions for the province. It is not surprising, then, that Dickie became centrally involved in Alberta's grand experiment with progressive education in the 1930s.

Between 1921 and 1935, Alberta was governed by the United Farmers of Alberta (UFA), a political party built on the principles of agrarian populism, group government and co-operation.[78] Education was a key concern for the party and there was a conscious desire to improve opportunities for rural children and support the teaching of co-operation in the schools. The United Farm Women of Alberta (UFWA), whose local and provincial leaders were often former teachers, played an important role in promoting the school reforms proposed by the progressive education movement in North America and England. The UFWA, for example, supported the Dalton Plan and encouraged its use in Alberta.[79] The convergence between the interests of the governing party and Alberta's educational leaders, several of whom had done graduate work at Teachers College, Columbia and the University of Chicago where they were influenced by the pantheon of American progressivists, resulted in the decision to bring progressive education to Alberta. An important outcome of this decision was the whole-scale revision of the school curriculum.[80] Designed under a UFA government, the new revisions were implemented with the support of another populist party, Social Credit, after the farmers lost the 1935 election.

According to a colleague in the Edmonton Normal School, Dickie was drawn into the curriculum revision process in the early 1930s by Fred McNally, the provincial supervisor of schools.[81] McNally, who became Deputy Minister of Education in 1935, had attended Teachers College, Columbia where he found John Dewey's lectures incomprehensible but enjoyed his course with William Heard Kilpatrick, "one of the greats both as a teacher and a scholar."[82] He liked Kilpatrick's project method and called upon Dickie, whom he had supervised while serving as principal of the Camrose Normal School, to speak to a conference of school inspectors about the methods of progressive education. Well-received by the inspectors, Dickie was then appointed in 1934 as one of three members of a committee assigned the task of drafting a framework for a new elementary school curriculum that would reflect an activity-oriented and integrated approach. The core committee supervising the work was almost wholly male in membership and the senior administrator assigned to over-see the revision process was Hubert C. Newland, the Chief Inspector of Schools, but the committee named to actually do the work was two-thirds female, with Olive Fisher of the Calgary Normal School joining her friend Dickie, along with William Hay, a school inspector.

In short order, this three-person committee presented a plan for curriculum re-organization to Newland. Central to the plan was the enterprise, the term the committee came up with to describe an inter-disciplinary, child-centred, activity method of education. Dickie herself saw the enterprise as "the co-operative achievement of a social purpose that a teacher presents to her class with a view to having them use it as an experience in intelligent social behaviour." [83] Newland "was well pleased with the vision of the plan" and believed it would provide "an opportunity for learning the ways of democratic living, since pupils and teachers would participate in the planning of the work to be undertaken."[84] The implementation process began in 1935 when 75 teachers from across the province were brought in to a summer school to learn about the new curriculum with the expectation that they would return to the field to proselytize their colleagues.

Over the next few years, Dickie was the most prominent activist in the cause of progressive education. A younger contemporary working in the Department of Education described her leadership in this way:

> Dr. Dickie did more than any other single person to make the implementation of the activity movement in Alberta education a reality. She wrote, she spoke, she demonstrated. She published, she edited, she revised, she evaluated. She gathered around her a group of energetic, young, competent teachers. In her classes, both during the academic years and during summer schools, she produced dozens of young enthusiasts who went out singly and in pairs to sell the gospel of the activity program. In a matter of a few short years, the "enterprise method" had reached into every corner of the province; into every teachers' convention; into every curriculum guide.[85]

Dickie's teacher education textbook, *The Enterprise in Theory and Practice*, first published in 1940, solidified her leadership in action, as did the many articles she published in a wide range of journals.[86] All told, it was Dickie's ability to think, write, work with others, and prepare useful teaching materials that proved crucial to attempts to implement progressive education reforms in Alberta. She was adroit in argument, able to shift ground easily to draw from the various strands of progressivism to make a case for each particular audience she addressed. She "sold" progressive education to teachers, school trustees, businessmen, and the women's organizations whose membership she enlisted in the cause.[87]

Although Dickie has been labelled variously as a pedagogical, child-centered or child freedom progressive,[88] her own life story and body of work reveal a woman who was also committed to traditional scholarship and the pursuit of knowledge. She did not see theory and practice as binaries and believed that children could come to learning with joy and pleasure but still master content and skills. Like feminist scholars of the late twentieth-century, Dickie was concerned with the interconnectedness of knowledge, with the stories of the silenced in history, and with the making of knowledge and the role of experience in that process. She was interested in using education to promote social improvement and thought this could be done by offering students active, purposeful learning activities designed to prepare them for democratic citizenship.

However, as she neared the end of her employment as a normal school instructor and faced retirement in 1944, Dickie began to appear less than sanguine about the likely success of the progressive experiment in Alberta. A tone of increasing desperation can be discerned in her writing as she resorted to expediency to fight for the curriculum she had worked so hard to develop. Particularly jarring is her turn towards emphasizing the vocational and social control dimensions of progressive education as she tried to mollify critics.[89] Only after retirement did she return to stating what had clearly been her goal all along: "to teach the young where and how to get information for themselves and how to use it to solve their social problems and make a useful contribution

Getting Things Done

to the solution of the problems of the community."[90]

There were real difficulties posed for the smooth implementation of progressive reforms. Access to a variety of learning resources, especially books, was essential, yet many schools lacked such materials. The enterprise method required well-educated and skilled teachers[91] but classrooms were too often staffed with poorly educated or young and inexperienced teachers, unable to cope with the demands of an integrated curriculum. World War II only exacerbated the problem.[92] Dickie, usually so supportive of teachers, was sharp in her condemnation of those she called "down-at-the-heel" conservatives who "do not, and will not, read."[93] In many cases, classrooms were filled with activity for activity's sake and little real learning took place, at least partly because the provisions for the professional development and re-education of teachers were inadequate. And, of course, many teachers resisted progressive education and disagreed with this new approach to schooling.[94]

At the same time, the Social Credit government became increasingly right-wing and more oriented to fundamentalist moralism and the administration in the Department of Education was changing and becoming more reliant on educational psychology to define educational purpose.[95] Elements of the business community and the media began an attack on progressive education that found support in the universities.[96] Some of the educators who had been strong supporters of progressive education changed sides.[97] Finally, even Dickie herself hinted at some second thoughts about the revised school curriculum. In the foreword to the 1950 history textbook, *The Great Adventure*, she commends the important work being done in social studies but admits that history "appears in bits and patches" and students "lose much of the significance of many social studies topics" and "leave school without ever having read a complete, connected history of their country."[98]

Conclusion

Dickie's work in curriculum reform in the 1930s and '40s came closest to modelling educational leadership as it is commonly understood in the educational literature. More than at any other point in her career, she moved to the centre of formal power in education and had the opportunity to shape the provincial school system as a whole. She worked indefatigably over a ten-year period for the implementation of the enterprise approach, using the full range of strategies commonly thought necessary to successfully introduce curriculum reform. It is hard to see how she could have done more. It is surprising, then, that in her brief autobiographical notes, Dickie makes no mention whatsoever of the work she did in curriculum revision or the part she played in Alberta's experiment with progressive education. Was she soured on top-down change-making or did she dislike the political machinations that went on behind the scenes? Did she come to realize that many educational leaders did not understand progressive education and consequently were not deeply committed to curriculum reform? Was she overcome with disappointment when she realized that her vision of change was becoming so watered down that it bore little resemblance to its original conceptualization? Or did Dickie come to realize that the curriculum and pedagogy she proposed were unattainable in the existing bureaucratic educational system? It is impossible to know but she certainly turned back to textbook writing with a vengeance when she retired in 1944 and said no more about the enterprise. Indeed, in her autobiographical notes, she emphasizes textbook writing as her major achievement in life, a fact which should encourage a further reconsideration of the way in which educational leadership is too often read as synonymous with educational administration.[99]

In 1925, Dickie offered the following words of advice to the students graduating from the Calgary Normal School. Almost certainly as a reference to her grammar classes and the use of comparatives and superlatives, she observed, "Play is pleasant; Work is pleasanter; Achievement is pleasantest of all."[100] She might have been speaking of her own life for while she could play and did so by golfing, hiking, climbing and travelling, she devoted the best part of her years to work. As a result, she achieved recognition as an author, an educator, and as a woman who provided "leadership and inspiration" to teachers.[101] Thus it was that Dickie exercised power. She claimed the right to be heard in the educational discourse, and moved into spaces where action mattered and where getting things done made a difference.

I wish to acknowledge the financial support of a Faculty of Education, University of Western Ontario Internal Research and Development Grant and the Social Sciences and Humanities Research Council of Canada Standard Research Grant No. 410-2000-0357.

Reprinted with permission from the Canadian Journal of Education *28 (4) (December 2005): 669-699.*

Notes

1. Jill Blackmore, *Troubling Women: Feminism, Leadership and Educational Change* (Buckingham: Open University Press, 1999); Carol Harris, "Innovative Leadership in Community Context: Elizabeth Murray and the History Plays in Tatamagouche, Nova Scotia," in Cecilia Reynolds and Beth Young, (eds.), *Women and Leadership in Canadian Education* (Calgary: Detselig, 1995), 173-192.
2. D.J. Oviatt to [P. Oviatt], 7 July 1970. Letter reproduced in R.S. Patterson, comp., *Progressive Education* (Edmonton: Faculty of Education, University of Alberta, n.d.).
3. Elizabeth Harris, telephone interview with author, December 2001. "Betty Don" Harris is Dickie's niece.
4. As a resident of Alberta, Dickie got the provincial vote in 1916 and, as the sister of someone in the armed forces, the federal franchise in 1917. She was not

Getting Things Done

recognized legally as a "person" in Canada until 1929. See Alison Prentice, *et al.*, *Canadian Women: A History*, 2nd ed. (Toronto: Harcourt Brace, 1996).

5   Women gained the right to supplicate for degrees at Oxford in 1920. See Paul Berry and Mark Bostridge, *Vera Brittain: A Life* (London: Chatto and Windus, 1995), 154.

6   Donalda Dickie, *The Enterprise in Theory and Practice* (Toronto: W. J. Gage, 1940). For histories of progressive education in Alberta see, R. S. Patterson, *The Establishment of Progressive Education in Alberta* (Ph.D. diss., Michigan State University, 1968); R. S. Patterson, "Progressive Education: Impetus to Educational Change in Alberta and Saskatchewan," in E. Brian Titley and Peter J. Miller, (eds.), *Education in Canada: An Interpretation* (Calgary: Detselig, 1982), 169-192; Nick Kach, "The Emergence of Progressive Education in Alberta," in Nick Kach and Kas Mazurek, (eds.), *Exploring Our Educational Past* (Calgary: Detselig, 1992), 149-174; Amy von Heyking, "Selling Progressive Education to Albertans, 1935-53," *Historical Studies in Education* 10, nos. 1 and 2 (1998): 67-84. Dickie receives only the briefest of mentions in all studies of progressive education in Alberta.

7   Carmen Luke and Jennifer Gore, "Introduction," in Carmen Luke and Jennifer Gore, (eds.), *Feminisms and Critical Pedagogy* (New York: Routledge, 1992), 2.

8   Carolyn Heilbrun, *Writing a Woman's Life* (New York: Ballantine, 1988), 31.

9   Andrew C. Holman, *A Sense of Their Duty: Middle-Class Formation in Victorian Ontario Towns* (Montreal & Kingston: McGill-Queen's University Press, 2000).

10 Charles G. D. Roberts and Arthur Leonard Tunnell, (eds.), *The Canadian Who's Who*, vol. 2, 1936-37 (Toronto: Murray Printing, 1936); University of Toronto Archives (UTA), School of Graduate Studies (SGS), Acc. No. A84-0011/026, Dickie, Donalda file, Application for Admission, 17 March 1926.

11 City of Cambridge Archives, Transcript of Dickie Family Grave Marker, New Hope Cemetery. The Harris interview indicated that new information has come to light recently which suggests that Dickie's father did not die in Australia in 1889, as his family concluded when he failed to return from a trip to that country. Rather, it appears he failed to inform his Canadian family that he was staying in Australia, where he re-married and started a second family.

12 Donalda Dickie, autobiographical notes, unpublished typescript in possession of family, n.d. Harris interview revealed that Dickie spent most of her vacations with her brother and his family, and that she provided financial support to the family during the Depression.

13 For comments on Dickie's understanding of children see, for example, "Who's Who Among Educationists," *Edmonton Bulletin*, 8 July 1936 and book reviews in UTA, Acc. No. A-73-0026/083 (94), Clipping File, Dickie, Donalda James. Information about working out comes from Harris interview. See, also, Holman, *A Sense of Their Duty* about the practice of children working in the homes of others in the Galt, Ontario region where Dickie was born.

14 Donalda Dickie, "Can We Teach Love of Country?" *Chatelaine*, April 1945, 57.

15 Ibid.

16 Laraine Sole, *Waverley: The Early Families* (Wanganui, NZ: H & A Print, 1996).

17 Harris interview; Dickie, autobiographical notes.

18 Saskatchewan Archives Board, Regina (SAB,R), Collection R-E 238, Regina Normal School Magazine: Souvenir number, 1901, 17.

19 Patricia E. Oviatt, *The Educational Contributions of H. C. Newland* (M.Ed thesis,

University of Alberta, 1970).
[20] SAB,R, Collection R-177.11, File 5: Certificates Granted by Dept. of Education, NWT 1903-1905; File 20: Inspector's Reports, 1899-1904; File 11: Index of Teachers, 1908-1927; School Officials' Registers, Westview S.D. No. 256.
[21] Dickie, autobiographical notes.
[22] Queen's University Archives (QUA), Office of the University Registrar fonds, Student Registers series, Locator #1161, Vol. 10.
[23] Dickie, autobiographical notes; SAB,R, Collection R-177.11, File 11: Index of Teachers, 1908-1927 and School Officials' Registers, Clarilaw S. D. No. 685. On university students going west each summer to teach see Rosalind Rowan, "The Eastern Student as the Western Teacher," *The School* 5, 2 (1916): 97-101.
[24] QUA, Office of Advancement, Advancement Business Office *fonds*, Deceased Alumni series, Locator #3599, Box 6.1, Donalda James Dickie.
[25] Arthur G. Dorland, *Former Days and Quaker Ways: A Canadian Retrospect* (Picton: Picton Gazette Publishing Co., 1965), 175-76.
[26] QUA, Queen's University Printed Collection, "Calendar of Queen's College and University, Kingston, Canada, For the Year 1909-1910."
[27] P. T. Rooke and R. L. Schnell, *No Bleeding Heart: Charlotte Whitton, A Feminist on the Right* (Vancouver: University of British Columbia Press, 1987), 10.
[28] A. B. McKillop, *A Disciplined Intelligence: Critical Inquiry and Canadian Thought in the Victorian Era* (Montreal: McGill-Queen's University Press, 1979).
[29] B. Anne Wood, *Idealism Transformed: The Making of a Progressive Educator* (Kingston & Montreal: McGill-Queen's Press, 1985).
[30] John Irving, *The Social Credit Movement in Alberta* (Toronto: University of Toronto Press, 1959), 10. R.D. Gidney first pointed out this connection between Aberhart and Dickie to me.
[31] Dickie, autobiographical notes.
[32] D. J. Dickie, "Dramatization as a Method in Composition," *The School* 1, 3 (1912): 185-188; "Teaching Canadian History," *The School* 3, 1 (1914): 37-41; "Methods of Teaching Canadian History," *The School* 3, 5 (1915): 337-340.
[33] Alberta Department of Education Annual Reports trace the re-location of normal school instructors. Dickie was at the Calgary Practice School in 1910, then employed at the Camrose Normal School in 1912, transferred to the Edmonton Normal School in 1920, Calgary Normal School in 1923, back to Edmonton in 1928, Camrose in 1933, Edmonton in 1935.
[34] Dickie, autobiographical notes.
[35] Pauline Adams, e-mail to author, 5 October 2001, conveying information about Dickie contained in the Somerville College Register.
[36] D. J. Dickie, "Life at an English University," Part 1, *The School* 6, 3 (1917): 213-217; Part 2, *The School* 6, 4 (1917): 274-277; Part 3, *The School* 6, 5 (1918): 346-349.
[37] Harris interview; Francesca M. Wilson, *Rebel Daughter of a Country House: The Life of Eglantyne Jebb, Founder of the Save the Children Fund* (London: George Allen and Unwin Ltd., 1967).
[38] Celia Jenkins, "New Education and Its Emancipatory Interests (1920-1950)," *History of Education* 29, 2 (2000): 139-151; Peter Cunningham, "Innovators, Networks and Structures: Towards a Prosopography of Progressivism," *History of Education* 30, 5 (2001): 433-451.
[39] "Who's Who Among Educationists."

Getting Things Done

40 Vera Brittain quoted in Heilbrun, 105.
41 The exact date of death is recorded on the dedication page of Donalda Dickie, *The Great Adventure: An Illustrated History of Canada for Young Canadians* (Toronto: J. M. Dent, 1950).
42 Adams, e-mail.
43 Harris interview.
44 UTA, SGS Acc. No. A84-0011/026, Dickie file.
45 Alberta Department of Education, *Annual Report, 1926* (Edmonton: King's Printer, 1927), 22.
46 Donalda J. Dickie, *Modern Practice in the Teaching of Composition* (Toronto: W. J. Gage, 1923); Donalda J. Dickie, comp., *The Canadian Poetry Book: A Book of Modern Verse* (Toronto: J. M. Dent, 1922); Donalda J. Dickie, *Learning to Speak and Write: Book 1, Grades I, II, III, and IV* and *Book II, Grades V, VI, VII, and VIII* (Toronto: Educational Book Company, 1924); Donalda J. Dickie, *Dent's Canadian History Readers*, 8 vols. (Toronto: J. M. Dent, 1924-26).
47 Donald Wright, "Gender and the Professionalization of History in English Canada Before 1960," *Canadian Historical Review* 81, 1 (2000): 29-66.
48 See, for example, R. S. Patterson, "Hubert C. Newland: Theorist of Progressive Education," in Robert S. Patterson, John W. Chalmers and John Friesen, (eds.), *Profiles of Canadian Educators* (n.p.: D.C. Heath, 1974), 289-290; H. T. Coutts and B. E. Walker, recorders, *G. Fred: The Story of G. Fred McNally* (Don Mills, Ontario: J. M. Dent, 1964). Newland went to the University of Chicago and earned a doctorate in 1932. McNally notes he was sent to Teachers College, Columbia on full salary but never completed his degree. There is no evidence to suggest that Dickie received any support from her employer to attend a doctoral program.
49 Mary Kinnear, *In Subordination: Professional Women, 1870-1970* (Montreal & Kingston: McGill-Queen's Press, 1995), 33.
50 Wright, "Gender and the Professionalization of History."
51 Beverly Boutilier and Alison Prentice, "Introduction: Locating Women in the Work of History," in Beverly Boutilier and Alison Prentice, (eds.), *Creating Historical Memory: English-Canadian Women and the Work of History* (Vancouver: University of British Columbia Press, 1997), 4.
52 Wright, "Gender and the Professionalization of History," 31. Wright notes the specific sexism of two professors who were involved in supervising Dickie's work.
53 See, Wright, "Gender and the Professionalization of History" and Alison Prentice, "Laying Siege to the History Professoriate," in *Creating Historical Memory*, eds. Boutilier and Prentice, 197-232.
54 Randi R. Warne, *Literature as Pulpit: The Christian Social Activism of Nellie L. McClung* (Waterloo: Wilfrid Laurier University Press, 1993), 186.
55 Dickie, autobiographical notes.
56 B. Anne Wood, "Canadian Citizenship for a Progressive State," in Keith A. Macleod, (ed.), *Canada and Citizenship Education* (Toronto: Canadian Education Association, 1989), 19-26; Ken Osborne, "Public Schooling and Citizenship Education in Canada," *Canadian Ethnic Studies* 32, 1 (2000): 8-37; Penney Irene Clark, *'Take It Away Youth!': Visions of Canandian Identity in British Columbia Social Studies Textbooks, 1925-1989* (Ph.D. diss., University of British Columbia, 1995).
57 Elizabeth Bailey Price, "Calgary Has Four Women Authors," *Canadian Bookman* 8, 3 (1926), 94.

58. Ken Osborne, "'Our History Syllabus Has Us Gasping': History in Canadian Schools—Past, Present, and Future," *Canadian Historical Review* 81, 3 (2000): 404-435; George S. Tomkins, *A Common Countenance: Stability and Change in the Canadian Curriculum* (Scarborough, Ontario: Prentice-Hall, 1986).

59. See, for example, Osborne, "Public Schooling and Citizenship Education;" Kenneth W. Osborne, *"Hard-working, Temperate and Peacable"—The Portrayal of Workers in Canadian History Textbooks* (Winnipeg: University of Manitoba, 1980); Neil Sutherland, *Growing Up: Childhood in English Canada from the Great War to the Age of Television* (Toronto: University of Toronto Press, 1997); Clark, "'Take It Away Youth!'"

60. Donalda Dickie, "The Anglo-Canadian Problem," *Canadians All* 3, 4 (1945), 13, 68-69.

61. The most sustained discussion can be found in Donalda Dickie, *All About Indians, Book 2, Dent's Canadian History Readers* (Toronto: J. M. Dent, 1925).

62. Donalda Dickie and Frederick S. Cooper, *We Talk and Write of What We Do* (Toronto: W. J. Gage, 1955), 95.

63. Donalda Dickie, comp., *Ships of Araby*, The Fifth Reader in the Far Horizons series (Toronto: J. M. Dent, 1936), 301.

64. Donalda Dickie, *The Great Golden Plain: A History of the Prairie Provinces* (Toronto: W. J. Gage, 1962), 194.

65. Ibid., 215.

66. Ibid.

67. Donalda J. Dickie and George Dill, *Two Little Indians* (Toronto: J. M. Dent, 1933); D. J. Dickie, *Joe and Ruth Go To School* (Toronto: J. M. Dent, 1940).

68. Donalda Dickie, *When Canada Was Young, Book 5, Dent's Canadian History Readers* (Toronto: J. M. Dent, 1925), 211.

69. Donalda Dickie, *In Pioneer Days, Book 6, Dent's Canadian History Readers*, rev. ed. (Toronto: J. M. Dent, 1927), 59.

70. Dickie, *Ships of Araby*, 103.

71. Thornton Mustard, introduction to *Junior Language, Book A*, by Donalda Dickie (1938; reprint Toronto: Gage, 1944), iii.

72. Donalda J. Dickie and Helen Palk, *Pages from Canada's Story* (Toronto: J. M. Dent, 1928). It is difficult to tell how many printings this book went through but I have been able to confirm the following publication history. Reprinting occurred in 1931, 1932 (twice), 1933, 1935. A slightly revised edition appeared in 1936 and was reprinted each year from 1937 to 1943. The book was "reset and electrotyped" and issued in 1947, revised and issued in 1949 and 1951, and then reprinted each year from 1952 to 1959 and again in 1961.

73. Donalda Dickie, *The Great Adventure: An Illustrated History of Canada for Young Canadians* (Toronto: J. M. Dent, 1950; reprinted 1951, 1952, 1953, 1954, 1955, 1956, 1957, 1958); (Edmonton: Alberta Education, 1977), sound recording. For reviews of this book, see, for example, UATA, A-73-0026/083 (94), Clipping File, Dickie, Donalda James; J. E. P., "Review of *The Great Adventure*," *Saturday Night* 66 (5 December 1950): 45; n.a., "La Grande Aventure," *La revue de l'université Laval* 7, 2 (1952): 187-189. On the Governor-General's Award see, Canadian Cultural Information Centre, *The Canadian Literary Awards, Part 1: Governor General's Literary Awards* (Ottawa: Author, 1966).

74. Donalda Dickie, Belle Ricker, Clara Tyner and T. W. Woodhead, comps., *Young Explorers*, *Gay Adventurers*, and *Proud Procession*, Canadian Parade Readers (To-

ronto: J. M. Dent, 1947; reprinted 1948, 1949, 1950, 1951, 1952, 1953, 1954, 1955, 1957) with teacher guides and workbooks; Sutherland, *Growing Up*, 217.

[75] "Dr. D. Dickie Retiring from Normal School; Widely Feted," *Edmonton Bulletin*, 5 June 1944. Glenbow Archives and Library, Library Clipping File, "Donalda Dickie."

[76] "Notes About Authors," *Chatelaine*, April 1945, 2.

[77] Harris interview.

[78] See, for example, Leroy John Wilson, "Perren Baker and the United Farmers of Alberta—Educational Principles and Policies of an Agrarian Government" (M.Ed. Thesis, University of Alberta, 1970); James Rennie Bradford, *The Rise of Agrarian Democracy: The United Farmers and Farm Women of Alberta, 1909-1921* (Toronto: University of Toronto Press, 2000); Tom Monto, *The United Farmers of Alberta: A Movement, A Government* (Edmonton: Crang Pub., 1989).

[79] L. J. Wilson, "Educational Role of the United Farm Women of Alberta," in *Shaping the Schools of the Canadian West*, eds. David C. Jones, Nancy M. Sheehan and Robert M. Stamp (Calgary: Detselig, 1979), 124-135.

[80] See, Patterson, "The Establishment of Progressive Education in Alberta"; von Heyking, "Selling Progressive Education."

[81] University of Alberta Archives (UAA), Acc. No. 69-29, Series 1, Box 4, Item 3/1, File 1, Interview transcript, W. D. McDougall.

[82] Coutts and Walker, *G. Fred*, 41.

[83] Dickie, *The Enterprise*, 125.

[84] UAA, Acc. No. 69-29, W. D. McDougall Collection, Box 4, 3/1, File 5, Donalda Dickie and Olive Fisher, "Some Events Leading to the Re-Organization of the Curriculum of the Department of Education of the Province of Alberta in 1933." Unpublished typescript, n.d.

[85] Oviatt to [Oviatt].

[86] Dickie, *The Enterprise*; see, also, articles by Dickie in a wide range of journals, including "New Lamp for Old," *Alberta School Trustee*, December 1939: 13-15; "Education via the Enterprise," *The School* 21, 9 (1940): 3-6; "Enterprise Education in Alberta," *Understanding the Child*, April 1940: 7-11; "Democracy and the Enterprise," *The School* 31, 6 (1943): 464-469; "Enterprise Education—Part 1," *The B. C. Teacher*, September 1940: 18-20 and Part 2, October 1940: 75-77; "A Comment on the New Course of Study for Elementary Schools," *The ATA Magazine*, November 1936: 35-36.

[87] Shelley Anne Marie Bosetti-Piche, *The Interest of Edmonton Club Women in Education, Health and Welfare, 1919-1939* (Ph.D. diss., University of Alberta, 1990).

[88] See, Patterson, "The Establishment of Progressive Education in Alberta"; von Heyking, "Selling Progressive Education"; University of Calgary Archives (UCA), UARC 86.034, A. L. Doucette *fonds*, Box 17, File 17.11, "Attitude Towards The Enterprise Curriculum." This document is an undated, anonymous assessment of the position on the enterprise taken by each of the normal school instructors. Here Dickie is put in the "child freedom group."

[89] See, for example, Dickie, "Democracy and the Enterprise."

[90] Donalda Dickie, "Improving Techniques in Social Studies," *The School* 33, 8 (April 1945): 673.

[91] Alberta Department of Education, *Annual Report, 1935* (Edmonton: King's Printer, 1936), 19.

[92] Robert S. Patterson, "History of Teacher Education in Alberta," in David C. Jones, Nancy M. Sheehan and Robert M. Stamp, (eds.), *Shaping the Schools of the Canadian West* (Calgary: Detselig, 1979), 192-207.

[93] Dickie, *The Enterprise*, 435.

[94] Patterson, "Progressive Education: Impetus to Educational Change;" R. S. Patterson, "Voices from the Past: The Personal and Professional Struggles of Rural School Teachers," in Nancy M. Sheehan, J. Donald Wilson and David C. Jones, (eds.), *Schools in the West* (Calgary: Detselig, 1986), 99-111.

[95] Patterson, "Hubert C. Newland"; Oviatt to [Oviatt].

[96] The attack most often cited is Hilda Neatby, *So Little for the Mind: An Indictment of Canadian Education* (Toronto: Clarke, Irwin & Co., 1953). See, also, W. G. Hardy, *Education in Alberta* (Calgary: Calgary Herald, n.d.). For a thorough discussion of the opposition, see Campbell A. Ross, "The Neatby Debate and Conservative Thought in Canada" (Ph.D. diss., University of Alberta, 1989).

[97] UCA, UARC 86.034, A. L. Doucette *fonds*, Box 1, File 1.5, General Correspondence. Material in this file indicates that Doucette, an instructor at the Calgary Normal School, had actively supported progressive education reforms, but later recanted.

[98] Dickie, *The Great Adventure*, vii.

[99] Blackmore, *Troubling Women*.

[100] UCA, UARC 0.2, Calgary Normal School Yearbooks, Box 1, File 1924-25, "The Comet," 9.

[101] UTA, Office of the President, Acc. No. A68-0007, Citation for Donalda James Dickie, 6 June 1952.

Sustaining the Fire of "Scholarly Passion"

Mary G. Hamilton (1883-1972) and Irene Poelzer (1926-)

DIANNE M. HALLMAN AND ANNA H. LATHROP

"Scholarly passion is caught by persons from persons," Mossie May Waddington Kirkwood once said while reminiscing on her long career at the University of Toronto. She was expressing the hope that, in the course of their studies, students might be inspired by at least one person "shot through with the love of truth."[1] This same hope animates our research; i.e., we search again for those whose passion inspires.

In her study of Mary Electa Adams and Mossie Mae Kirkwood, Alison Prentice held that the close examination of individual scholarly women shed light on commonalities and controversies in the relatively brief history of women in higher education and the professoriate.[1] Our interest is in women whose scholarly passion is suffused with feminist fire, women who have spoken their truth about the patriarchal foundation of society, and have worked through professional education to build new visions of the future based on dignity and justice for women. We, too, focus on the lives of individual women—Mary G. Hamilton (1883-1972) and Irene Poelzer (1926-)—for, even with the burgeoning research on academic women, much can be understood about the complex weave of women's history in higher education by touching the rich texture of particular lives. Our subjects, two Canadian women who promoted a feminist perspective in higher education in their respective contexts, were scholars in the broadest and deepest sense: they were/are scholars of life. Theirs was/is a love of learning that includes dedicated study of an intellectual discipline as well as many other creative, spiritual, and recreational pursuits. If women had had a renaissance, they might be called Renaissance women.[2]

Mary G. Hamilton, a physical educator, worked in the first half of the twentieth century. She was principal of the Margaret Eaton School from 1926 to 1934. Margaret Eaton, a school of higher education for women in Toronto, Ontario, was the first in Canada to offer intensive training for women entering the profession of physical education. Hamilton established one of the first camps for girls in Algonquin Park, a wilderness preserve in central Ontario, and developed a feminist vision of wilderness training for women in programs of professional preparation. She believed that young women should be physically strong and prepared to meet the most challenging circumstances. Anna Lathrop traces Hamilton's career, drawing out the collegial supports that helped Hamilton enact her vision of an empowering education for women.

Irene Poelzer's career as a university educator spanned three decades during the second half of the twentieth century. She initiated and developed a feminist discourse in the College of Education, University of Saskatchewan, creating courses for both pre-service teachers and graduate students that prepared them to challenge sexist practices in society, and to undertake research from a feminist perspective. She thus made this the first college of education in Canada to incorporate a women's studies focus.[3] A sociologist, historian, philosopher, and poet, Poelzer encouraged students and colleagues to make their "scratch on the wall," to struggle for justice.[4] Through an in-depth personal interview with her, Dianne Hallman reveals Poelzer's energetic work to foster supportive networks for women as the key antidote to the chilly climate of academe.

Taking Prentice's essay on "Scholarly Passion" as a point of departure, we examine continuities and discontinuities in the career paths of our subjects in relation to that of Adams and Kirkwood. Comparison is instructive for we see plainly how gender continues to shape the world of higher education and teaching. Prentice reveals "two very different scholarly women."[5] Adams, a late nineteenth-century academic nomad, assumed teaching and/or leadership positions in one American and six Canadian educational institutions over her winding, frequently interrupted career. While some of these ladies' colleges and seminaries offered a measure of university training, none offered degrees or the kind of advanced studies available to privileged men in universities and seminaries. While Adams predicted that "women would gain 'university privileges' in her time," she "was excluded from playing a significant continuing role in this triumph."[6]

Kirkwood was one of the exceptional women who did achieve a university teaching position early in the twentieth century. A graduate of University of Toronto's Anglican Trinity College (B.A. 1911; M.A. 1913; and Ph.D. 1919), she also taught there during the First World War and, when the end of the war ended her employment, she found another position at the non-denominational University College. Here she taught English and served as dean of women, even after marriage in 1923, and the subsequent birth of children. In 1929 she gave up her administrative role, at least in part because of objections to her marital status, but in 1936 she assumed the same position in her old college, Trinity. Aided by the labour shortage created by war, and with the support of mainly male relatives and colleagues, Kirkwood managed to combine "the roles of dean, English instructor, faculty wife and mother," and maintain her university career for over 40 years.[7]

As different as Adams's and Kirkwood's careers were, what was possible for either of them was framed by their identity as women. The academy was (and to a fair extent still is) the world of privileged men: "an institution that has been predominantly male and that, until recently, has been run entirely by men alone, cannot be understood in isolation from the central fact of women's marginality to its functioning, or subordination within its governing structures."[8] Both women laboured intensively, yet on the periphery: Adams in institutions premised on a separate and, at least as far as credentials were concerned, inferior education for women; Kirkwood in administrative structures hived off from the centre of power. While their familial obligations were different, with Adams remaining single and Kirkwood marrying, they both shouldered extended family responsibilities beyond what would be expected of men. Their occupational trajectories more closely resembled Inga Elgqvist-Saltzman's "winding tracks" as moves and disruptions to accommodate family needs resulted in career paths that deviated significantly from the "straight lines" of men's, although the later Kirkwood's was more straightforward and stable than Adams's.[9]

To better understand these gendered career paths, Prentice alludes to an important study of American women's entrance into the professions from 1890-1940. In *Unequal Colleagues*, Penina Migdal Glazer and Miriam Slater identified four strategies that aspiring professional women used to manage their careers in response to the discrimination they faced: "superperformance, subordination, innovation, and separatism."[10] Individual women may have combined or changed strategies depending on their particular circumstances; often the strategies overlapped. Many women gained professional credibility by working harder than their male counterparts, either in separate or coeducational institutions. Separate institutions, such as Mount Holyoke, provided "isolated splendor" where women could develop their intellectual and professional aspirations in a woman-centred community.[11] The separate institutions of Adams's isolation likely lacked the splendor of Holyoke; yet they provided her a measure of economic independence and intellectual stimulation. Still, for much of her career, her status was that of a subordinate and her attempts to forge an innovative affiliation between Brookhurst, the college she founded with her sister Augusta, and Victoria College failed. Prentice describes Kirkwood's career as an amalgam of these strategies: superperformance in her administrative, teaching, and familial roles; subordination "both to individual men and to men's expressed interests;" innovation in her capacity to find new jobs and create new roles for herself; and separatism in her role as dean of women in the separate spaces of women's residences.[12]

Drawing further on the analysis of Glazer and Slater, Prentice notes that, like other late nineteenth-century, early twentieth-century academic women, Adams

Dianne M. Hallman and Anna H. Lathrop

2.1. Mary G. Hamilton. Courtesy of Monica Jenset.

and Kirkwood failed to reproduce themselves: "their immediate tasks were too many and their resources too few."[13] We wonder if our subjects had better success. Did they help open the way for another generation of women into institutions of higher learning and the professoriate? Did their work assist the integration of women as "equal partners in Canadian institutions of higher learning"?[14] Did their strategies of career management vary significantly from those of Adams and Kirkwood? Did the supportive networks that Hamilton and Poelzer deliberately nurtured in their respective settings sustain a scholarly life? And did their conscious articulation of a feminist concern for the empowerment of women ignite a contagion of scholarly passion? Or, were the tasks too many; resources too few?

Mary Grace Hamilton's quest for a role in higher education began 60 years after Mary Electa Adams's. Despite Adams's hope that women would gain access to university privileges in her time, Mary Hamilton's educational possibilities were still limited. As Prentice suggests, by the end of the century, options for young women whose social class and personal aspirations allowed them to pursue higher learning, included a network of private schools, seminaries, academies and convents—women's institutions and colleges that were subordinate to the institutions of higher education for men and subsequently relegated to the margins of mainline educational history.[15] Of the

Sustaining the Fire of "Scholarly Passion"

existing institutions of higher education, only universities, designed to educate young men for the professions, were considered sufficiently advanced to warrant public funding. Although women slowly gained access to these institutions by the end of the nineteenth century, the coeducational university environment was not welcoming.[16] During the first decade of the twentieth century, the advantages and disadvantages of separate educational institutions for women persisted as a topic of heated debate.[17] Most of the few women who entered the coeducational university environment pursued a degree in arts, which generally limited them to employment in teaching, library, and secretarial work—unlike their male counterparts who entered careers in the church, the civil service, and business. Given this set of circumstances, Hamilton opted for a professional life of education and service that kept her within the nineteenth-century model of separate educational institutions for women.

Described by her friends as a "quiet woman of practical vision,"[18] Mary Hamilton grew up in the small town of Fergus, Ontario. Her grandfather, George Colquhoun Hamilton, was one of the original settlers who emigrated from Scotland in 1834. Her father, Thomas Hamilton, was born on the family homestead. Following an education in Edinburgh he returned to Fergus, began a career in business, and married Sarah Graham from Tilsonburg, Ontario. Mary was the second of five children, born in 1883. Raised in a Presbyterian home, she recalled an athletic childhood that was encouraged by her father, an accomplished curler, who traveled to Scotland with the first curling team to compete for Canada internationally.[19] She loved horses, the outdoors, and rode at country fairs.

Hamilton's early interest in physical activity, coupled with her desire to teach, led her to Boston where she attended the Sargent School of Physical Training. Here she received a two-year teaching diploma. In the absence of professional physical education programs in Canada, many Canadians sought summer courses and diploma certification programs either in the United States or England.[20] Given nineteenth and early twentieth-century views of women's unique anatomy and limited physiological ability, physical education for women evolved as a separate and distinct area of professional preparation within these specialist colleges and training institutions. By the turn of the century, women's health and education reform brought employment opportunities for those who were certified to teach physical education to girls and women in schools, academies, and YWCAs. With certificate in hand, Hamilton returned to Canada and accepted a position with the YWCA in Kingston, Ontario. Shortly thereafter, in 1909, Hamilton moved to Toronto where she was hired to teach physical education at Bishop Strachan School, and Branksome Hall, two private schools for girls.

While in Toronto, Mary Hamilton met Emma Scott Raff, the enterprising young principal of The Margaret Eaton School of Literature and Expression, a private women's academy established in 1901. Funded and supported by Margaret Eaton, the wife of department store magnet Timothy Eaton, the school offered a "professional and practical education for women"[21] in literature, dramatic art, and physical culture. In the school's curriculum, classes in physical culture—primarily dancing and gymnastics—were designed to complement dramatic training. Scott Raff believed that the revival of Greek plays demanded a balance between mental development and physical perfection.[22] She also argued "all culture should bring with it breadwinning power."[23] Scott Raff asked Hamilton to teach classes in gymnastics, games, and social dance. By 1910, Hamilton was appointed head of the work in physical education at the school. She lived in the women's residence at Annesley Hall, Victoria College, as did Emma Scott Raff. Here, Mary Hamilton entered a vibrant women's network that included women interested in the arts and culture, as well as those who taught physical education in private girls' schools and YWCAs.

For the next 35 years Mary Hamilton remained affiliated with the Margaret Eaton School. Emma Scott Raff and Mary Hamilton became good friends. Reminiscent of Patricia Palmieri's analysis of the social networks among women at Wellesley College, the staff and students of the School of Literature and Expression, later renamed The Margaret Eaton School, were remarkably homogeneous.[24] Faculty and students of the school were closely bonded. In addition to the school curriculum, they took part in theatre productions, social work, patriotic fêtes and discussion clubs.[25] The Alumnae Association, established in 1913, was particularly active. In 1925, when the T. Eaton Company threatened to close the school due to financial difficulties, the alumnae successfully lobbied to keep the school open. Emma Scott Raff and Mary Hamilton were known affectionately by the students as, "Auntie Em and Ham."[26] Scott Raff and Hamilton clearly took pleasure in each other's company. They often took drives in the country together, "far from the haunts of men."[27] One young graduate of the school, Dora Mavor,[28] also became close and the three women remained life-long friends.

In 1915, the school formalized the division between dramatic art and physical education, and Scott Raff appointed Mary Hamilton director of the Physical Education Department. By this time, the school boasted that their graduates filled positions as teachers of physical education, expression, public readers, interpreters of drama on the professional stage, supervisors of playgrounds, workers in settlements, and workers in YWCAs.[29] Within a decade, Scott Raff reported to the board that the school did not have enough teachers to supply the demand.[30]

In 1924, angered by allegations of financial mismanagement by the school's board of trustees, Emma Scott Raff resigned her position. In 1926 the school reorganized with an exclusive focus on physical education, and Mary Hamilton became Scott Raff's successor. As principal, Hamilton believed that it was important to stay current with the latest professional developments in the field. She wanted her young graduates to "be competent to organize and take charge of every branch of physical training for girls."[31] She spent a number of summer vacations in the United States and England investigating the latest trends in

Sustaining the Fire of "Scholarly Passion"

physical education. By the early 1920s, Hamilton was convinced that the camping movement for girls would begin to flourish and provide important career opportunities for the physical education graduates of the school. She believed the school needed to broaden its curriculum and offer courses in camp counselor training.

Fired by the vision of creating the first camp counselor training centre in Canada, in 1924 Hamilton traveled 200 miles north of Toronto to Algonquin Provincial Park. With $75, she leased a parcel of land, formed a charter company, and arranged for camp buildings to be erected on White's Lake. Camp Tanamakoon became the third camp for girls in the province.[32] Each September, Hamilton brought the junior and senior students from the Margaret Eaton School for a month-long training course. She taught wilderness education, canoeing, and campcraft skills. Three- or four-day overnight canoe trips, complete with challenging portages, were a mandatory part of the curriculum. Mary Hamilton's goal was to train young women to be "staunch and rugged and unwilling to acknowledge defeat by weather or circumstance."[33]

During the summer months, Tanamakoon operated as a summer camp for girls between the ages of eight and eighteen.[34] Many of the students of the school, once trained, were hired as camp counselors for the summer. Each fall, the staff of the Margaret Eaton School joined Mary Hamilton at the camp. In addition to outdoor skills, dramatic training was also added to the curriculum. Hamilton was joined by her close friend, Dora Mavor, who organized the construction of an outside theatre.[35] Mavor was involved with dramatic work at the camp during the summer months between 1930 and the 1950.[36] From the students' perspective, the camping experience was tremendously successful and served to further increase loyalty to the school. Hamilton advertised the camp counselor training as "the only course of its kind in Canada."[37]

During the early years of her camping experience, described as her "lone wolfing period,"[38] Mary Hamilton was joined by two other friends who owned and operated girls' camps: Mary S. Edgar and Ferna Halliday. Hamilton, Edgar, and Halliday formed an alliance as the first female directors of girls' camps in the province. In 1922 Mary Edgar established Glen Bernard, in Sundridge, Ontario, and in 1925 Ferna Halliday established Camp Oconto, in the Rideau Lakes district, near Kingston.[39] These three attended camp conferences and spent holidays together. Eventually, according to Hamilton, they were "taken in hand"[40] by the directors of the boys' camps. She recalled, "After a few years of being a law unto ourselves, working alone and running things as we chose, the directors of the boys camps took us under their wings."[41] In 1933, they joined Taylor Statten, A. L. Cochrane and H. E. Chapman to form the Ontario Camping Association.[42]

Reflecting the dominant social themes of Christian reformism and Canadian nationalism, Mary Hamilton's girls' camp incorporated many of the rituals that were characteristic of camps run for boys. Opening prayers, the national anthem, and flag-raising ceremonies began each day. On Sunday, outdoor chapel services were held. Hamilton, a follower of the Oxford Group,[43] advocated a philosophy of Christian outreach, community living, and unselfish leadership. She believed that camp life could help initiate "a new social order— a pattern for the right kind of world."[44]

Although parts of this "pattern" reflected traditional gender expectations with regard to service and community, the inclusion of wilderness experiences for girls and women challenged these stereotypes. As C. F. Plewman recalled of the period, "No one in their right senses would have thought of asking a girl to rough it in the out of doors."[45] Clearly, Hamilton's vision of a new social order included the right of girls and women to experience the physical demands of the wilderness and, like young boys and men, the joy of physical exertion. In the words of one popular Tanamakoon camp song,

> Strap a compass and knife and axe to your belt
> There's is a thrill in the woods to be felt
> When you chop and you swing,
> You can hear your axe ring
> Oh the call comes to hearts that are true.[46]

Mary Hamilton, like Mary Electa Adams before her, experienced the privileges and restrictions of a scholarly life lived within the separatist model of higher education for women. The Margaret Eaton School was an example of innovative separatism: a women's academy, carved out on the margins of the economic empire of the T. Eaton Company and the intellectual empire of the University of Toronto. Like other women's academies, it was not afforded the same recognition that degree-granting institutions were given. The two-year Margaret Eaton School diploma was not recognized by the Ontario College of Education, and subsequently, Margaret Eaton graduates were not allowed to teach in the public schools. As a result, Hamilton forged networks with private girls' schools, YWCAs, and with other girls' camp directors to create opportunities for the graduates of her school. This restriction was a severe limitation; one that eventually contributed to the absorption of the Margaret Eaton School by the University of Toronto in 1941. When the school was merged with the University of Toronto, the two-year diploma gave way to a three-year degree in health and physical education, and the distinctive characteristics of the school disappeared. The camp experience ended, the teaching components of the programme were dropped, and the curriculum shifted to a higher concentration in science and health theory with less emphasis on activity. The Margaret Eaton School was one of Ontario's last private academies for women to give up its distinct curricula.

Hamilton's metaphor of the "lone wolf" probably captures her experience of living on the periphery of a male-centred scholarly academy. However, by valuing close relationships with her students and the collegial synergy of her colleagues, she was part of a movement that proved women could create a

2.2. *"Miss Hamilton and Mrs. Geddes," Camp Tanamakoon photo album.
Courtesy of Monica Jenset.*

cohesive intellectual and social community outside the domain of universities. Hamilton would have believed that scholarly passion was caught from persons by persons, and worked to extend the parameters of this possibility to include both academic and wilderness contexts. Like Adams, Hamilton also remained single, achieving an independent lifestyle that included supportive relationships with women. Challenging nineteenth-century notions that single women were considered to be women "adrift,"[47] Hamilton's ambitions for herself and her graduates included the mandate to take charge, find useful employment, *and* be able to paddle a canoe.

With the notable exception of programmes like the girls' camping movement, the separatism that had marked women's colleges, reform organizations, and suffrage societies during the late nineteenth century generally declined from the 1920s onward as women, optimistic about the opportunities opened to them with enfranchisement, sought integration in mainstream political and educational institutions. As seen in the case of Margaret Eaton, separate institutions themselves were sometimes absorbed into universities, often in the name of progress or necessity, and lost their distinctive characteristics. When Irene Poelzer began undergraduate studies at the University of Saskatchewan in the late 1940s, coeducation had become the norm in universities, and had been affirmed in this university's founding documents: "no woman shall, by reason of her sex, be deprived of any advantage or privilege accorded to male students of the University."[48] Still, the coeducational university environment may have been no more welcoming to women than it was in the nineteenth century. Women represented only about 25 percent of undergraduate enrolment nationwide and they were severely under-represented in some colleges and programmes of study.[49] Moreover, women's enrolment in graduate schools had been in decline since the 1920s. Only a very few held jobs as university professors, and they were concentrated in the lower ranks.[50]

Irene Poelzer is in some ways an unlikely candidate for the professoriate. Except for a brief sojourn in Oregon, she grew up in small German-Catholic enclave in rural Saskatchewan. Because of widespread poverty during the 1930s and '40s, few children could take advantage of the educational opportunities in the St. Peter's abbacy; Grade VIII would have been the terminal point for most children during the 1930s and '40s. Born in 1926, Irene was the fifth of Michael Poelzer's and Elizabeth Hinz's twelve children. Her father, a farmer, had almost no formal education. By contrast, her mother was relatively well educated, having received the Governor-General's gold medal in Grade XII and taken Normal School training to become a teacher. That her parents were not only able to provide, but insisted upon Grade XII and at least one-year post-secondary education for all twelve children is remarkable, especially in light of the difficult economic times and exigencies of war.[51]

Upon completion of her Grade XII by correspondence, Poelzer studied at the University of Saskatchewan, graduating in 1950 with a Bachelor of Arts in English and Philosophy. That same year she followed a centuries-long separatist tradition of education available to Roman Catholic women who seek a life of scholarship and service; she took up a religious vocation. Gerda Lerner and others have illuminated the historical role of the convent in providing scholarly-minded women opportunities for higher learning, leadership, and meaningful work.[52]

While it seemed very natural to Poelzer to take up the consecrated life (several of her sisters and cousins joined religious congregations), the chance for further intellectual development united with her religious commitment in making this an attractive option:

> having the education made a difference because I saw how a lot of other girls my age would get married when they were seventeen, sixteen, you know, and they would have babies, and work on the farm, drudgery and all this ... and the thing is, I had a taste of the intellectual, and so....[53]

And so, inspired by a chance visit to the school in Sedley, Saskatchewan, where Lorettos taught, Poelzer decided to go to Toronto, Ontario, and join the Institute of the Blessed Virgin Mary (also known as Loretto Sisters), a teaching congregation dedicated to women's education.[54]

As Sister Ruth, Poelzer taught for several years in Ontario including the Motherhouse and Loretto College School in Toronto, and a convent school in Fort Erie. Eventually her community sent her back to Saskatchewan to take up

2.3. Irene Poelzer, 1999. Courtesy Irene Poelzer

teaching and the principalship of the Sedley school. With the support of her congregation, Poelzer's desire for further formal study was realized during the 1960s. She completed her Bachelor of Education at the University of Saskatchewan, and then was the first student to graduate with a Masters in the Foundations of Education in 1967. By 1969 she completed a M.A. in English at the University of Seattle as well. Like Kirkwood, she loved both Philosophy and English. For Poelzer it was a toss up as to which of the two subjects she would choose for her Ph.D. She attributes her decision to go with Philosophy (with Sociology as an additional area of study) to two professors in education who served as mentors. She most admired one's dialogical method of teaching and the other's ability to cut through to the real issues in any situation or debate. Most importantly, she saw teacher educators as having a greater capacity to bring about social change because of the ripple effect: they taught students who would in turn be teaching large numbers in the schools. By contrast, in her view, English professors had ivory-tower offices and little impact on the outside world.[55]

These same education professors modelled the kind of person that Poelzer wanted to be as a teacher in the university. She followed Chet Bowers from the University of Saskatchewan to the University of Oregon to take Ph.D. studies under his supervision. She thought that he was not only an excellent philosopher but an incisive critic of capitalism, high technology, and other issues that resonated with her own concerns for justice. Poelzer also was very positively influenced by Doris Dyke, the only female professor in the Department of Educational Foundations (University of Saskatchewan). To see an intellectual, highly competent woman in a leadership position (Dyke became department head) was encouraging for Poelzer. Women rarely achieved this status in the

60s: "...very few women, on campus had anything except... sessional [appointments]."[56]

In 1970, two years before Poelzer completed her doctorate, Dyke invited Poelzer to return to the department to teach and her community agreed. Except for occasional leaves, she remained there for 23 years. The relative proportion of female faculty stayed pretty much the same during this time. When Poelzer assumed this position, 23 of the 118 full-time positions (19.4 percent) were held by women; when she retired in 1993, women held fourteen of the 73 full-time positions (19.1 percent). In 1993 only two women (including Poelzer) had achieved the rank of full professor compared to 39 men.[57]

While by 1970 women of privilege had made substantial gains in access to university education, many were critical of the knowledge generated and disseminated therein. Poelzer was acutely aware of the inequity of education where women's knowledge grounded in experience was not valued:

> a terrible injustice has been done to women, because we have built up the code of knowledge, or the body of knowledge, on only half of the human race's experience, on how [men] understand, or what ... *they* have learned. And then they give it us and they say, this is knowledge.[58]

Poelzer sought to redress this imbalance by developing and teaching a six-credit course entitled Women and Education. Its purpose was to examine knowledge and society from the perspectives of women. Students explored the relation between experience and knowledge and were encouraged to question whose experiences were included in the knowledge they were learning to become teachers. They studied women's contributions to history and education, they learned about sexism and sex-role stereotyping, and they considered how social institutions such as the church, family, law, and the media maintained discrimination against women.

This course was the first of its kind in a College or Faculty of Education in Canada, and was approved with considerable reluctance. Its marginality was assured for several years because it was not deemed a satisfactory elective to fulfill programme requirements. With students not allowed to count it against their requirements, the course could have been jeopardized by lack of enrolment.[59] Fortunately, Poelzer's reputation for innovative, dialogical teaching methods drew curious students and the course was a success. As well, at the graduate level, Poelzer developed new courses with a similar women's studies focus so students could complete a M.Ed. with a specialization in women and education.

Poelzer worked hard to break down barriers and build bridges among women, remembering those who were the most marginalized not just on campus, but in the wider community. In the late '70s, she taught Aboriginal women in the newly developed Northern Teacher Education Programme (NORTEP), a course of study designed to prepare northerners, especially Métis and status Indians, to teach in northern communities.[60] Her work here prompted field research that she hoped would give voice to the concerns of Métis women and "help them overcome many of the obstacles that keep them from realizing a fair share of the benefits that accrue from the development of the north's natural and human resources."[61] The project, undertaken with her sister Dolores (a sociologist at Humboldt State College, California, and also a woman religious), involved interviews with 86 Métis women which then formed the basis of their co-authored book. To assess the importance of this work for the Métis women themselves is difficult. Its significance may lay more in bringing a silenced group to the attention of the academic community which had rarely troubled itself to learn anything about the lives of its neighbours whose land and knowledge had long been appropriated, and whom it now purported to include.

Poelzer's second book also focused on a group whose work had, until recent times, received short shrift in the historical record: women teachers. Observing that women numerically dominate teaching, but historically are under-represented in positions of educational leadership, Poelzer examined the social attitudes about women that served to relegate them to the lower ranks of the profession and make invisible the work they did. She states,

> ...because of the vast difference between their gender-roles, the participation, and hence the contributions, of men and women are vastly different. They cannot be understood or valued from only one perspective, and thus, it is unjustified to use only the male norm.[62]

The chapters document the varied ways the province's early women teachers contributed to the improvement of education and the growth of the province.

Another example of her outreach to the wider community was the development of the Women's Educational Summer Institute (WESI), a summer programme of both credit and non-credit courses that drew women from across the province to attend lectures and films on various themes related to women, as well as workshops on financial planning, self-defence, and health. Operating under the direction of an advisory board made up of representatives from several provincial agencies, and eventually incorporated into the Extension Division, the institute's most enduring legacy was the support network it created for farm women.[63]

During Poelzer's career, the term "chilly climate" had connotations beyond Saskatchewan's weather.[64] It came into currency in the early '80s to describe the inhospitable atmosphere for girls and women in educational institutions. Poelzer initiated a number of informal activities that gave people across the campus an opportunity to meet, discuss issues particularly salient to women, watch videos over lunch, and generally make connections. These groups were open to "anyone who wanted to come" and some men did; not surprisingly, women formed the majority.[65] She abrogated the hierarchical distinctions within the university by encouraging people from diverse working groups—students, support staff, faculty, administrators—to participate in venues outside her own college. Another instance of informal organizing occurred in the early '90s when a female colleague in the College of Education was enduring intense sexual harassment. Poelzer rallied all women there from cafeteria staff to assistant dean to give support. Before their first meeting, Poelzer received a threatening phone call from a man reminding her of the Montréal massacre,[66] a reference to the December 1989 murder of fourteen women by woman/feminist hater Marc Lépine at the École Polytechnique. Thus began regular meetings where women shared their experiences of negation, harassment, and other gender-based problems within the workplace.

While Poelzer's work to support women is abundantly evident, her own sources of sustenance are more difficult to discern. For the first eight years of her appointment, she was connected to the Loretto community; however, no one else in the Saskatoon convent where she resided was engaged in university teaching so it is doubtful that she could share details about her work with assurance that others understood.[67] Guided by the vision articulated in Vatican II and called to embrace a radically different conception of the consecrated life, Poelzer left the Lorettos in 1978 and joined a non-canonical organization, Sisters for Christian Community (SFCC). SFCC is a loosely-organized community of self-supporting members who are committed "to promote and witness Christian Community ... in whatever work or living structure [they] penetrate and permeate." Although belonging to a community that "transcends distance,"[68] Poelzer was nevertheless geographically isolated from other SFCC members and, however stimulating and loving these connections, she had to build supportive networks in Saskatoon on her own.

Her mentor, Doris Dyke, left the department shortly after Poelzer's appointment. They remained close friends but no longer shared day-to-day interactions. Other colleagues, both female and male, figure highly in her conversations as providing friendship and emotional buffer zones. Yet the sense of kinship and solace among women scholars devoted to shared goals that characterized Wellesley, Margaret Eaton, or Kirkwood's women's residences at University College is noticeably absent from Poelzer's descriptions. Still, she would likely have eschewed this separatist ideal, preferring to confront patriarchal structures (and patriarchs) in everyday exchange, and teach for personal transformation in men's and women's lives. While Hamilton saw herself as a lone wolf, Poelzer saw herself as a gadfly whose sting might have made people squirm, but brought forward the underlying issues for discussion. Drawing inspiration from her teacher mother, Poelzer remained firmly optimistic about the power of teaching to elicit change: "If you make your scratch on the wall, in 200 years if everyone makes a scratch, the wall comes down."[69]

As "women's studies" was slowly recognized as a legitimate field of study, debates about whether it should be housed in a separate department or integrated throughout faculties animated university campuses.[70] In 1992 the senate of the University of Saskatchewan approved a proposal for a department of women's and gender studies to be housed in the College of Arts and Sciences.[71] Poelzer viewed this decision as a mistake. She believed a separate department would isolate and trivialize feminist scholarship, and other departments and professional colleges would then do little to take into account women's perspectives and knowledge in their respective fields. However, she did not have the opportunity to see the unfolding of this unit's work or to redirect the university towards her integrationist vision. In 1993, under the terms of the collective agreement between faculty and the university, she was forced to retire.

Like Adams, Kirkwood, and Hamilton, Poelzer expended enormous energy throughout her career on the work at hand. Like them, she worked to create community that nurtured justice, possibility, and scholarly passion. She is far more straightforward than Kirkwood about the sexism in societal structures and the obstacles facing women in the realization of their academic and personal dreams. Her own reflections on her career reveal the earthy humour that typifies her respect for women's traditional work and undercuts academic pretentiousness:

> Now when I look back on it [career], it was like a woman in a house, or running a farm or whatever. And you know, the kids have to be taken care of and the garden has to be done, and the laundry has to be done and the spring cleaning, the windows have to be done, and the meals have to be made. I'd just go ahead and do it. And so on campus I saw these things about women, particularly, women students ... and I said well, we have to do something here.... I didn't sit down and plan and say, well this will be a career project for me or something like that, because I really wasn't interested in that. And so, it was just all part of my professing at the university.[72]

Prentice's study of Adams and Kirkwood provides snapshots of two women educators in higher education at the end of the nineteenth, beginning of the twentieth century. Kirkwood was able to realize a university career that Adams, barred from entrance, could scarcely dream possible. Our subjects stand at the two ends of the twentieth century, one working within the separatist tradition like Adams; the other sustaining a university teaching career for twenty-three years, achieving the highest rank. Innovation and superperformance characterize both Hamilton's and Poelzer's career, as evidenced by their pioneering of new programmes and the very high levels of personal dedication to their work and the relationships that evolved from it. And yet, subordination is an ongoing reality. Given the hundred years or so that separate Adams and Poelzer, the changes wrought for women in higher education are not as great as one might expect.

While universities were opened to women in Adams's time as she predicted, very few were able to partake of its privileges; not until the 1960s did the percentage of women's undergraduate enrollment approach men's. A few women began to achieve teaching positions in universities during the First World War as Kirkwood did. By 1931, women constituted nineteen percent of full-time university teachers, but their numbers dropped during the depression and even more so during the 1950s. In spite of the huge expansion of universities during the 1960s, when Poelzer began university teaching in 1970, women made up only thirteen percent of professors nation-wide. By 1992, her final full year of teaching, 20 percent of Canadian professors were women, a gain that is less spectacular when the widespread downsizing of the '80s is taken into account.[73] Is this snail's pace progress towards equality a failure of scholarly passion? We think not. Both Hamilton and Poelzer, in their different contexts, consciously articulated an education aimed to empower women. While difficult to measure the impact of their work in terms of numbers seeking entrance to graduate school (or wilderness training), their teaching and passion for life had immeasurable effects on individual scholars and oriented them toward nurturing, loving communities.

Prentice closes her article with reference to the contemporary (1990) status of feminism within the academy, insisting "on the right to hand on to a new generation of women—and men—our gift of a feminist vision."[74] We, too, insist on that right, but as professors who began their careers during a decade marked by restructuring of public education toward a market-driven research agenda and increased performance measures, we wonder if the academy is the right venue to place our gift. With the increasing commodification of intellectual inquiry into numbers of refereed articles in the competition for grants, tenure, promotion, and merit pay, is there time or energy left to build the connections and caring that foster curiosity and engagement? Perhaps we should take our cue from Hamilton, climb into canoes, and commune with each other in the bush. Scholarly passion is not caught from a computer screen, it is "caught by persons from persons."

Notes

[1] Alison Prentice, "Scholarly Passion: Two Persons Who Caught It," in Alison Prentice and Marjorie Theobald, (eds.), *Women Who Taught: Perspectives on Women and Teaching* (Toronto: University of Toronto Press, 1991), 269.

[2] See Joan Kelly-Godol, "Did Women Have a Renaissance," in Renate Bridenthal and Claudia Koonz, (eds.) *ecoming Visible: Women in European History* (Boston: Houghton Mifflin, 1977), 137-164.

[3] Don Cochrane, "A Tribute to Dr. Irene Poelzer on her Retirement," College of Education, University of Saskatchewan, 23 April, 1993. Unpublished text of an oral tribute in author's possession. Based on a survey of 55 teacher training institutions in Canada, Cochrane found that "...no college of education in the country had an undergraduate course of this nature earlier than we did at the

Sustaining the Fire of "Scholarly Passion"

University of Saskatchewan (only McGill and Dalhousie universities also offered courses in 1974 at the undergraduate level; most universities did not catch up until the '80s and '90s)."

4   Irene Poelzer, interview by author, 25 July 2000.
5   Prentice, "Scholarly Passion," 259.
6   Prentice, "Scholarly Passion," 267.
7   Prentice, "Scholarly Passion," 273.
8   Prentice, "Scholarly Passion," 276.
9   Inga Elgqvist-Saltzman, "Why Are We Standing Still? Reflections from History," in Alison Mackinnon, Inga Elgqvist-Saltzman and Alison Prentice, (eds.), *Education into the 21st Century: Dangerous Terrain for Women?* (London: Falmer Press, 1998), 26.
10 Penina Migdal Glazer and Miriam Slater, *Unequal Colleagues: The Entrance of Women into the Professions, 1890-1940* (New Brunswick, NJ: Rutgers University Press, 1987), 14; Prentice, "Scholarly Passion," 273.
11 Glazer and Slater, *Unequal Colleagues*, 25.
12 Prentice, "Scholarly Passion," 273.
13 Prentice, "Scholarly Passion," 274.
14 Prentice, "Scholarly Passion," 277.
15 Prentice, "Scholarly Passion," 260.
16 Women gained access to the University of Toronto as early as the last quarter of the nineteenth century. Augusta Stowe, the first woman to graduate from a Canadian medical college in 1883, recalled her struggle in the coeducational university environment as a path "not strewn with roses." See, Anne Rochon Ford, *A Path Not Strewn with Roses: One Hundred Years of Women at the University of Toronto: 1884-1984* (Toronto: University of Toronto Press, 1985), iv.
17 In 1908, a senate committee of the University of Toronto, arguing on behalf of the "special" needs of women's higher education, voted in favour of segregation and the establishment of separate colleges for women. The University of Toronto alumnae successfully convinced senate to reverse this decision. See " Report of the Committee Appointed to Enquire in Regard to a Possible College for Women," *University of Toronto Monthly*, 9, 8 (June, 1909): 286-289; and also "Reply of the Alumnae," *University of Toronto Monthly*, 9, 8, (June, 1909): 289-91.
18 Victoria University Archives (VUA) 90.064/3/19, "Director of Physical Education, Reports Regarding Women's Use of the Gymnasium," Winter, 1909.
19 Mary S. Edgar, "Among Ourselves," *Canadian Camping* 8 , 3: 17.
20 Helen Gurney, *The CAHPER Story: 1933-1983; Fifty Years of Progress* (Ottawa: The Canadian Association of Health, Physical Education and Recreation, 1983), 3.
21 *The Margaret Eaton School of Literature and Expression Calendar*, 1908-1909, 10.
22 Dorothy N. R. Jackson, *A Brief History of Three Schools* (Toronto: T. Eaton Company Ltd., 1953), 10.
23 Emma Scott Raff, "Canadian Women in the Public Eye: Mrs. G.G. Nasmith," *Saturday Night* (Sept. 11, 1920): 26.
24 Patricia A. Palmieri, "Here was Fellowship: A Social Portrait of Academic Women at Wellesley College, 1895-1920," *History of Education Quarterly*, 23, 1 (Summer, 1983): 63-67.
25 Emma Scott Raff's studio functioned as an alumnae centre where meetings were held each month. See Jackson, *The Three Schools*, 11.

[26] Elizabeth Pitt Barron, interview by author, 25 March 1994. Pitt Barron graduated from the Margaret Eaton School in 1925. See Anna H. Lathrop, "Portrait of a 'Physical:' A Case Study of Elizabeth Pitt Barron (1904-1998)," *Historical Studies in Education/Revue D'Histoire De L'éducation*, 11 (2) (Fall/automne 1999): 131-146.

[27] "Emma Scott Raff to Dora Mavor," *Dora Mavor Moore Papers* (UTF-DMM) 207/60 (October 24, 1912), Thomas Fisher Rare Book Library, University of Toronto.

[28] Dora Mavor (later Moore) was a graduate of the Margaret Eaton School of Literature and Expression in 1912. She was the first Canadian to enter the Royal Academy of Dramatic Art in England and later became one of Canada's most successful amateur dramatists. See Paula Sperdakos, "Dora Mavor Moore: Her Career in the Canadian Theatre" (Ph.D. diss., University of Toronto, 1990).

[29] *Margaret Eaton School Calendar* 1916-1917 to 1922-1923, 8-10.

[30] "Report to the Director from Emma Scott Raff Nasmith" (November 4, 1918), Eaton Collection (PAO-EC) 22/6/1, Provincial Archives of Ontario.

[31] *Margaret Eaton School Calendar*, 1926-1927, 5.

[32] Other girls' camps had been established by Fanny Case, an American, in the early 1900s, and Mary Edgar in 1922.

[33] Mary G. Hamilton, *The Call of the Algonquin: A Biography of A Summer Camp* (Toronto: The Ryerson Press), 174.

[34] In 1925, 35 campers attended Camp Tanamakoon. By 1933, this capacity increased to 125. See, Hamilton, *Call of the Algonquin*, 18, 53.

[35] UTF-DMM, 207/ 29, "Tanamakoon."

[36] UTF-DMM, 207/ 29, "Miscellaneous" and "Tanamakoon."

[37] *Margaret Eaton School Calendar* 1932-1933, 5.

[38] Mary G. Hamilton, "Questions and Answers on Recorder," personal papers of Mary G. Hamilton. In files given to the author by Monica Jenset, nd.

[39] Don Burry, "The Early Pioneers of the Camping Movement in Ontario," in Bruce W. Hodgins and Bernadine Dodge, (eds.), *Using Wilderness: Essays on the Evolution of Youth Camping in Ontario* (Peterborough: Trent University, 1992), 84.

[40] Hamilton, "Questions and Answers on Recorder," nd.

[41] "Letter from Mary Hamilton to Adele Epps" (November 6, 1963), Ontario Camping Association (TUA-OCA), 72-007/ B7/ 7, Trent University Archives.

[42] Edgar, "Among Ourselves," 18.

[43] The Oxford Group was a Protestant evangelical movement founded by F.N. Buchman (1878-1961) in the late 1920s. See, F.L. Cross, *The Oxford Dictionary of the Christian Church* (Oxford: Oxford University Press, 1974), 1019.

[44] Hamilton, *Call of the Algonquin*, 167.

[45] TUA-OCA, 72-007/ 2/ 11, C.F. Plewman, "The Pioneers of Ontario Camping," 5.

[46] National Archives of Canada (NAC), 98-2218, "History of Tanamakoon, Sound Recording of Camp Tanamakoon's 50th Anniversary; 1925-1975," Gingerfoot Productions, Toronto, 1975.

[47] Diana Pedersen, "'A Building for Her:' The YWCA in the Canadian City," *Urban History Review* 15, 3 (February 1987): 227.

[48] The University Act of 1907, cited in A.S. Morton, *Saskatchewan: The Making of a University*, revised and edited by Carlyle King (Toronto: University of Toronto Press, 1959), 15.

[49] *Report of the Royal Commission on the Status of Women in Canada* (Ottawa, ON: Information Canada, 1970), 168.

Sustaining the Fire of "Scholarly Passion"

50   Ruth Roach Pierson and Marjorie Griffin Cohen, *Canadian Women's Issues, Volume II: Bold Visions, Twenty-Five Years of Women's Activism in English Canada* (Toronto: Lorimer, 1995), 163.

51   Poelzer, interview.

52   See Gerda Lerner, *The Creation of Feminist Consciousness: From the Middle Ages to Eighteen-seventy* (New York: Oxford University Press, 1993); Marta Danylewycz, *Taking the Veil: An Alternative to Marriage, Motherhood, and Spinsterhood in Quebec, 1840-1920* (Toronto: McClelland and Stewart, 1987).

53   Poelzer, interview. One sister joined the Maryknoll Congregation and two joined the Congregation of the Sisters of St. Joseph of Peace, congregations that pushed the traditional boundaries of mission for women religious.

54   On the origins of the Lorettos or "The English Ladies," see Elizabeth Rapley, *The Dévotes: Women and Church in Seventeenth-Century France* (Montréal & Kingston: McGill Queen's University Press, 1990), 28-34. Sedley was a "public" school in a community where Roman Catholics formed the majority. The board arranged for the Loretto sisters to teach there. In Saskatchewan, legislation provided for the founding of "public" schools in cases of either a Catholic or Protestant majority, and "separate" schools for a Catholic or Protestant minority.

55   Poelzer, interview.

56   Poelzer, interview.

57   *University of Saskatchewan Calendar*, 1970-71, p. J-2-3; *University of Saskatchewan Calendar*, 1992-93, p. 129. The figures for the 1970-71 faculty are inflated by "representatives of other Faculties or Departments." I thank Rick Schwier and Barry Brown for their help in ascertaining the number of women on faculty.

58   Poelzer, interview.

59   Cochrane, "A tribute."

60   NORTEP was established in 1977. For information regarding teacher education programs for Aboriginal peoples, see Catherine Littlejohn and Robert Regnier, *Aboriginal Teacher Education, Mission Statement and Background Paper* (Saskatoon, SK: University of Saskatchewan, 1989).

61   Dolores T. Poelzer and Irene A. Poelzer, *In Our Own Words: Northern Saskatchewan Métis Women Speak Out* (Saskatoon: Lindenblatt and Hamonic, 1986), p. xvi.

62   Irene Poelzer, *Saskatchewan Women Teachers, 1905-1920: Their Contributions* (Saskatoon: Lindenblatt and Hamonic, 1990), 6.

63   Angela T. Wong, "A Review of the Women's Program" (Report prepared for the Division of Extension and Community Relations, University of Saskatchewan, Saskatoon, 1986); Poelzer, interview; and Glenis Joyce, Extension Division, interview with author, 7 September 2000.

64   Roberta Hall and Bernice R. Sandler, *The Classroom Climate: A Chilly One for Women?* (Washington, DC: Project on the Status and Education of Women, Association of American Colleges, 1982).

65   Poelzer, interview.

66   Poelzer, interview.

67   For a general discussion of the tensions for women religious in professional work in secular contexts, see Elizabeth Smyth, "Professionalization Among the Professed: The Case of Roman Catholic Women Religious," in Elizabeth Smyth, Sandra Acker, Paula Bourne, and Alison Prentice, eds., *Challenging Professions: Historical and Contemporary Perspectives on Women's Professional Work* (Toronto: University of Toronto Press, 1999), 234-254.

[68] Lillanna (Audrey) Kopp, *Sudden Spring: 6th Stage Sisters: Trends of Change in Catholic Sisterhoods, A Sociological Analysis* (Waldport, OR: Oldtown Printers, 1983), 60.

[69] Poelzer, interview.

[70] See "The Canadian Women's Studies Project," *Atlantis: A Women's Studies Journal* 16, 1 (1990); *Final Report of the Ad Hoc Committee of the Committee on Academic Affairs on the Status of Women's Studies at the University of Saskatchewan* (Saskatoon, SK: University of Saskatchewan, 1989), 20.

[71] See "Department of Women's and Gender Studies: History," http://www.usask.ca/wgst/etc/history.htm, retrieved 21 May 2002.

[72] Poelzer, interview.

[73] Anne Innis Dagg, "Hiring Women at Canadian Universities: The Subversion of Equity," in Jacqueline Stalker and Susan Prentice, (eds.), *The Illusion of Inclusion: Women in Post-Secondary Education* (Halifax, NS: Fernwood, 1998), 109-111.

[74] Prentice, "Scholarly Passion," 277.

And Gladly Teach?

The Making of a Woman's Profession

MARJORIE THEOBALD

In 1998 the report of the Australian Senate inquiry into the status of teachers was published under the title, *A Class Act*.[1] It is in many ways an admirable report; it recognizes that teachers are the most important asset in our schools. It contains statistics on women's position within the teaching profession that should not surprise us. They comprise 77 per cent of teachers at primary the level, 53 per cent at the secondary level, a minority at the tertiary level, and they are under-represented in leadership positions across the board.[2] In other ways too, the report makes disturbing reading. It makes the claim that:

> All is not well in the teaching profession, and it is generally agreed that there is a widespread crisis of morale amongst the teachers. The status of the profession is disturbingly low. Perceptions in the community about the low tertiary entrance requirements for teacher training, and the low status accorded in this country to children, contribute to this state of affairs. As well, the feminisation of the profession ... means that prejudiced views about the value of women's work are also a factor. Few teachers recommend a teaching career to their own children or their brightest students. Some are even ashamed to admit to being teachers. While teachers themselves value their work they believe it is not understood, appreciated or supported in the general community.[3]

The findings of the Senate Inquiry disturbed me, but they did not surprise me. As a historian I know that we discover the woes of the teaching profession over and over again. I have a collection of these pronouncements, dating back to the 1860s. Most teachers in most decades believe that they live in uniquely troubled times.

Marjorie Theobald

As a historian of women, however, there was one aspect of the report, which did surprise me. In the evidence given to the inquiry there is a plea from a group of women educators not to lose sight of the "collective history of the systematic disadvantage of women and the understanding of how it continues to operate in the restructured system."[4] The response of the report is, in my view, disappointing. It urges that:

> The focus should be on re-establishing and reasserting the value of education and those who practise it, and of recognising and rewarding the skills good teachers bring to their task. A rise in status will follow. In this context, undue emphasis upon gender issues is, in the Committee's view, a diversion from the main game.[5]

Since I did not offer to give evidence to the inquiry I cannot complain. Yet I felt an old-fashioned sense of outrage; at every historical moment in the history of the teaching profession, gender has been a central dynamic. Beliefs about the proper relationships between men and women, and the differing material realities of their lives, come in across the grain of notions such as professionalism, status and merit. We cannot somehow wipe the slate clean and assume that no such dynamic is at work in the present. What happened to women teachers in the past is therefore important to our current understanding. It is in this spirit that I want to visit some aspects of my research on the history of women and the teaching profession in Australia.

The Australian teaching profession as we understand it today was called into existence by key policy decisions made in the nineteenth century. In the last quarter of that century, all Australian colonies legislated for centralized State systems of elementary education, beginning with Victoria in 1872 and ending with Western Australia in 1893.[6] Though they are sometimes known as the "free, secular and compulsory" acts, there was sufficient variation in the fine print to defeat this categorization. The intention, however, was clear enough. All colonies created departments of education under a minister of the crown, withdrew effective power from local authorities and parents, withdrew state aid from church schools, separated secular instruction from religious instruction, abolished fees and mandated attendance.

Consumed as they were with the need to resolve the conflict between church and State on the education issue, I doubt that legislators, church men, and other protagonists gave much thought to the other consequences of these momentous Education Acts—that is, the building of schools to house the children who were now obliged to attend, and the recruitment of teachers who were to implement this grand design of Protestantism to render all children literate and good. The colonial legislatures had, by accident, called into existence the mass profession and the consequences of that began to dawn slowly in the 1870s and '80s. Women would have to be recruited in large numbers, trained in some rudimentary way, paid for the work which they had traditionally done with

And Gladly Teach?

children free of charge and, most disturbing of all, granted the status of public servants when that status was granted to men.

The Catholic Church in Australia came to the same conclusion via a different route.[7] After those same "free, secular and compulsory" Acts cut off state aid to their schools, the bishops recruited overseas Orders and restructured their primary schools around the Parish priest and the female teaching Orders. I respect what Catholic women have done in the education of their flock but the fact remains that the Catholic Church, like the secular State which had deprived it of funds, marshalled the teaching labour of women to its own advantage and for the least possible cost. The staffing of secondary schools was a different story and I will return to that.

I want to suggest that these nineteenth-century women teachers were the captive canaries in the coalmine in the movement known as the emancipation of women. The very notion of women as salaried intellectual workers went against the right order of things. By definition a lady was neither salaried, nor intellectual nor professional. The teaching profession emerged in the same decades as the Australian feminist movement that fuelled up in the 1880s and, though there was no necessary cause and effect, an emerging professional class of women became the target of anxieties concerning women's new demands for equality with men. It was not an accident that by the end of the century legislation ensured that women teachers taught under the male governance of head teachers, inspectors, and the men at head office; they were minimally trained as pupil-teachers; confined to separate and unequal career paths; denied access to headships; paid at best four-fifths of the male rate; and subject to informal and formal marriage bars.[8] The terms under which women were to be tolerated in the teaching profession were clear. They were to teach briefly, on low salaries, with minimal prospects for advancement, before fulfilling their "natural destinies" as wives and mothers.

Under these ground rules, by the end of the nineteenth century, a three-caste system of female teachers had emerged: young women who taught briefly before marriage and never taught again; married women who for reasons of personal misfortune taught as temporaries in schools where nobody else would take the job; and the spinster teachers who, having by general consent failed to find husbands, were in for the long haul. These three castes were clearly visible when I began teaching in the 1960s.

Nevertheless, these teaching women had one thing in common; at whatever social level they emerged, they were the high achievers. In the one-teacher bush school, the smartest girl in grade eight became the pupil-teacher; the top student of the country high school and country convent school went on to the regional teachers' college; and women graduates of Australia's universities overwhelmingly became teachers. As high achieving women a certain ambiguity swirled around them, and it is to that "certain ambiguity" that I will now turn.

For those who wish to retain the status quo, educating women has always been a risky business, especially when that education carries with it the possibility of economic independence. By and large, the conservative opponents of women's higher education in the eighteenth and nineteenth centuries got it right. They feared that women educated on a par with men would not wish to marry or make troublesome wives if they did. And all demographic studies from the 1880s onwards tell us that highly educated women are less inclined to marry and have fewer children when they do marry. The *Age* cartoonist Leunig is of the opinion that they also make less than adequate wives and mothers. Underpinning those demographics are a psychology of independence and a sense of entitlement to a better life.

The same fears concerning the education of women can be observed in the brutal Taliban regime until recently in the ascendancy in Afghanistan where women have been denied education and the right to work for a living. The deficiencies of another culture are easier to spot than our own, but a fall in the birthrate can still generate a moral panic in Australia. When the Australian Bureau of Statistics released the bad news in April 2000 the media took up the issue with enthusiasm. As Fiona Stewart commented in the *Age*: "It has been the stark gulf in procreation trends between tertiary-educated and 'other' women that has caught the public's imagination."[9] Professor Jerzy Zubrzycki declared that this accelerating trend in fertility decline "should be linked with a moral crisis eroding the foundations of family and public life ... [and] a selfish narcissism that contributes to undermining the family unit."[10]

Thus the Western liberal democratic State has inherent difficulties with the educated woman. No-one now disputes women's entitlement to equality of education with men, but should they shirk their responsibilities to give birth, the ground begins to move under our feet. These tensions go back to the beginnings of women's higher education in Australia. There was no shortage of liberal-minded men willing to sponsor women into the colonial universities of Melbourne, Sydney, and Adelaide in the 1880s, among them Charles Pearson in Victoria, William Windeyer in New South Wales, and Samuel Way in South Australia.[11] Indeed there was no organized feminist movement in Australia when women were admitted to the Universities of Melbourne and Sydney in 1881 or when the first academic secondary schools for girls were established: Presbyterian Ladies' College, Melbourne in 1875; Brisbane Girls' Grammar School in the same year; the Advanced School for Girls, Adelaide in 1879; and Sydney Girls' High School in 1884. The same is true of the Married Women's Property Acts passed in those decades.

Yet the ensuing woman suffrage movement, in effect a demand by women to enter the public world of men, proved to be far more contentious than a few bluestockings doing Arts degrees.[12] The assumption was that if women were permitted to meddle in the affairs of men they would soon desert the private sphere of home and family. As the Australian colonies groped their way towards federation in 1901 the birth rate was falling, there were fears of the Asianization of white Australia, and a psychology of war had seeped into the colonial consciousness as conflict between Britain and Germany loomed ever closer. These are the preconditions for a "back to the kitchen" rallying cry in any era. It is small wonder that votes for women were argued through on the essentially conservative grounds of women's capacity for "public housekeeping"—that is, that women had special moral qualities developed in the private sphere which they would now employ to spruce up the public sphere.

Even so, a link was quickly made between women's demand for citizenship and the new educational opportunities that they had enjoyed since the 1880s. Newspaper editors, clergymen, and even directors of education argued that this education business had gone too far. The emphasis in the debate shifted from whether women *could* succeed in masculine education (proved beyond doubt by their conspicuous success in recent years) to whether they *should* succeed, given their destinies as wives and mothers. The Edwardian era produced insistent discourses around the desirability of marriage, the sanctity of marriage, and the separate spheres of men and women within marriage. Put another way, in the same decades that professional life became a possibility for women, formal and informal marriage bars emerged to block the way. It still astonishes me that, by and large, the marriage bars held firm until the 1970s when they became the prime target of the second women's movement. Against this background the women's profession of teaching has been shaped and reshaped. Now I want to take a closer look at my three-caste system of women teachers.

The Revolving Door

By far the most numerous were the women who entered teaching through a revolving door; that is, they taught for a short time, then married, never to return. A psychology of transience developed early in the teaching profession and it has endured. Though this psychology of transience was the inevitable result of the marriage bars, it was soon turned against the women themselves. After all, why invest heavily in women when they will only marry and leave the profession? It was this mindset which slowly eroded the training of primary teachers from its high point under two outstanding principals, Dr. John Smyth at Melbourne Teachers' College and Dr. Alexander Mackie at Sydney Teachers' College in the first decades of the twentieth century.

I have great respect for these young women who went through the revolving door in and out of teaching. Everybody knew but nobody said that they were recruited to staff remote bush schools where nobody else would teach. In 1910, Alfred Williams, director of education in South Australia, wrote to Elsie X, then teaching at Keyneton:

> In consequence of the very low attendance at Keyneton it is necessary that I should transfer you elsewhere, at any rate, temporarily. I propose to send you to Yorke's Peninsula, until the June vacation, to take charge of the two half time schools at Koolywurtie and Minlacowie. Immediately I receive word that the building at the latter place is ready I will wire you to proceed.

You will therefore make your arrangements and be ready when called upon. You will go by steamer [from] Juno to Stansbury and thence per coach to Minlaton, where you will be met by Mr. Fred Edwards, with whom you will lodge.[13]

All did not go smoothly. Elsie found that she was expected to travel seven and a half miles to and from the Koolywurtie school on horse back (horse-back riding was an accomplishment which she did not possess) and to share a bedroom with two of her pupils, the Edwards daughters, aged fourteen and seven years. Apparently these sleeping arrangements were tolerated by the Department, as the pro forma which Williams had devised for those intending to board the teacher inquired whether she was to share a room and if so, with whom? Young teachers walked unsuspecting into mine fields of local feuds and ancient enmities. Aloise X of Boowillia School was unaccountably persecuted by a family who encouraged their children to defy her in the school. At length the chairman of the Board of Advice wrote to the Department:

The ... trouble as far as Mr. Dee is concerned appears to be in the following, as far as we can ascertain, Miss X is not a Catholic and he would like a Catholic teacher ... and she is engaged, or about to be, to a Mr. Harding, a young farmer of very good standing and reputation, who is Mr. Dee's neighbour and against whose family Mr. Dee had a law suit at one time, which Dee lost, and as he cannot avenge himself otherwise he is trying to do it through Miss X by annoying her in every way he can.[14]

At its most elemental this encounter with frontier life implicated the young woman teacher in the culture clashes between Aboriginal and white settler Australians as railway construction pushed north towards Alice Springs and west across the Nullabor Plains. In 1920 Alice Ferber wrote from Oodnadatta to the Department in Adelaide that the white parents at the school were insisting that she exclude the children of mixed Afghan, Aboriginal, and Chinese descent on the grounds that they were "known to be suffering from the effects of venereal disease in their parents."[15] Courageously, in the circumstances of a small country town, Ferber refused. She was vindicated when Dr. Gertrude Halley, first medical inspector for the South Australian Education Department, visited Oodnadatta and reported that the children in question were healthy and better dressed than the white children. Education Departments around Australia had no legal right to exclude these children, but they were duplicitous in the extreme, ignoring instances where parents had successfully excluded the children and scapegoating teachers caught in the middle. Alice Ferber married in the next year and left the service. Another young teacher, Mary Bennett, was so appalled by what she witnessed while teaching on the black-white frontier in Western Australia that she devoted her life to advocacy of the black peoples' cause.[16] In 1933 she travelled to Britain to speak on the issue to the British Commonwealth League, and the subsequent coverage in the British press embarrassed the Australian Government into appointing a royal commission into the treatment of indigenous Australians in Western Australia.[17]

Young women teachers suffered unwelcome sexual advances, even rape, by the men of the households in which they boarded; others broke down from the sheer loneliness and hardship of their lives. In extreme cases, some committed suicide. In belated recognition of their plight most Australian States appointed female welfare officers in the interwar years. But most young women coped and there is ample oral history to testify that they did indeed see teaching as an interlude between school and marriage. Under the circumstances, a psychology of transience was no bad thing. An engagement ring on the finger could be used as a talisman against infant mistress, headmaster, and inspector. Nor should we assume that the experience of "being a teacher" ended with resignation from the Department upon marriage. Women who had been teachers insisted that their own children be well educated. Teacher activist Florence Johnson and her married sister, ex-teacher Minnie McNaughton, were instrumental in the foundation of the Victorian Federation of Mothers' Clubs in 1925, a development greeted with alarm by the Victorian Education Department.[18] Minnie's lifetime commitment to the Federation and the welfare of children in State schools began a tradition in which ex-Premier of Victoria Joan Kirner is a distinguished example. Ex-teachers wrote books for children, taught in Sunday schools and enlivened the local Country Women's Association. So pervasive is the figure of the ex-lady teacher in Australian society that Patrick White, winner of the Nobel Prize for Literature, endowed his hero Stan Parker with a teacher mother who "did not go much with the other women" and read him Shakespeare, dooming him to his quest for grace in the unlikely setting of Castle Hill.[19] Indeed it was generally accepted that when the young lady teacher married into a farming family both the standard of the gene pool and the standard of agriculture rose significantly.

Temporary Married Women Teachers

It took me some time to understand that marriage bars in the various teaching services were formalized only when the informal bars came under challenge. Thus in Western Australia a marriage bar was instituted by regulation during World War I when it became apparent that married teachers would be needed to replace men going off to the front. All States used married women as a reserve army of temporary, cheap and malleable labour, peaking of course in wartime.

The working of the marriage bar is best documented in the case of New South Wales where a formal ban was not instituted until 1932.[20] Until that time the Department had relied upon informal sanctions. During the Depression of the 1930s women began to stay on after marriage in greater numbers, sparking a political row over the fate of the unemployed exit students from Sydney Teachers' College. The conservative Stevens government faced a concerted campaign against the legislation, led by the women's caucus of the New South Wales Teachers' Federation and the Sydney feminist movement led by Mrs. Jessie Street. The case was eloquently put by teacher and labour activist Clarice McNamara:

> The case for the women teachers is the case for all womankind. Legislation like the Married Women Teachers Act is the first step towards putting back the clock of emancipation and self-respect for every married woman who wants to enjoy economic independence, and that widening of mind and vision that comes with following a career outside the home .... The great and noble army of fighters and writers for the cause of women's rights—the Olive Schreiners, the Pankhursts and the Rose Scotts—would weep in despair to behold the retrogression of such legislation as the NSW Married Women Teachers Act.[21]

The Act was not repealed until 1947.

The documentation generated by the Act reveals the often-harrowing circumstances that led women to accept the oppressive conditions of temporary service offered by the New South Wales Education Department. Subsequent to the Act, all married women could apply for temporary employment, but they were subject to a hardship clause under which they were required to fill out yearly statutory declarations giving in detail the economic grounds for their applications. These statutory declarations, some thousands of them, have survived in the State Archives of New South Wales.[22] They provide a snapshot of New South Wales society in the depth of the Depression of the 1930s. Women teachers had married into all strata of the social structure, from the Macquarie Street medical establishment to the poorest share farmers in remote corners of the State. As supplicants to the Public Service Commissioner, the women were obliged to give intimate details of their circumstances that they pleaded should remain confidential. Many were supporting unemployed or irregularly employed husbands, children, and other relatives. Others were supporting husbands incapacitated in World War I. Mrs. X had three teenage children. The sole means of support from her husband was a war pension for partial blindness contracted while serving with the Australian Imperial Force. From her meagre teacher's salary she was paying off a home. Mrs. Y's husband had been in sugar farming before enlisting. His experiences as a prisoner of war had caused a "serious nervous derangement ... which takes the form of great depression and uncontrollable weeping ... aggravated by the position of dependence into which circumstances and economic conditions have forced him." Only when her position as a teacher came under threat did he apply for a war pension. Many women testified that they had returned to teaching only when their husband's health had broken down. Other women wrote that they had married and outlaid money in buying and establishing homes on the understanding that their positions were permanent. Some were obliged to admit that their marriages had broken down, a cause for shame and secrecy in the interwar years.

For the most part, the need to appear before the Public Service Commissioner as supplicants tempered the anger many must have privately felt. One exception was Thelma Hitchcock, headmistress of Parramatta Girls' Public School, active in both the Teachers' Federation and the United Associations of Women in support of the married women. She was more forthright:

> I desire to protest forcibly and emphatically against your wickedly unjust proposal to dismiss me, a proved and experienced teacher of twenty-five years experience. I have committed no offence nor broken any regulations. Neither have I failed in any respect to carry out the duties of my position. I have been assured by numerous inspectors that my work is done well. Yet I am to be subjected to the indignity and shame of a summary dismissal. My chosen career is to be ended thus depriving me of the results of twenty years' striving to obtain the position I now hold—that of mistress [head] of a first-class school.

In all States during World War II, women who married were routinely offered employment on a temporary basis, and this continued into the 1950s when the postwar baby boom and the flood of immigration strained both State and Catholic systems to bursting point. In each State the removal of the marriage bars was grudging (1947 in New South Wales, 1956 in Victoria, later in the other States), and only achieved when the percentage of married women employed as temporaries assumed the status of a public scandal.[23]

The Spinster Teachers

Inevitably, the most conspicuous and contentious group were the spinster teachers in for the long haul. From the 1880s to the 1970s, generations of a potential female intelligentsia were gathered into the teaching profession. With nurses they were the prototype of the professional woman in Australia, yet they are scarcely noticed in the new history of twentieth century women that is currently being written both in Australia and overseas. I want to look briefly at some of that new history, work that in a variety of ways explores the question of women's identity in twentieth-century Australia.

Marilyn Lake, in her recent book *Getting Equal*, is concerned with the nature of women's political activity after the vote was won.[24] To those of us working on the history of women teachers' politics, the connections are potentially exciting. Lake's work is implicitly grounded in a search for continuity between the women's movement of the turn of the century (the suffrage movement) and the women's movement in the 1970s. My generation of women, the footsloggers of the second women's movement, had no sense of continuity with former generations of feminist woman and no appreciation of what they had achieved for us. Our sense of discontinuity was complete. Marilyn Lake now argues against this assumption of historical discontinuity. She argues that post suffrage women did indeed take up that pledge to housekeep in the public sphere. It is now clear that the interwar years produced another generation of feminist leaders. Many of them were, significantly, married women with independent means: Jessie Street in New South Wales; Bessie Rischbieth in Western Australia; Edith Jones in Victoria. There was a flowering of women's organizations, among them the National Council of Women, the United Associations of Women and the Australian League of Women Voters. They were concerned to educate women to exercise their new rights as citizens of the democratic State and to fight for the rights of all women, married and unmarried, to full equality with men. Thus Lake argues that a specific politics of suffrage transformed itself into an eclectic politics of citizenship. She also identifies an enduring dilemma for women: was the achievement of full equality with men to be achieved through a separate "women's" politics (implicit in those organizations) or through a politics of social class and therefore of party affiliation alongside men?

In contrast, Drusilla Modjeska explores the question of women's identity in the post suffrage era by looking at the lives of Australia's women artists and writers in the interwar years: among the artists were Margaret Preston, Thea Proctor, Clarice Beckett and Grace Cossington Smith; among the writers were Miles Franklin, Eleanor Dark, Katharine Susannah Prichard and Christina Stead. I am interested in Modjeska's work because it deals with a female intelligentsia, alongside the teaching women, sometimes converging, mostly diverging, but sharing the characteristics of a sub-culture of women with the potential to challenge the dominance of men in the intellectual and cultural spheres. In her two studies, *Exiles at Home* and *Stravinsky's Lunch,* Modjeska makes a case for what she terms a crisis of masculinity caused by the devastation of World War I—that catastrophic sacrifice of a whole generation of young men who did not return, and the physical and psychological trauma of many who did (glimpsed briefly in those statutory declarations).[25] In this historical and cultural space, she argues, an extraordinary generation of creative women emerged, producing the most interesting and challenging Australian art and literature of the period. In Modjeska's words, they

> inhabited a psychic space, carved out with difficulty, between intimate lives lived largely without the support of men, and public lives that claimed for them an identity as modern and independent .... With their city studios, their exhibitions and their visibility in women's magazines these artist-women undercut the stigma of the spinster, and made good lives for themselves.[26]

She makes a similar case for the women writers of the period. Modjeska is only one of a number of writers, most recently Frank Moorhouse,[27] to suggest that in the aftermath of World War I the Western nations were more open to what are termed the "feminine" values of caring, values manifested in the League of Nations, the anti-Fascist movements and the peace movements which, like Modjeska's flowering of a female aesthetic, were snuffed out by World War II and the Cold War.

Where Marilyn Lake is concerned with the political history of women in the twentieth century and Drusilla Modjeska with their cultural and creative history, Sheila Jeffreys is centrally concerned with the depiction of women as sexual beings in the twentieth century. In her wonderfully titled book *The Spinster and Her Enemies* Jeffreys is not specifically concerned with Australian society.[28] She argues more generally that women who live without men are regarded differently in different historical periods. She argues that the early twentieth century was singularly inhospitable to the woman alone, that the sexologists such as Havelock Ellis demonized the single woman in new ways— the "dried out prune" theory of the celibate woman, if you like. This is the psycho-medical work necessary to those discourses surrounding the desirability of marriage to which I referred earlier. Underpinning Jeffreys' work is the astute observation that it is not sufficient to put in place marriage bars, but to invade the inner life of young women, instilling a horror of spinsterhood that in turn is mapped on to the independent, professional woman. The relevance of this work to my spinster teachers should be obvious.[29]

These texts allow us to think about women teachers in some intriguing ways. It is, I think, an unintended effect of Lake's political history to overlook the women teachers. They did not need to be educated for citizenship. They were not asking for entry to the public sphere or knocking on the doors of a new profession. They were fighting old battles on familiar terrain; indeed in the same decades that Modjeska suggests were more hospitable to women, teachers experienced a backlash against their demands for equality within the profession as the men returning from the war re-asserted their status—assisted, of course, by repatriation legislation which also gave them precedence over men who did not enlist.

Women teachers' politics had a long history.[30] The Victorian Lady Teachers' Association (VLTA) was formed in 1885, among the first women's industrial unions in Australia, to protest against their grossly unequal treatment under the *Public Service Act* of 1883. They took their first petition to Parliament in 1886. The marriage bars of 1889 and 1894 expelled hundreds of their foundation members, including their president, Mrs. Lucy Tisdall. Savage Depression economies of the 1890s degraded the conditions of all teachers, but women were the hardest hit; they did not regain their four-fifths salary entitlement until 1918. By that year, according to their own meticulous calculations, the majority were doomed to spend a lifetime in the lowest classification on salaries below those of barmaids and stenographers. Across the decades they organized and they fought—petitions to Parliament, approaches to local members, deputations to minister and director, letters to the press. The detailed archival research upon which I base these claims is

Marjorie Theobald

*3.1. Florence Johnson, teacher, feminist and union organizer.
Courtesy State Library of Victoria.*

depressing in the extreme. They were consistently betrayed by their male colleagues who feared that equal pay and equal career structures would degrade their own conditions. The VLTA affiliated reluctantly with the main teachers' union in 1907, and walked out again in protest in 1908, affiliated again in 1920 and broke away in 1924, significantly by this time known as the Victorian *Women* Teachers Association (VWTA).[31] In 1937 Phebe Watson led over 600 women out of the South Australian union to form the Women Teachers' Guild. Both the Victorian and the South Australian women were well aware that the British National Union of Women Teachers had seceded from the National Union of Teachers in 1920.

President of the break away VWTA, Florence Johnson, was indeed a twentieth-century woman in search of a life larger than teaching.[32] Born into a working-class family in Port Melbourne in 1884, she was appointed a pupil-teacher at South Preston State School in 1900. As the Victorian Education Department had been savagely restructured during the economic depression of the 1890s this was the worst possible time to enter the profession. Florence never went to teachers' college and was deeply suspicious of those who did; she was never promoted beyond the fifth class. She was active in the VLTA by 1908, the stormy year in which the women walked out of the union. Her family history of labour activism and the material conditions of her teaching life produced in Johnson an outspoken, sometimes arrogant militancy which was a complete break with the genteel ways of the VLTA. In a palace coup in 1926 she drove from the VWTA an old guard of women who were distressed at her confrontationist tactics and mistrusted her agenda to align teacher politics with the Labor Party.[33] Outrageously for the times, Johnson repeatedly called for a royal commission into the administration of the Education Department. Not surprisingly, she was detested by Director of Education, Frank Tate, by then at the end of his career and in hopes of a knighthood. She was also detested by the leadership of the Victorian Teachers' Union whom she publicly branded as weak, vacillating, and sycophantic. Johnson twice resigned from the Department to take up paid positions as a union organizer and established her credentials as a fiery and effective public speaker on behalf of working women and men.[34] In 1927 Johnson stood unsuccessfully as an independent Labor candidate for the seat of St Kilda.[35] She was deeply hurt by the failure of the Labor Party to endorse her candidature, given the presence on the Central Executive of two prominent feminists, Jean Daley and Muriel Heagney. Women's organizations involved in the politics of citizenship promoted several woman as parliamentary candidates in these years, among them prominent members of the teaching profession Martha Simpson in New South Wales and May Mills in South Australia. Dorothy Tangney, elected as a Labor senator for Western Australia in 1943, was a schoolteacher.

In each State women did remain within the unions, forming sub-branches around their sectional interests: infant mistresses, women assistants and so on. Hettie Gilbert became president of the Victorian Teachers' Union during World War II; Ruth Don became president of the Queensland Teachers' Union in 1951. For other women their union activism was integral to a wider politics of the left that Modjeska suggests was infused with the values of the feminine. This was an alignment for which they sometimes paid dearly. In 1932 Beatrice Taylor, a teacher at the Paddington Junior Technical School, was suspended by the New South Wales Education Department for speaking from the public platform about her trip to Russia as a member of the first Friends of the Soviet Union delegation.[36] A public campaign was mounted on her behalf led by the Beatrice Taylor Defence Committee under the leadership of Sam Lewis and the New South Wales Teachers' Federation. At a Public Service Board inquiry, Taylor was skillfully represented by Clive Evatt and the case against her collapsed. In 1954 Margaret Kent Hughes was escorted from the premises of Fort Street Girls High School to give evidence before the Royal Commission on Espionage;[37] Principal of Flemington Girls' High School, Doris McRae, suffered a similar public humiliation when her name was submitted to the 1949 Victorian Enquiry into Communism. Though she was exonerated by an Education Department inquiry she chose to resign and continue her activism outside the system.[38]

Lucy Woodcock was senior vice-president of the New South Wales Teachers' Federation for three decades, though she never became president. Her causes and affiliations are also a snapshot of the left intelligentsia in the interwar years. For much of her career she was also headmistress of the Erskineville Public School, where she was not afraid to comment publicly on the pitiable condition of the families and the children in her constituency. Woodcock retired in 1953 and, at a time when most of us are contemplating the quiet life, she embarked on a full-time career as a feminist and activist. In 1956 she succeeded Jessie Street as president of the United Associations of Women. Not surprisingly, Lucy Woodcock has an Australian Security Intelligence Organization file of over a thousand pages.[39]

I want to make a plea for the inclusion of women teachers' activism in the wider history of women's politics in the twentieth century. At the very least, it is clear that their activism did converge with the politics of citizenship that Marilyn Lake has restored to the historical record. Women teachers' organizations and individual teachers were active within the National Council of Women, the Pan Pacific Women's Conference, and the Australian Women Graduates Association, among many other organizations. As with the campaign against the *New South Wales Married Women Teachers Act* they made common cause with the wider feminist movement when the opportunity arose. They also had to choose between a separate women's politics and a common front with their male colleagues. A women's caucus within the teachers' unions led inevitably to a sense of frustration that the men did not take their concerns seriously; a separate women's politics outside the union risked marginalization and fragmentation, especially after access to arbitration was granted to the teaching profession. Florence Johnson's sometimes frenetic activism, which eventually undermined her health, demarcates the limits of hope for women's politics in the interwar years.

Yet they also give us a different perspective on women's political activity in the twentieth century. Women teachers worked within State bureaucracies that were obliged to reproduce inequality by the rule book. The documentary evidence of their dealings with the women is voluminous. The code is hard to crack but there are rich pickings in the archives of the education departments for those who want to understand the strange fate of feminism between those two women's movements.

For women like Lucy Woodcock, Phebe Watson, and Florence Johnson political activism helped to sustain what was, in Drusilla Modjeska's terms, a distinctive sub-culture, which undercut the stigma of the single woman. Their activism gave them a sense of purpose beyond the frustrations of the teaching life; it created networks of women which went beyond the confines of the school; there was mutual support in hard times; friendships lasted for a life time; lives were shared in the woman-centered world sensitively explored by Barbara Falk in her recent biography of headmistress of Melbourne Girls' Grammar School Dorothy Ross.[40]

Against the odds, women who were gifted artists, musicians, and writers taught in schools and still belonged to the world that Modjeska claims for creative women in the interwar years. Dymphna Cusack published several novels while teaching in New South Wales high schools.[41] Her play, *Morning Sacrifice*, was a barely disguised depiction of her own experiences teaching in girls' schools, the identity of the loathsome headmistress and her sidekicks a matter for lively conjecture at the time. Flora Eldershaw taught at Presbyterian Ladies College, Croydon, when she was writing her novels with Marjorie Barnard, and was also president of the Fellowship of Australian Writers.[42] Amy Witting tried but failed to write a novel while teaching in New South Wales high schools.[43]

Drusilla Modjeska's claim for the ascendancy of feminine values in the interwar years could also be made for educational thinking and practice in the same decades. Collective remorse at the horrors of World War I and the subsequent rise of fascism and nazism encouraged a belief that schools had a role to play in educating future citizens who would ensure that these things did not happen again. That cluster of ideas under the rubric of "alternative education" re-emerged strongly in the interwar years and women were leaders in this movement. Kathleen Gilman Jones and Dorothy Ross at Melbourne Girls' Grammar, Constance Tisdall at Rosbercan, Margaret Lyttle at Preshil, and Winifred West at Frensham were only the most prominent of the women whose passion for education shaped their lives and drew others into their sphere.[44]

In the conventional setting of the school, however, an aesthetic of the teaching life was more difficult to achieve. There was dissonance between the teacher as the 'modern woman' and the actual work of teaching. The requirement of celibacy and the demand for self-censure in behaviour, dress, and demeanor in women teachers were increasingly at odds with the greater freedoms won by women after World War I. Generations of school girls experienced on a daily basis an ambivalence towards these women who were often the only independent women they knew, but who remained, incontrovertibly, old maids.

Beatrice Faust captures this ambivalence in her memoir of the teachers at MacRobertson Girls' High School in the 1950s:

> Most of the MacRob staff were outstanding and I could give a score of vignettes of lovable, admirable, or simply memorable women ... Miss Bowden, tall, rawboned and withered, wore a black suit and a bowler hat that seemed eccentric except that it suited her individuality. She must once have had a pink and white rose-petal complexion and her voice was as delicately refined as an etching in dry-point. She had a wonderfully lucid mind that inspired respectful imitation in some of us, although others found her pukka British aloofness so intimidating that they could not learn from her. ... Some sixth-formers polarised around Mrs. Dow ("Frow"), who was blonde, bosomy and romantic. Others gravitated to Miss Anchen

who was brunette, thin and intellectual. Both taught English and both were splendid teachers. I enjoyed Mrs. Dow, but I modelled myself on Miss Anchen ... Here was another lucid, meticulous, resilient thinker. If Frow Dow was Dionysian, Mollie Anchen was Apollonian.[45]

Gwyn Dow would have liked that, I think.

Though the girls at MacRob did not know it, behind the eccentric Dr. Jean Bowden stood generations of scholar spinsters reaching back to the beginnings of that movement for the higher education of women that I spoke about earlier. The profession of secondary teaching was indeed grounded in the emancipation of women. The early girls' schools and the elite State high schools reaped a rich harvest of female graduates, many with Honours and Masters degrees. They were recruited from a higher social class; by historical accident they were steeped in the romance of feminism; they were inclined to equate the emancipation of women with the attainments of scholarship; and they remained, defiantly, single.

A small aristocracy of these women came from the Mecca of women's education in the Empire, Cambridge University.[46] Charles Lilley, who founded Brisbane Girls' Grammar School in 1875, recruited through Girton College, and there were several Cambridge women on the staff in the nineteenth century. Andrew Harper of Presbyterian Ladies' College, Melbourne, visited the women's colleges personally and recruited Charlotte Pells who later became head of Brisbane Girls' Grammar School. Maryborough Girls' Grammar School appointed a Newnham woman, Caroline Darling, who is described in the diary of her friend Beatrice Webb as coarsened by the vulgarity of a small Australian town.[47] Emily Hensley of Newnham was principal of Janet Clarke Hall and the founding principal of Melbourne Girls' Grammar School, which she called Merton Hall and where she was followed in 1914 by another Newnhamite, Kathleen Gilman Jones.[48] As late as the 1930s James Darling's sister Margaret, another Cambridge woman, was offered three prestigious headmistress-ships while she was staying with him at Geelong Grammar.[49]

Other graduate teachers did not have the luxury of full-time university study. It is salutary to realize that the women who rose to the top in the Victorian State service—women like Christina Montgomery, Julia Flynn, and Mary Hutton—completed degrees while teaching in the classroom.

For these spinster scholars the secondary school was dangerous territory. In the teeming life of the secondary school a love of scholarship is often the first casualty. These women kept up with their field as best they could, wrote textbooks, supported subject associations, and served on curriculum committees and examination boards. This was also the first generation of women teachers to understand that the precious gifts of celibacy, feminism and scholarship had limited appeal to the Australian schoolgirl. Unlike Modjeska's artists and writers they could not separate their lives from their task as teachers. As Beatrice Faust reminds us, in the hothouse of the all-female school the exchange between teacher and taught was negotiated on a daily basis. Bodies were judged, clothes were scrutinised; withered cheeks and bowler hats had no part in the imagined future.

But the scholar spinsters did achieve a kind of coterie feminism, reaching across the classroom to the girls who could imagine a future of independence and achievement. What they could not be expected to achieve single-handed was that explosion of women's consciousness which ignited the women's movement of the 1970s.

Conclusion

I want to return now to the Senate inquiry that so annoyed me in 1998. By now it should be apparent why committees of inquiry do not seek out my testimony on matters of current concern. With my fellow historians I have never acquired the art of the dot point summary or the bottom line. But I hope I have established that it is impossible to understand the teaching profession if we do not understand that gender is an important dynamic. A genderless, one-size-fits-all teacher will not do. In a profession that depends crucially upon the labour of women, it is imperative that policy makers understand the wider context of women's lives. Members of the Senate inquiry might protest that things have changed, that the ruthless policing of women teachers into categories of "married" and "unmarried" is a distant memory. With all other women, teachers are protected by equal opportunity legislation that forbids discrimination on grounds of marital status and mandates equal pay for equal work. Women have access to reliable contraception and the stigma of the working mother has all but disappeared. Married women are now central to, not marginal to, the teaching profession. But this is simply to say that the context for women's work in teaching has changed, and it is this new context that must be understood. For one hundred and fifty years we have taken for granted the presence of women in our schools, but we are now on dangerous ground. As other avenues are open to them, they are no longer hostage to the profession. High achieving girls have already left teaching. The Catholic Sisters have also left. The nurses have demonstrated what happens to a woman's profession when conditions become degraded and there are other options for intelligent and well-educated women.

And finally, I offer my research as a tribute to women teachers in the past. I make no spurious claims of sisterhood with the women whose lives I have appropriated, nor do I assume that they would wish to know themselves as I have depicted them. And I hope that women teachers in the future will remain as they were in the past: truculent, enigmatic and elusive.

Notes

[1] *A Class Act: Senate Inquiry into the Status of the Teaching Profession*, Australian

Government Printer, Canberra, 1998. This chapter was first written and delivered as the Fink Memorial Lecture at the University of Melbourne in 2000. This accounts in part for the personal style in which it is written. There is, however, a more compelling reason for my presence in the chapter. I began my career as a school teacher and I am coming to the end of it as a feminist academic who writes about the history of school teachers. I am therefore writing about myself. I now agree with Theodore Zeldin that history is in some sense autobiography. This in no way compromises the meticulous archival research upon which my work is based or the meanings which I draw from those sources. Feminist historians will recognize the wider debates on the meanings of subjectivity and objectivity that have informed our work over the last two decades. To create my history in a personal register and then to step back and disguise it in the third person would be unnecessary and dishonest. I thank the editors for their forbearance in this matter.

[2] Ibid, ch. 5, p. 23.
[3] Ibid, ch. 1, p. 1.
[4] Ibid, ch. 6, p. 20.
[5] Ibid, ch. 5, p. 26.
[6] A. G. Austin, *Australian Education 1788-1900: Church, State and Public Education in Colonial Australia* (Melbourne: Pitman, 1961).
[7] R. Fogarty, *Catholic Education in Australia 1806-1950* (Melbourne: Melbourne University Press, 1959).
[8] M. Theobald, *Knowing Women: Origins of Women's Education in Nineteenth-Century Australia* (Melbourne: Cambridge University Press, 1996) ch. 5.
[9] *Age*, 6 April 2000.
[10] *Age*, 29 November 2000.
[11] Theobald, *Knowing Women*, ch. 3.
[12] Marilyn Lake, *Getting Equal: The History of Australian Feminism* (Sydney: Allen and Unwin, 2000).
[13] GRG/18/2, Schools Correspondence, no. 1634, 1910, Public Record Office of South Australia.
[14] Ibid, no. 2460, 1910.
[15] For a fuller discussion of this case see M. Theobald, "The Afghan Children of Oodnadatta: Gender and Ethnicity in the History of Australian Education," *Paedagogica Historica*, 37, 1, 2001, pp. 211-230. "Afghan" was the generic name bestowed on the men who came to nineteenth-century Australia from Afghanistan and India to establish camel transport in the semi-arid and desert regions. They were crucial to the pastoral and mining industries, and in the construction of the overland telegraph and the railways that eventually replaced them. Chinese Australians had been present in large numbers since the gold rushes of the 1850s. The immigration of both groups was severely curtailed under the *Federal Immigration Restriction Act* of 1901. Denied the right to bring wives and families to Australia many intermarried or co-habited with Aboriginal Australians. Their mixed race children were seen as a threat to the future of the preferred white Australia.
[16] Fiona Paisley, *Loving Protection? Australian Feminism and Aboriginal Women's Rights, 1919-1939* (Melbourne: Melbourne University Press, 2000), passim.
[17] Royal Commission into the Status and Conditions of Aborigines in Western Australia, 1934.
[18] *Victorian Federation of Mothers' Clubs Quarterly Review* (December 1944): 10.

[19] Patrick White, *The Tree of Man* (Harmondworth: Penguin, 1967 ed.), 11-12.
[20] For a detailed account see M. Theobald and D. Dwyer, "An Episode in Feminist Politics: The Married Women (Lecturers and Teachers) Act, 1932-47," *Labour History* 76 (1999): 59-77.
[21] Ibid, p. 63.
[22] Public Service Board records, 8/1187A, Married Women Teachers' Statutory Declarations, State Archives of NSW. All material below is from these files.
[23] I have been unable to find evidence of a formal marriage bar in Tasmania.
[24] Lake, *Getting Equal*, passim.
[25] Drusilla Modjeska, *Stravinsky's Lunch* (Sydney: Picador, 1999); *Exiles at Home: Australian Women Writers, 1925-1945* (Sydney: Angus and Robertson, 1981).
[26] Modjeska, *Stravinsky's Lunch*, p. 185.
[27] I refer here to Frank Moorhouse's recent League of Nations novels with their female hero, Edith Campbell: *Grand Day* (Sydney: Random House, 1997), and *Dark Palace* (Sydney: Random House, 2000).
[28] Sheila Jeffreys, *The Spinster and Her Enemies: Feminism and Sexuality, 1880-1930* (London: Pandora Press, 1985).
[29] For an overview of feminist theorizing about female sexualities, see *Resources for Feminist Research/Documentation sur la recherche féministe*, 19, 3 & 4, (1990), Special issue: Confronting Heterosexuality.
[30] Theobald, *Knowing Women*, ch. 5.
[31] The name of the teachers' union and the roll call of its affiliates changed several times in these years, but it became the Victorian Teachers' Union in 1926. There is room for debate as to whether the VWTA was a direct descendent of the earlier VLTA. The breakaway women claimed that it was; their enemies claimed that it was not.
[32] At the point of secession in 1924 Johnson was paid women's organizer for the main teachers' union, and she continued as paid organizer/secretary for the VWTA. She later became president. For an account of her career see James Mcdonald, "Florence Johnson: Melbourne's Forgotten Feminist," *The Victorian Historical Journal* 51, 3 (August 1980): 131-48.
[33] As I have been unable to locate the records of the VWTA or its predecessor, the VLTA, my account of this episode is taken from Victorian Public Record Series 10537, Teachers' Associations files, item 62, 1926-29, Victorian Public Record Office. I have also used accounts of the episode in the *Argus* and *Age* from November 1926 to April 1927. The leadership group defeated by Johnson was led by Annie Fleming and Edith Coleman.
[34] For Johnson's career as an organizer for the Public Service Union I used the *Public Service Journal*, and for her career as women's organizer for the teachers' union I used the records of the Victorian Teachers' Union and its predecessors housed at the Butlin Archives at the ANU.
[35] Sources on Johnson's candidature are scarce. I used chiefly the daily newspapers for January-April 1927 and the Minutes of the Central Executive of the Victorian ALP, 1922-1928, MS 10398, State Library of Victoria.
[36] Theobald and Dwyer, "An Episode in Feminist Politics," 65.
[37] *Royal Commission on Espionage*, (Petrov Inquiry), Transcript of proceedings, pp. 2421-5, evidence by Margaret Kent Hughes, 8 March 1955.
[38] S. Fabian and M. Loh, *Left-Wing Ladies: The Union of Australian Women in Victoria, 1950-1998* (Melbourne: Hyland House, 2000), 26.

[39] For Lucy Woodcock's years in the NSW TF I used their papers in the Butlin Archives at the ANU. For her presidency of the United Associations of Women I used their papers in the Mitchell Library. Her ASIO file is in the National Archives of Australia, series A6119/87 (vol. 1), 2031 (vol. 2), and 2032 (vol. 3).

[40] Barbara Falk, *D. J.: Dorothy Jean Ross, 1891-1982* (Melbourne: Melbourne University Press, 2000), see especially ch. 6.

[41] Dymphna Cusack, *A Window in the Dark* (Canberra: National Library of Australia, 1991).

[42] Maryanne Dever, "Flora Sydney Eldershaw," *Australian Dictionary of Biography* (Melbourne: Melbourne University Press, 1996), 85-86.

[43] Amy Witting, *Faces and Voices: Collected Stories* (Melbourne: Viking/Penguin, 2000), xi.

[44] Rosbercon, Preshil and Frensham were privately owned schools founded by Tisdall, Lyttle and West respectively in the interwar years.

[45] Beatrice Faust, "Eggshell Psyche" in P. Grimshaw and L. Strahan, (eds.), *The Half-Open Door: Sixteen Modern Australian Women Look at Professional Life and Achievement* (Sydney: Hale and Iremonger, 1982), 238.

[46] Details of this Cambridge diaspora in Australia are from the published registers of the two colleges: *Newnham College Register, 1871-1971*, Newnham College, Cambridge, 1979; *Girton College Register, 1869-1946*, Girton College, Cambridge, 1948. See also Theobald, *Knowing Women*, ch. 4.

[47] N. and J. Mackenzie, eds., *All the Good Things of Life: The Diary of Beatrice Webb: Volume Two, 1892-1905* (London: Virago, 1986), 91.

[48] R. McCarthy and M. Theobald, eds., *Melbourne Girls' Grammar School: Centenary Essays, 1893-1993* (Melbourne: Hyland House, 1993), chs. 1-3.

[49] Peter Gronn, "Sister of an Educated Man: Margaret Robertson Darling at Corio, 1931-33," *History of Education Review* 20, 1 (1991): 4-21.

Cecilia Fryxell

The Life of a Swedish Educator

INGA ELGQVIST-SALTZMAN

How can teachers' life stories and documents from a local history of schooling be useful in the training of teachers for a new century? This question initiated a three-year project at Rostad, Kalmar Teacher Training College[1] in southern Sweden some years ago. Two researchers keenly interested in women's educational history and involved in current educational reform work turned to archives of the local educational history in collaboration with 20 education students.[2] The project, *Kalmar Teachers in Time and Space*, was a continuation of a course of research on generations of teachers trained at the local teacher training college focused on women teachers' lives, training, work, and status in society. The aim of the new study was to link historical sources with current developments in teacher training: the work of teachers in a 150-year perspective; the relationships among teachers, children, parents, and society, and the changing view of knowledge and pedagogy. In each year of the three-year project, the study focused on a particular theme linked to the life and work of a representative teacher.[3]

When the students, who are now active teachers in the Swedish comprehensive school system, evaluated their experiences in the project, they reported that historical perspectives were a great asset in their training. They found the historical roots of many contemporary educational questions that they themselves faced. They reported that a biographical approach made history comprehensible and concrete. Many expressed surprise over the wealth of knowledge they found in "old fogeys." Several students took particular interest in the pedagogical instructions to student teachers, dictated by Cecilia Fryxell, one of the main figures the project had chosen to focus on. These instructions were contained in a student's notebook from the mid-1850s. Despite the great difference in time and educational conditions, her advice

Inga Elgqvist-Saltzman

4.1. *Cecilia Fryxell during the heydays of Rostad.
Courtesy of the Museum of Kalmar.*

resonated with student teachers of today.

Cecilia Fryxell's power to catch the interest of different generations of Swedish student teachers inspired me to introduce her to an international audience in order to link her to the ongoing and promising work on women educators.[4] This chapter presents excerpts from Cecilia Fryxell's lessons as well as elements of her life and career and the educational and social context that shaped them.

Cecilia Fryxell's Instructions to Student Teachers

Cecilia Fryxell's "black box" contains archival material that have been preserved for decades in the cellar of Kalmar Teacher Training College.[5] The box contains several notebooks from lessons in the mid-1800s, letters, transcripts, and drafts as well as photographs collected by former principals of the College who wished to document the historical significance of Cecilia Fryxell's life and work.

Notebooks contain Fryxell's thoughts about key competencies for a teacher. These include both pedagogical elements of classroom management and instruction and character education for the students and the teacher. She instructed:

> Knowledge and talents alone do not make a competent schoolmistress. A schoolmistress may possess both knowledge and talent without for that reason possessing gifts for either teaching or education…
>
> All a schoolmistress's knowledge and talents are therefore like a locked-up treasure, a dark glass which does not admit light, or like a person whose speech organs are paralysed, if she cannot communicate them.

These wise words were written down by one of the students in the teacher training class that Cecilia Fryxell started at a time when Sweden had no formal training for women teachers and a time when girls' education generally was deficient and considered to be the duty of the family, without any state obligation.[6] The student's notes allow us to follow the rest of the lesson and learn what the gifts of communication are:

> The gift of being able to think correctly
> The gift of being able to think clearly
> The gift of being able to talk correctly, clearly and vividly
> The gift of having a friendly, understanding and patient love in order to be able to bring oneself down to the level of the children's thoughts.

Fryxell concludes:

> The gift of communication is thus one of a competent schoolmistress's required gifts. She must communicate to the children not only her own thoughts but also others' in a distinct and lively manner. How could she do this without being able to think plainly, clearly and distinctly herself?

The girl's notes continue:

> These gifts can to some extent be possessed by nature, but they must be consecrated, strengthened and enhanced by exercise, and it is certain that what is lacking can be achieved through the prayer of faith.

Cecilia Fryxell was a deeply religious woman. This is reflected in her description of a schoolmistress's daily tasks:

To teach and educate, which includes having an influence on the will-power and heart of the girls, of the children, so that their minds may be shaped to receive the knowledge of faith and truth and their hearts will be willing to do good so that they may lead a Godly life.

The instructions start with the importance of an ability to communicate education. This is followed by Fryxell's interpretation of the gifts that education in itself implies:

The gift of admonition
The gift of having a firm will
The gift of having an even temper
The gift of instilling trust
The gift of love and patience
The gift of wisdom.

Cecilia Fryxell let the girls write down the meaning of these gifts. As regards admonition her message is:

There are admonitions that scarcely make any impact on the mind, much less the will. They may be ever so long and ever so broad, or be filled with biblical language and fine maxims, yet are mere talk without pith, force, or end. In contrast, there are admonitions that go through marrow and bone even if they consist of but a few words. Those who just cry "Lord, Lord" may have moral talk, to be sure, but they do not have the gift of admonition. But those who increasingly penetrate into the word of God, who enter with increasing sincerity into His will and practise increasingly doing the will of the Holy One, they have and obtain the gift of admonition. *One word* from the mouth of a person who *walks in the truth* has more effect than a whole sermon from others.

The gift of instilling trust inspired the following reflection:

No position, no recommendations, no friends and patrons can help the schoolmistress who does not have the trust of the children and the parents. Unless the schoolmistress has the trust of the children, she can scarcely coerce, let alone educate.

Fryxell warned her students:

A distorted opinion of the means to acquire the children's trust is also to flatter them and teach them to have self-will as a way to win them. Yet this has precisely the reverse effect, and the proper trust must be won in a completely different manner.

The most important attributes were to have love for the children and to show it. Cecilia Fryxell talks about the divine love that is so strong that it educates the teacher and through her the children:

> This love includes patience, in this divine love there is such strength that it educates that of the teacher and through her that of the children, and every single person who has been educated in the true sense of this word has been brought up through this love.

The gift of wisdom meant being able to distinguish between the children's different hearts and dispositions and being able to treat each one according to its different nature—to be able to punish correctly and to reward correctly, at the right time and in the right way.

As an experienced teacher, Cecilia Fryxell knew about difficulties and disappointments: "A teacher and educator, however, can possess all these gifts and still not win trust, since prejudice, ill will, and the scorpion stings of slander impair and even conceal it, and then God alone can help."

The notes on classroom discipline from Cecilia Fryxell's mid-nineteenth century teacher training class had for today's students a contemporary ring: "Everything good begins and thrives in tranquillity, and the same is true of good instruction. When teaching and learning, there *must* be quiet."

She continued:

> Yet tranquillity is of two kinds: the *outer tranquillity*, when all external tumult, all loud, unnecessary talk and laughter, all noise when coming and going are avoided, and so on; and the *inner tranquillity*, when the vehement desires and passions are silent, the disorderly inclinations of selfishness and self-will are suppressed when floating and diverted thoughts cease and the attention of the mind is wholly directed towards what it is supposed to be directed towards and is thus open to every good impression.

Fryxell regarded outer tranquillity as a consequence of the inner tranquillity:

> but inasmuch as the instruction cannot wait until the children's hearts have come to rest ... the aim of school discipline is to achieve this outer tranquillity. A schoolmistress must therefore, when she commences her vocation, at the start of every day and at the start of every lesson, resolutely see to it that the necessary tranquillity prevails in the children, not the silence of death and the grave, as with the undertaker, but the silence of life and activity which prevails in those who are able to arouse and display the powers implanted in them by God.

While the notes contained strategies such as having a small bell at hand, the key message communicated was the necessity for the teacher herself to possess the inner tranquillity.

Continuing one's own education was another important theme:

> To study and further search for instruction is also an indispensable property of a competent and skilful schoolmistress.... Without a delight in studies she is lazy in learning and sluggish in letting herself be taught.

> In instruction and in the teaching profession no one is ever fully skilled, and she who is not ashamed to be a disciple of the truth will therefore be a competent teacher, and she who allows herself to be educated in life by the Holy Spirit will be a competent educator.

The Life Story of Cecilia Fryxell

Who was the woman behind these 150-year-old instructions that so appealed to student teachers of Kalmar today? What were her sources of inspiration? What shaped her own teaching career? Let us take a look at her background and her own way to teaching.

When Cecilia Fryxell was born in western Sweden in 1806, Sweden was a sparsely populated country on the northern periphery of Europe, considered backward particularly with regard to women's education. Cecilia's life story is interwoven with great social and cultural development partly due to great popular national movements.

Cecilia Fryxell's extended family included important Swedish school reformers, educators, teachers and clergymen. An uncle, Anders Fryxell, was a famous scholar of Swedish history and an early advocate of comprehensive schooling for all children. Another male relative Elof, was a co-founder of Stockholm's *Wallinska flickskolan*. Founded in 1838, this was one of the first schools for girls.

Cecilia's personal history also contains tragic elements. Alcoholism cost her father his position as head of the county constabulary. As a result, the eight-year-old Cecilia, the oldest of five children, was placed with the family of a clergyman uncle. Aunt Lena, the clergyman's wife, taught her and her three girl cousins, Ulla, Betty and Ellika, to read, write, and perform various domestic tasks. While the girls received all their education at home in accordance with the custom of the time, the male cousins were sent to be educated at the secondary school in the nearby city and at the University of Uppsala. The girls were, therefore, able to draw upon some of the scholarship in this intellectual home, with a great many talented young people around. Cecilia was not the only foster-child. One foster-brother, eleven years older than Cecilia, became particularly important for her educational development.[7]

Thanks to her foster-brother, the eighteen-year-old Cecilia was offered a position as governess at the estate of Svaneholm, the home of industrialist Count Uggla, where her foster-brother was employed as a tutor. Letters tell us that although Aunt Lena was grateful for the opportunity for employment for the young Cecilia, she was also anxious that her education was insufficient to teach the young girls of the estate. "She is not advanced enough to bear the name of a governess," she writes in a letter to the countess, "and if you should find Cecilia to be too useless for you, I shall be content to take her back at any time."

Preserved correspondence between the tutor and the young governess over three decades show how her foster-brother assisted when Cecilia's own knowledge ran short. Readers of our days get a feeling of how dependant our governess was on the informal teaching her half-brother provided. The letters contain advice concerning books to read, corrections of language, and answers to questions from Cecilia such as: "What kind of country is Australia? Nora wonders what the star is that is visible just after the sun has set in the west. Is it a comet?" The young Cecilia soon developed into a good teacher and became a beloved friend of the countess and her family. She prospered in the cultural environment. Her musical ability and her fine singing voice, were very much appreciated as one duty of the governess (as well as that of the tutor) was to entertain with music and reading aloud. Long distances and bad roads made the industrialists' mansions into lodging houses for nobility travelling on business to markets and cities. Libraries were built up on these estates, which were centres of the industrial community in their regions, and which gradually became cultural centres.

Cecilia served as an estate governess for 20 years. During this period of her life, she established connections with the cultural elite that benefited her later in life when she established her schools. The famous Swedish poet Geijer wrote poems that he was anxious to let her perform. Troili, a famous Swedish painter, drew a portrait of the young Cecilia which is one of the treasures of the Kalmar Teacher Training College.

The young governess with her graceful and witty personality was praised, and she soon became a favourite among young gentlemen. However the barriers of class and social status did not allow for an alliance between a penniless governess and a baron. Cecilia met with disappointment in love, which according to her biographers, made a profound impression on her life.[8]

By 1841, Cecilia was tired of the transient life of a governess and she wanted a new mission in life. Like many others, she was attracted to the popular nationalist Non-Conformist Church Movement, and joined in 1841 the newly founded Swedish Missionary Society.[9] This was a time when severe coercive laws were in force in order to preserve the uniformity of the Swedish Lutheran Church. Until 1860, switching to any other religious congregation was punished with exile. The *Conventicle Act* did not allow people to assemble in small circles outside the Swedish State Church for Bible studies. The religious movement pleading for other forms of affinity and exercise of piety embraced all classes—even members of the Swedish Royal Family. In 1859, at a national meeting of clergy, the Archbishop of Sweden warned about the religious fervour that was causing discord in society. "It is seething and sizzling everywhere," he complained.[10]

Most important for Cecilia Fryxell's religious and educational development was her meeting with the Swedish missionary Peter Fjellstedt, at that time agent for the Basel Mission, the oldest European Protestant Missionary Society. They met when Fjellstedt was travelling around Sweden to arouse interest in and raise money for the sake of Missions. Cecilia Fryxell who had joined the newly erected Swedish Missionary Society was eager to take part in the growing missionary work among the Laplanders in northern part of Sweden. She turned to Fjellstedt for advice how to proceed. Fjellstedt however, who had become very impressed by the Swedish governess' gifts and refinement, brought new ideas. He informed her that a Women's Committée had been created at the Basel Mission planning to send women teachers to India to help missionary wives in their work in founding girls' schools. Fjellstedt considered Cecilia Fryxell to be an excellent candidate for this new mission and asked her for permission to put in an application to the Basel Mission for her. This meant that Cecilia would be the first Swedish woman to enter into foreign missionary work, which at that time mainly was considered a male matter.

After a great deal of deliberations, the 37-year-old Cecilia Fryxell in May 1845—not without fear—embarked upon her travel to Basel. Letters to her friends in Sweden testify to some kind of disappointment. Although she was devoted to follow the calling of her Lord she felt some uncertainty concerning her future task. There was in fact great diversity of opinon on women's role in missionary work at that time, particularly at the Basel Mission, which was characterized by a very patriarchal structure. The Women's Committé had great difficulties in realizing the project of sending out female missionary workers, not least to send out unmarried young women.

Another difficulty had to do with health matters. Cecilia Fryxell, who was of delicte frame, fell ill in Basel. Some of her new friends were afraid that she was not strong enough for the hard work on a missionary field in foreign countries. Her Swedish friends asked her to return home. With reluctance, Cecilia, in consultation with Fjellstedt, decided to give up her plans for missionary work abroad and instead devote herself to the home mission. Her particular mission was defined as founding girls' schools in Sweden.

Cecilia Fryxell's stay in Switzerland offered the former governess an opportunity to develop her teaching abilities. There is evidence in the archival sources that she got to know several of the famous educationalists of that time. She was particularly interested in Christian Heinrich Zeller, who has been named the foremost representative of pietist pedagogy[12] and whose training college for teachers targeted teaching poor children.[13] Evidence suggests that Cecilia Fryxell taught there for a time as an 1866 notation by one of her students records: "What is the most remarkable teacher training college in a Christian spirit? The teacher training College in Beuggen in Baden opened and directed by C. H. Zeller." Fryxell's instructions to student teachers are highly influenced by Zeller.

Cecilia's new mission in life was to start girls' schools in Sweden and she prepared herself by visiting girls' schools in Germany on her journey back to Sweden. Oral tradition recalls that in Gnadau she was offered the post of principal of a school, but declined. Her Christian brothers and sisters in Sweden had other plans for her. Upon her return to Sweden a teaching position was arranged at the Moravian girls' school in Gothenburg, one of the few schools for girls in Sweden.[14] She held this position for about a year while plans for a school of her own were made.

A School Enterprise is Started

The great need for girls' schools that offered a broader curriculum than the accomplishments offered in available boarding schools (offering mainly French vocabulary, needlework, and piano lessons) was also felt by the leaders of the revival movement. Girls' schooling was considered an important instrument in their work. A new partner in Cecilia's strivings in founding a girls' school was Peter Wieselgren, who besides being one of the leaders of the revival movement, was the founder of another important national movement of that time, the Swedish temperance movement. Wieselgren was planning a girls' school in Helsingborg, in southern Sweden, where he was going to take up a position as vicar. He had personal reasons for his engagement in the school project—he was eager to give his four daughters a good education.

The curriculum was planned in cooperation with two of Cecilia's old friends and benefactors, Peter Fjellstedt and countess Eva Heikensköld. In 1847 the plans for a school were to be realized. The archives reveal that the school planners had great ambitions. Wieselgren was planning to take care of religious instruction, Cecilia aimed to teach history following the story-telling methodology developed by her relative, Anders Fryxell. Natural history as well as writing and arithmetic were to be provided with the aid of teachers from the established boys' secondary school in Helsingborg, while literature and the arts were to benefit from visits to museums and other institutions of fine arts in nearby Copenhagen in Denmark. Native teachers in English, German, and French were to be hired. A house with a garden was rented for the school and advertisements were published in the local newspaper and in the paper published by the revival movement. However, parents seemed to be reluctant to send their daughters to Cecilia Fryxell and her school. There was a rumour that she was going to train the girls to become missionaries and send them abroad. The school had to start on a much smaller scale than originally planned. However, very soon new rumours in the city reported that Cecilia Fryxell was a great teacher. Within three months her students had increased in number from six to 40. Later on one of the students described the education "as a current of life bringing a reawakening and creative force to every receptive soul."

In 1852 Cecilia was offered a chance to expand her school. Her good friend and former employer, Eva, now remarried to Count Gösta Lewenhaupt, invited Cecilia to move her school to the city of Västerås in central Sweden. The count and countess were leading figures of the revival movement in central Sweden and eager to see that Cecilia Fryxell's educational ability was used to spread enlightenment to all "dark regions" in Sweden.

They offered to relocate her school to the great manor house, Carlslund, into which they just had moved.

In September 1852, Cecilia, in company with her women teachers and pupils, embarked on an eight-day sea trip via Gothenburg and Göta Canal to Stockholm and on to Västerås. Among the pupils were three of the Wieselgren sisters, nine, eleven, and thirteen years of age. Thanks to extant diary notes from one of the Wieselgren sisters, Emma, we can get an impression of the great undertaking.[15] The travel days were at the same time lessons on geography. The girls had an opportunity to test their knowledge of English, since an English doctor and his wife happened to be their travelling companions.

A month later Cecilia and Eva were ready to open the girls' school at Carlslund—a school that was soon to develop into one of the most respected and famous schools for girls. The enterprise has been described as "one of the most venturous and most successful enterprise for girls' schooling in our country."[16] The school's prospectus for 1857 states its aim "to direct the children to Jesus Christ, our Saviour. The school pays more attention to general education, based on God's word, than to any particular measure of knowledge."

In the beginning the school was set up on the ground floor of the estate while the count and countess lived above. All meals were served in the private dining room where students and teachers dined together with the Lewenhaupt family and guests. When the school increased in numbers a special building was erected on the property.

The girls' school consisted of three classes. The subjects taught in the upper classes of the girls' school were: Bible Knowledge, Catechism, General History and Swedish History, Geography, Arithmetic, Grammar with Swedish Essay-writing, French, German and English including grammar, essay-writing and pronunciation. The first language was German, which was followed after three months by French and finally English. It was not common to teach English in girls' schools at this time. The archival sources provide information concerning methodology in language training as well as in the teaching of history, geography, and religion. The sources also document the books used in different subjects and the fee schedules.

In addition to the girls' school, the school at Carlslund offered one preparatory class for children aged three to seven; one burgher class which did not provide language training; one class for orphans (without cost). Most remarkable was however a class for teacher training that Cecilia Fryxell instituted in order to manage the lack of trained teachers for girls' schools. Several students from her teaching class went on to found girls' schools in different parts of the country. Alumnae of the school included prominent school principals in

Gothenburg, Stockholm, Enköping, Gävle, Västerås and Luleå. For seven years Cecilia Fryxell led the school at Carlslund. These were important years in the history of Swedish girls' schools, especially in the pioneering of teacher training.

An interesting glimpse of what it really meant to be a girl at Carlslund, far away from home, is provided by the diary of one the Wieselgren sisters, Emma, who stayed with Cecilia for three years. (The preserved diary covers half a year in 1856.)[17] The school day started when the girls were woken up at six o'clock. One hour was devoted to homework before breakfast at seven followed by morning prayer. The school day contained seven lessons with ten-minute breaks. The religious spirit at the school seems to have been overwhelming. Religious talks were common: entertainment often consisted of listening to sermons and prayers. One letter from the twelve-year-old Emma to her father contains a burning question being discussed at the school. "When do you have to know that you are a child of God? Is it important to know the time and hour of the conversion?" Her father answers his daughter with a long scholarly exegesis of the state of grace. The diary also contains glimpses of happiness and joy. An excursion to Stockholm together with Cecilia Fryxell with lots of visits to prominent members of the revival movement is one such event. Emma's devotion to the school and to "dearest Mademoiselle Fryxell" is obvious, although from time to time she is upset due to reprimands for not being humble and submissive enough to the teachers.

Due to the long distances, most of the girls spent all year at the school. The intimacy is striking: teachers and pupils shared dormitories. Cecilia Fryxell had the custom of letting the youngest and newly-arrived pupils sleep near her, "to be able to reach out a motherly hand but also to get to know their personalities." Sickness and early death were constant threats in those days. The oldest of the Wieselgren girls had to be sent home before her education was finished. The school register describes her situation as being "very bad, little hope of life." The youngest of the sisters died suddenly at home in Helsingborg six months after having spent four years at the Carlslund school. Letters from Emma's mother (very few are preserved as she was ashamed of her poor writing and asked her daughters to destroy the letters immediately) show a mother's worry for her daughters' physical health, even though she trusted Cecilia Fryxell, "the motherly friend, who is more than a mother and father."

Rostad: A New Field of Action and a Home of Her Own
In a letter dated January 1858 Cecilia wrote:

> It has grown like the leaf in springtime this move to Calmar. The beautiful Rostad is mine, I am the owner of this little patch. I had quite a lot of money saved, and many people assisted me too.... I cannot say for certain when the move will take place, perhaps next autumn. Everything has happened

Inga Elgqvist-Saltzman

4.2. Rostad 1860 (detail) reproduced on cover of notebooks used by students. Courtesy of the Museum of Kalmar.

so strangely, it all seems to be drawing so steadily in that direction.

The letter was addressed to Emma Wieselgren, who had finished her education and was living in Helsingborg, assisting her father in his adult educational activities. Two months later, a new letter told: "At little Rostad everything is being put in order and already more children than there is space for are applying for entrance."

Unknown to Cecilia, some people belonging to the circle of pietists in Calmar had been working to found a girls' school in the city, described as "a place of great ungodliness." When a small estate and former out-of-town restaurant came up for sale, some citizens, in collaboration with the pietist leader Fjellstedt, bought it and invited Cecilia Fryxell to move her school to the place called Rostad. Cecilia came to see the place and as the letters to Emma show, she was delighted. Cecilia, who now was 52 years old, found Rostad appropriate for a home and a school of her own. She arranged that one of her former students took over the school at Carlslund and moved to Calmar together with some of her teachers and students. In 1859 the local newspapers announced that Cecilia Fryxell had moved her girls' school to Rostad. A music teacher and some new native-speaker teachers of language, one from Switzerland, were appointed as well as a housekeeper, a female cook, and a coachman.

Up to this time Rostad was known as an amusement park and a popular destination for excursions among the citizens of Calmar. The plans to erect a pietist school at this place were met with disappointment and hard feelings in the city. The bishop and most of the clergy had religious reasons to be suspicious of the new school. Cecilia Fryxell was known as a member of the revival movement, which was feared. It would take some time before the bishop allowed his daughter, who later on became one of Cecilia's favourite teachers, to attend her school.

Cecilia Fryxell and her school enterprise soon overcame the scruples of the citizens of Calmar. A letter from 1873 to Peter Wieselgren, with whom she started her first school, tells about the development:

> The Lord has provided me with a pleasure. A big house in a beautiful park. He has installed me as matron of 50-60 persons. The school building contains 50 full-board students and as many day students. The business is going well ... and my health is still unbroken....

Rostad, where Cecilia lived until her death in 1887, was the first real home of her own. Here, she could gather around her relatives and friends, and she could set up a school according to her own ideas, capitalizing on previous experience.

Photographs, prospectuses, and notebooks give a good picture of life at Rostad. Many routines were the same as at Carlslund, for example the habit of teachers and students sharing rooms. However, there seems to have been a more cheerful and lighter spirit at Rostad. A chorus of voices affirm how pleasant the stay at Rostad was and how lively and interesting Cecilia's lessons were. Cecilia was known for her great linguistic skills; she had a complete mastery of several European languages. The subjects she preferred to teach were religion and history. The small children's introduction to the Bible seems to have been her particular interest. Her pupils' notebooks give some impression of her famous educational ability. Notes from a history lesson in 1866 "on the restoration of equilibrium in Europe and further vicissitudes" show how she was able to bind together Swedish and general history, political science, religious instruction and women's history into a whole that was quite fascinating even for student teachers of the 1990s.

Cecilia was critical of lessons learnt by heart. She declared: "This school is not a dispensary where gallipots are displayed containing passive knowledge but an elixir of all those gallipots named all-round education."

Her education aimed at character building for this life and the next. Her aim was to foster honest, industrious, competent young girls with a Christian attitude to life. It has been said that Cecilia Fryxell's greatness consisted in her ability to shape character.

Information to parents on the conditions of the school tell not only about which books were used but also how many underbodices, vests and skirts the girls were expected to bring along—with a request from the principal to send plain, hardwearing clothes. The school seems to have been very particular about health matters. Daily walks for one hour were prescribed. Summer bathing in the sea was available. Homework was restricted to one hour. The fare was simple; interestingly enough, Cecilia Fryxell was convinced that meat was not good for young girls: "meat incites their blood and irritates their nervous system."

The Rostad school was at the same time a centre for missionary work in southern Sweden. Several of the leading men of the Non-Conformist Church and missionaries visiting Sweden received lodging at Rostad, in a room called "the prophet's chamber." One of them described Rostad as "an oasis in the wandering in the wilderness." Cecilia's devotion to religion was great and described as a warm, light faith. A boy who attended her Sunday school, which was open for boys as well, described her as follows: "when you meet her in the street it is as if the sun starts shining."

Cecilia, who once started to train for missionary work abroad, had an unexpected opportunity to practise missionary work on a young Zulu girl, Sara, who strangely enough had arrived in Kalmar in the company of a family of a tradesman. Cecilia Fryxell took care of Sara's Christian education when it was decided that Sara, who was pregnant, was to stay in the city. In 1865 Sara was christened in Kalmar Cathedral during a solemn ceremony which can be followed in a special booklet published by the missionary society.[18] The publication contains a conversation between Sara and her teacher, Cecilia Fryxell. The seventeen-year-old Sara told the very sad story of how her family had been slaughtered by the Boers and how she had been kept as a slave before she was taken care of by the tradesman. The ceremony ended with Sara disclaiming her old gods and confessing her belief in Jesus, the Saviour. After her christening Sara came to Rostad to be Cecilia Fryxell's personal assistant, and she stayed there until Cecilia's death.

Several histories of the colourful and temperamental Sara can be found among the preserved notes. The citizens of Kalmar recognized the traditional red headgear she always wore when she was sitting beside Cecilia in the small coach from Rostad drawn by the horse Rolf, when the ladies from Rostad went to the marketplace to make their purchases. Sara's daughter was given free education at Rostad. She later on became a music teacher in Kalmar. Sara as well as her daughter have their graves beside Cecilia in the local churchyard.

Sunday school, morning prayers, missionary evenings were thus important elements of daily life at Rostad, but the Rostad school also became famous for great parties in the beautiful park. One day in spring "when the park appeared in all its splendour," a common birthday party for all students was celebrated with music, games, and newly written songs. St Cecilia's Day in November was celebrated as a music day when the music teacher and the students showed parents and invited guests what they had learnt. Many children in the city of Kalmar would long remember the great Christmas party at Rostad, with the crib on Holy Innocents' Day. Cecilia composed a poem:

Månn någon nånsinn fanns　　Can anyone conceive
Som djupet fatta kan　　　　The splendour so profound
Av Rostadfesters glans　　　Of Rostad festivals

The heart of Rostad was the drawing room. Every afternoon at six o'clock the school day was completed in this room where students and teachers gathered, doing needlework, reading aloud, and practising their knowledge of foreign languages. Quite often Cecilia played her piano and students could now and then admire her singing voice. Late in the evening Cecilia would sit at her desk penning letters to friends and also reports to the parents on the progress of the schoolgirls. The drawing room was also the place where Cecilia received her many friends as well as parents.

The End of an Era and the Beginning of Another

For eighteen active years Cecilia Fryxell was the principal of Rostad, which obtained an reputation as one of the best girls' schools in Scandinavia. Several young girls from proprieted classes received their education at Rostad. Students came from all over Scandinavia and even a few from the USA. In 1877, when Cecilia was in her 70s she made a decision that was considered a very remarkable event. She decided to donate her school and her property to the state in order to provide proper premises for the local training college for elementary school teachers. Since 1842 when compulsory school attendance was introduced in Sweden, teacher education was an obligatory task for the community. The training College in Calmar was one of the few where women were admitted. The principal was a good friend of Cecilia Fryxell and kept her well informed about the difficulties the college met in its strivings to train women teachers for the emergent elementary school for the public. Becoming a teacher in the elementary school did not have high status, and the teacher training colleges had difficulties recruiting students. Housing conditions of the college were poor.

Cecilia Fryxell had always shown a great interest in teacher education. Zeller's educational programme for teachers for the poor children in Switzerland had—as mentioned before—been one important source of inspiration in her own work. The work with training teachers for girls' higher schooling that Cecilia started at Carlslund had partly missed its mark when a State Training College for Women started in Stockholm in 1860.[19]

The donation of Rostad provided a boost for the development of the local teacher training. In September 1877 a jubilant troop of young student teachers could take possession of the halls and the park of the beautiful Rostad property. The teacher training college, which retained the proper noun of Rostad, was soon to be known as an outstanding teacher training college. In some periods during the twentieth century the college was even considered a centre for educational research in Sweden. The principals of the college were long eager to connect to ideals and traditions from Cecilia Fryxell's school. The notion of the school as a home with responsibility for the entire student was a main component in the famous Rostad spirit,[20] which linked generations of student teachers together.

Cecilia Fryxell continued living at Rostad for seven years after the donation. She resigned from teaching but was from time to time asked to perform tours of inspection to schools in the neigbourhood of the city. In 1887, she was followed to her grave by many friends and citizens of Calmar who had learned to love and respect the woman who came to their city to take over their amusement park of Rostad and made it into a loving home for many young people. Grateful students have raised a gravestone with the inscription: "We remember your acts for the faith and your work in love."

To Sum Up

Cecilia Fryxell, whose life and work has been described in detail in this chapter, is a prominent figure in the local educational history of Kalmar. Even though her girls' schools were groundbreaking in the transitional period between girls' boarding schools and the rise of secondary schools for girls and her teaching class at Carlslund was pioneering work in women teachers' education in Sweden, Cecilia Fryxell is however not well known among educational researchers. Her name is not to be found in general textbooks on educational history. In my own research[21] gradually the life and work of Cecilia Fryxell has come to fascinate me. Cecilia Fryxell has inspired me to focus on connections, interplay and how the history of different educational institutions flows into each other. In my Swedish material I have found evidence of interesting cooperation among educationists across boundaries of gender class and nations, and I have found surprising social and regional mobility and international exchanges of ideas. Women's role in transitional periods of time has come to interest me. I have also found a local perspective helpful in the deconstruction of general categories. The interplay between Cecilia and the leading men in the revival movement was mutually beneficial. To date, educational research has failed to pay attention to this interplay and its consequences for the curriculum in girls' education.

From an international perspective it would be of interest to relate the curriculum Cecilia introduced in her Swedish girls' schools to the curriculum of girls schools in other parts of the world. For example, how did the "female accomplishment curriculum" Marjorie Theobald[22] found in early Australian schools compare with that of Swedish schools? Another question is whether the dual function of her educational institutions as girls' schools and missionary centres is to be found in other parts of the world?

My essay started with a question about the usefulness of teachers' life stories and archival sources drawn from the local history in the training of teachers of today. The life story of Cecilia Fryxell proved to be quite useful in our KaPe Project. The students were able to use their newly acquired historical knowledge to discuss current educational problems in a deeper and more nuanced perspective.[23] They found it inspiring to trace the historical roots of their own teacher training and to find that the history of teaching had interesting local aspects. The Teacher Training College in Kalmar, with traditions from Cecilia Fryxell's time, is now part of a University. In Kalmar, as in many new universities, natural science and technology have high priorities. As a modern institution striving to attain higher status, historical traditions particularly those derived from association with a former girls' school, are not always considered an asset. The positive response students gave to the project presented in this chapter may however suggest that the woman with the great educational ability we have met here still seems to be able to play a role in Swedish teacher education! Her life story provided a good framework for debates on everlasting educational questions. New life was given to questions on teachers' relationship to students, questions on trust and confidence and how to bring about a good environment for teaching and learning. Cecilia Fryxell's own winding route to teaching raised interest for questions of equality in educational conditions and curriculum matters. The students received insight into teaching as "a great profession" and had their eyes opened to the fact that women's and men's educational history was not the same.

Notes

[1] Kalmar is an old city situated in southeast of Sweden. The name was formerly spelled as Calmar.
[2] The two researchers were Anna Henningsson-Yousif and the author.
[3] The first year was thus called Dahm's year after O. E. L. Dahm (1812-1883), the first principal for the local teacher training institute and a famous author of textbooks for the elementary school. The second year was called Fryxell's year after Cecilia Fryxell whose work is described in this article. The third year of the project was called Wigfors's year after Fritz Wigfors who was senior master of mathematics and psychology at Kalmar Teacher Training College (1919-1953) and one of the foremost figures in educational reform work at that time.
[4] In earlier research on Swedish women and women teachers, I have had the advantage of drawing from the research of international scholars such as Alison Prentice, Jane Martin, Alison Mackinnon, Marjorie Theobold. A book collection in honour of Alison Prentice, who has been a great inspiration to me in all my research, seems to offer a very good opportunity to present this piece on the history of women's education in Sweden.
[5] The material is so far uncatalogued and does not have further accession numbers.
[6] See Christina Florin and Ulla Johansson, *Där de härliga lagrarna gro.*, (Stockholm: Tid, 1993), 105-131 and 181-203. See also article by Florin and Johansson, "Education as a Female Strategy," *Journal of Thought* 6, 1-2 (1991): 5-27. Christina Florin's dissertation *Kampen om katedern* (Umeå University: Umeå Studies in the Humanities, vol. 82, 1987), deals with the gender history of teaching 1860-1906. Gunhild Kyle described in her dissertation from 1972 the development of Swedish girls' school during 1800.

Inga Elgqvist-Saltzman

7   Johan Magnus Malmstedt, a younger half-brother of the author Anna Maria Lenngren.
8   See biographies: Karin Häggström, *Cecilia Fryxell, Rostad Elevförbunds årsskrift, 1947, Kalmar* (Stockholm: Korsblomman, 1884); Vera Wigforss, *Cecilia Fryxell, En märkeskvinna inom pedagogik och missionsarbete i 1800-talets Sverige*, (Kalmar: Rostads elevförb, 1960).
9   There is a story of how she was reawakened when she found her newly repaired pair of dancing shoes wrapped in an issue of the Missionary Paper published by the Englishman George Scott.
10 See Gunnar Westin, *I den svenska frikyrklighetens genombrottstid—svensk baptism till 1880-talets slut. Kyrkohistoriska uppsatser* (Stockholm: Westerberg, 1963).
11 See Carl Anshelm, *Peter Fjellstedt*, (Stockholm: Svenska Kyrkans Diakonistyrelses förlag, 1957).
13 See Gustaf Kaleen, "Fackundervisningen vid våra folkskoleseminarier 1865-1914," *Årsböcker i svensk undervisningshistoria* 158 (1978): 142.
13 See Christian Heinrich Zeller, *Lehren der Erfahrung fur christliche Land- und Armen-Schullehrer* (Basel: Bahnmaier, 1865).
14 Before 1840 only eight girls' schools were registered in Sweden compared to at least 22 between 1840 and 1870 (Alice Quensel, 1942).
15 See Hervor Widding, *En liten stjärna och hennes krets* (Borgholm: Mikas Förl, 2000).
16 See Axel Johansson, *Religiösa folkrörelser i stad och bygd* (Vestmanlands läns Tidnings AB Tryckeri Västerås, 1964).
17 See Widding, above.
18 *Tal wid en hednisk flickas dop. Andliga sånger*, (Kalmar: Missionsförening, 1865).
19 It seems however that Cecilia Fryxell constantly was consulted in matters concerning teaching. In a letter to a friend Cecilia Fryxell in 1870s complained that she was deluged with inquiries concerning women teachers and disappointed that the state teacher training college could not supply the demand for good teachers for the emerging girls schools in Sweden.
20 The particular Rostad spirit characterized by unity and responsibility for oneself and other people left traces in former pupils' society, in a yearbook which from time to time had a reputation as an important educational news service. Class letters, class meetings, and festivities following traditions from Cecilia's days were other tokens of the spirit.
21 In the Rostad-Project, sponsored by the Treasury Fund, an interdisciplinary research group followed three generations of women teachers. The research resulted in several reports, summarized in Elgqvist-Saltzman, *Lärarinna, Kvinna, Människa* (1993). In the 1990s a new project (*Women Actors in Educational Practice*) sponsored by HSFR gave me an opportunity to lengthen the temporal perspective to include the time of Cecilia Fryxell and follow the first generations of Kalmar teachers. *Women in the Educational Web* is the name of the current project sponsored by HSFR.
22 See M. Theobold, *Knowing Women: Origin of Women's Education in Nineteenth-Century Australia* (Melbourne/Cambridge University Press, 1996).
23 See the final report of the Kape-project: *Kalmar-pedagoger i tid och rum* (Department of Education, University of Kalmar, 1999).

II.
Regulating Women:
Social Work, Teaching and Medicine

A Passion for Service

Edith Elwood and the Social Character of Reform

CATHY JAMES

Over the last 30 years feminist historians of education have documented, with sensitivity and insight, women's efforts to gain entry to the halls of Canadian academe, and their subsequent (and continuing) struggles to achieve parity with their male colleagues. This generation of scholars has charted, as well, the admission and subsequent struggles of some Canadian university women who entered the "learned" professions, and the movement of others into what came to be known as the "helping" professions. The endeavours of Canadian women reformers in the early twentieth century have also been an important focus of feminist research in the past few decades.[1] Taken as a whole, the close interconnections between these three areas of inquiry are clear, as is their continuing relevance to current concerns in feminist scholarship. Indeed, a number of new and fascinating questions have arisen in recent years. Some of the most compelling of these queries focus on issues of meaning and significance in the lives of the women who participated in the social reform movement in early twentieth-century Canada. What, for example, did it actually mean, for the people involved, to "re-form" individuals, communities, or urban environments? And what influence, if any, did professional aspirations have on the way that reformers defined their role and their task?

One way to address questions like these, as Alison Prentice noted more than a decade ago, is through biography. By looking closely at the lives of individual women who actively engaged in work that they themselves defined as vital and transformative, we can begin to get an idea of the complex meanings of, and relationships between, women's higher education, professionalization, and progressive social reform. One potential candidate for such a study is Edith Elwood McLaren.[2]

A member of the first generation of women to graduate from the University of Toronto's Trinity College, Edith Elwood was an educator, community leader and social work pioneer. She began her career as a teacher, and subsequently became one of the first Canadians to take an active role in the settlement house movement—a major international initiative in community education and social activism. As a resident staff member and then headworker of the first Canadian settlement, Evangelia House, Elwood helped to create in Toronto a network of community services that eventually became integral to the modern welfare system. She later galvanized local women's and reform groups to organize a similar network in Ottawa. In the process she helped to lay the groundwork for a new profession in Canada—social work—as well as the administrative structure of the modern welfare state.

While her efforts as a social work pioneer make Edith Elwood a particularly intriguing subject for a life history, the biographer's task is complicated by the fact that relatively few of her writings or other records detailing her ideas, activities, and opinions have survived. There are fragments here and there. After her death in 1931, some admirers from a literary group she presided over put together a short pamphlet outlining her life and work. About 30 years later a group of social workers collected reminiscences about her from former members, volunteers, and staff of Evangelia House in the course of putting together a manuscript on the history of the Canadian settlement movement. Her alma mater's student newspaper, *The S. Hilda's Chronicle*, reported on her activities from time to time, as well as on life at Evangelia House more generally. Elwood's name also appears frequently on the executives of several women's clubs, social workers' groups, and reform organizations, and some of her addresses to these organizations have survived as well. Pieced together, these fragments create a picture that, though incomplete, offers a unique perspective on the life of a university trained, professionally oriented, Canadian settlement leader and progressive social reformer.

Several contexts helped to shape Elwood's life and career. One context, of course, is the expansion of opportunities in higher education for women in English Canada. Long the preserve of young men seeking entry into the learned professions, by the 1880s Ontario universities had been forced, by a combination of economic, social, and political factors, to open their doors to female scholars. By the time Elwood and her fellow co-eds were crossing that threshold in the 1890s, women in academe had become an established fact, though their place there remained, nevertheless, somewhat tenuous and vulnerable. As a result, many women students felt it necessary to prove themselves worthy of their opportunity to study. Another, overlapping context is the growing need of middle-class, Anglo-Canadian women to earn a living. Financial need had long impelled working-class women into paid employment, and by the late nineteenth century it was drawing an ever-increasing number of their bourgeois counterparts into the workforce as well. Limited, for the most part, to teaching in either public secondary or private schools, many female university graduates actively searched for alternative occupational choices. A third context, closely related to the other two, is the changing landscape of poverty relief and social welfare in the early twentieth century, which attracted a number of these new job seekers and encouraged them to create their own employment alternatives. Elwood was one of these.

My goal in this study is to shed some light on the forces that shaped Elwood's life and career. I hope, as well, to offer some insight into what social reform meant to her and women like her by examining what she actually did as a settlement worker. Actions, as the saying goes, speak louder than words, and Elwood's speak more loudly than most. I intend, too, to elucidate her role in the professionalization of social work, one of the leading white-collar occupations for Canadian women, outside of teaching. It is an aspect of the history of social work of which few modern-day scholars are aware, and it highlights, among other things, the significance of women's networks in the professionalization of what had long been considered women's work. But Elwood's life story, I will suggest, illuminates more than just the history of Canadian social work; it offers, as well, to broaden our knowledge about the history of women, of social reform, and of the formation of the welfare state in Canada.

Edith Constance Elwood McLaren was born on May 12, 1875, into a solidly upper-middle-class family in Goderich, Ontario. Her mother, Marion Whales Watson, was American-born, most likely a member of one of the many wealthy American families who summered in this picturesque little town situated on the shores of Lake Huron.[3] Edith's father, John Yeats Elwood, was both a barrister and the clerk of the high court in Goderich, which was also the county seat.[4] Her many uncles were prosperous lawyers, businessmen, government officials, and clergymen, and her paternal grandfather, Archdeacon Edward L. Elwood, M.A., was one of the most prominent figures in the early history of Goderich.[5]

The long serving rector of St. George's (Anglican) Church, Archdeacon Elwood also appears to have been a formative influence in Edith's life. He was well known for his commitment to community education and interfaith cooperation, serving for many years as trustee of the local public high school, and collaborating with his Catholic, Presbyterian, and Methodist counterparts (rare in the fractious religious environment of nineteenth-century Ontario), to establish a number of local interdenominational institutions. These included a branch of the Young Men's Christian Association, the Goderich Mechanics' Institute, and the local literary society. A scholar, Elwood often lectured publicly on a wide range of subjects, including geometry, astronomy, nature and revelation, and political science.[6] Although no written records of his personal opinions on the education of women have survived, given that members of his family were actively involved in academically-oriented, elite women's private schooling, and given that at least two of his granddaughters were among the first cohort of women to gain access to higher education in Ontario, it seems likely that he supported the expansion of women's educational opportunities.[7]

Whatever position the Archdeacon might personally have held on the subject of women's education, the women of Goderich were nevertheless largely excluded from the many clubs, associations, and societies that he and his counterparts helped to set up. Like the majority of middle-class women in small-town Ontario, the central preoccupation outside the home for Goderich matrons and their daughters was volunteer work on behalf of poor women and children, virtually always performed under the aegis of the church. Typical of many towns and cities in Southern Ontario, between 1866 and 1882 Goderich boasted a Ladies Benevolent Society and Ladies Aid societies in each of the mainline churches, including St George's. Few other women's organizations existed in the town apart from some small, private groups devoted to women's "self-improvement."[8] Altogether, one can identify an important cultural tension within the world in which Edith was raised. On the one hand she grew up in a family that valued service, religious tolerance, education, and neighbourly cooperation; on the other she lived in a social world that was rigidly divided along gendered lines, effectively restricting women's public activities and non-domestic interests.

Few details exist regarding Edith's childhood and early schooling. She was the youngest of four children, with two brothers, Edward Lindsay and John, and a sister, Mary.[9] Her father died suddenly of "congestion of the lungs" (possibly pneumonia) at the age of 38, four months after Edith was born.[10] Though tragic, his untimely death placed Edith's mother in a position of independence unusual among the middle-class women of her town—an independence that certainly must have shaped Edith's perceptions of women's agency and autonomy. Marion Elwood never remarried, and raised her children on her own.

Although members of the Elwood family were involved in Anglican women's private education, Marion sent Edith, and likely Edith's brothers and sister as well, to the public high school in Goderich. High schools, as Robert Gidney and Wyn Millar have pointed out, were part of a then newly restructured secondary level of education in Ontario.[11] In these new institutions, boys and girls were educated together in a scholastic environment clearly intended to prepare the best students for further academic and professional training. The school evidently had a strong impact on Edith, for she credited both the principal, Dr. Strang, and the modern languages teacher, Miss Charles with "turning her thoughts and inclinations towards a university career."[12] They certainly equipped her to write the university entrance examinations, which included Latin, Greek, Mathematics, History and Geography, English, Divinity, Physics, Chemistry, French, German, and Italian.[13]

Edith Elwood matriculated into the University of Trinity College, in Toronto, in October 1893.[14] At that time women had been present as students in the college for about ten years, although their status as full members of the Trinity community was still in dispute. Their introduction into Trinity came in stages: in 1883 the college allowed women to write examinations and receive certificates, but did not permit them to attend classes or to take degrees until 1885. One of the first women to register as a full-time Trinity student in 1885 was Ethel Middleton, Edith's cousin.[15] Middleton and her fellow women students soon discovered that although Trinity purported to allow women to take degrees on the same basis as men, the college council, and some of the faculty, did not accept fully the idea of coeducation. Persistently uneasy on the subject, the council decided to establish St. Hilda's College, a separate institution for Trinity women, in 1888.[16] The university then attempted to institute a policy of separate classes for men and women in pass level courses, and co-educational classes for those doing honours. It was only in the face of financial exigency that the college authorities finally abandoned this cumbersome and expensive arrangement in 1894.[17] St. Hilda's College, however, continued as a distinct residential college for women at Trinity, with its own administrators, its own rules and regulations, and its own student culture.

For the women of Trinity, life at St. Hilda's was carefully structured. From the waking bell at 7:00am to lights-out at 11:00pm, women students, like their male counterparts at Trinity proper, followed a regular routine of classes, study, and exercise, punctuated by chapel services on Sundays and saint's days. At 9:00am each weekday morning Ellen Patteson (later Rigby), St. Hilda's principal, escorted those students who were taking honours to Trinity for their classes and stayed waiting for them until the morning session concluded at 1:00pm, after which she ushered her charges back to St. Hilda's for lunch and an afternoon of study and recreation. Women in the pass course were instructed at St. Hilda's in the afternoons; Patteson taught French and German, and Clara Brett Martin, who later became Canada's first female lawyer, taught mathematics for a few years after she graduated from Trinity in 1890.[18] Otherwise, until the college did away with separate instruction in 1894, Trinity faculty came over to St. Hilda's to repeat the lectures they had given in the morning to the men. As Ethel Middleton recalled in 1903, with so few students in each class, "lectures had to be prepared for, perhaps more assiduously than now; for one did not care to go to a possibly tête-à-tête lecture with a grave and severe-looking professor without having made some attempts to unravel the hidden mysteries contained in the work at hand."[19]

The students of St. Hilda's were not, of course, solely occupied with classes and study. In an era in which sports were becoming an increasingly important aspect of student culture, athletically inclined women at Trinity had their own ice rink and hockey team by the early 1890s. They had access to the Trinity lawn tennis courts as well, though it is not clear how many of them actually took advantage of the opportunity.[20] Many apparently preferred more tranquil pursuits like boating and picnics along the Humber, or inter-collegiate club meetings and informal get-togethers. In addition, students at St. Hilda's regularly organized "nice little supper parties, [and] afternoon teas in our rooms, at which certain of the male persuasion used to present themselves, though uninvited."[21] Female undergraduates also attended various teas and dances over at Trinity.[22]

Other than at chaperoned social functions, college policy placed severe limitations on contacts between male and female students, though contemporary accounts of life at St. Hilda's indicate that these strict rules were not strictly enforced. Co-eds were, according to the rules, prohibited from even conversing with fellow undergraduates of the opposite sex anywhere on the grounds or in the buildings of Trinity. Women students' use of the telephone was also monitored and restricted, as were their movements outside the college after dinner; they could only be out one to three evenings per week depending on their year, and always had to be in by 10:30. Male visitors were officially permitted only on Friday evenings and at St. Hilda's monthly receptions.[23]

The concern for the proper deportment of Trinity women was part of a much larger and more persistent issue: many people both in and outside the college continued to question the wisdom of educating women in the university long after they had been admitted, arguing that higher education would render women "unsuitable" for the domestic sphere. On several occasions both the students and the principal of St. Hilda's had to defend themselves from this kind of criticism. As Ethel Middleton observed,

> At that time we had to fight our way inch by inch, as the *profanum vulgus* was only too ready to cry down higher education for women on the ground that it unfitted them for home duties. Only by means of ocular proofs, such as cakes, etc., made by our own hands, were we able to dis-illusion them of such old-world ideas.[24]

"Old-world ideas" continued to perturb Trinity's women for many years, however, exerting a subtle but nonetheless significant pressure on them to justify their scholarly pursuits.[25]

Women persisted at Trinity nevertheless, and when Edith Elwood arrived in 1893 she seems to have moved fairly comfortably into the social and academic routines of college life. Like many of the first generation of women to attend university in Canada, she specialized in modern languages—that is, French, Italian and German.[26] Her academic record was exceptional; in 1896 she graduated at or very near the top of the class in all her courses, standing I-1 in Divinity (and beating out, in the process, all the prospective clergymen in her year) and receiving a governor-general's award as head of college.[27] After graduation—again like many others in the first generation of university women—she took a one-year teacher training course in order to obtain the specialist's certificate in French and German that would qualify her to teach in Ontario secondary schools.[28] Rather than seeking a position in the public system, though, she and two other Trinity alumnae, Georgina Potts and Alice Woon, instead joined Elwood's cousin, Ethel Middleton, who was then teaching at the St. Mary's Institute, a private Episcopalian girls' school in Dallas, Texas. The four women maintained their ties to St. Hilda's, however, returning to Toronto each June to attend the meetings of the newly formed St. Hilda's Alumnae Association, of which Middleton and Elwood were president and vice-president, respectively.[29]

In the summer of 1902 Ethel Middleton and Edith Elwood came back to Toronto to establish their own private girls' academy, the Parkdale Church School. The two women quickly secured an affiliation with the Bishop Strachan School, where Middleton had lived for a year while she attended Trinity College in 1886.[30] Elwood became the school's vice-principal. According to reports in the *S. Hilda's Chronicle* and reminiscences of former pupils, she was a well-liked, progressive teacher who especially highlighted girls' athletics.[31] At the same time, she was deeply concerned about the problems facing the private-school teacher. A founding member and later president of the University Women's Club, she presented a paper on the inadequacy of wages for private school teachers at the club's inaugural meeting in April 1903.[32] Later that year she and Ethel obtained their M.A. degrees from Trinity—at that time a relatively simple exercise requiring only that the applicant pay a ten-dollar fee and hold a Bachelor of Arts degree for at least a year prior to the application.[33] Though many considerations no doubt prompted the move, it seems likely that the decision to acquire the M.A. was at least in part tactical—a stratagem the two decided upon as a means to raise their salaries by enhancing their credentials.

Beyond her teaching and administrative duties at Parkdale, Edith devoted a great deal of time to a number of women's voluntary organizations. She continued, for example, to participate actively in both the St. Hilda's Alumnae Association and the University Women's Club, sitting on the executives of both organizations from their early years. In the context of a society that still at times expressed outright hostility toward highly educated women, groups like these provided university alumnae with a crucial source of encouragement, intellectual stimulation, and sense of belonging.[34] As Anne Firor Scott has pointed out, women's clubs offered their members the collective support that made it possible for individual women to develop leadership skills and to function effectively in the public sphere.[35] At their monthly meetings the members of Toronto's University Women's Club organized social events, lectures, and reform work, reported on the findings of their community-oriented studies and research projects, and engaged in discussions on everything from their housing and employment prospects to their duty to improve the educational opportunities and the living and working conditions of women across the country and in all walks of life.[36]

It was within this context of collective action, discussion, study, and report that the settlement movement entered Edith's circle. Indeed, the very first paper read before the University Women's Club was entitled "Settlement Work in London, England." Its author was St. Hilda's recently appointed principal, Mabel Cartwright. Cartwright, a graduate of both Cheltenham Ladies' College and Lady Margaret Hall, Oxford, had had some experience in British women's settlement work while studying in England.[37] In her talk, and in the article she subsequently published from it, Cartwright argued forcefully that as far as university women were concerned, knowledge and service must go together. In connection with this, she pointed out that the growth of women's higher education everywhere "has been accompanied by the establishment of women's settlements."[38]

Cartwright's argument was carefully constructed to work at two different levels. By linking voluntary social service and post-secondary schooling for women, she attempted to validate women's higher education in rather traditional terms. Essentially, she was arguing that academic training helped middle-class women to fulfill more effectively their traditional feminine role: offering assistance to poor women and children. At the same time, by directing university women to the settlement movement she was introducing them to one of the most dynamic international social movements of the early twentieth century, a movement that set out to challenge many previous assumptions about the nature of poverty and the way it ought to be addressed.[39]

For movement proponents, there were two important points that set settlements apart from other social agencies. The first was that settlements, ideally, did not dispense charity, though they did help their neighbours to obtain relief from other sources, and they did, in times of great need, offer other kinds of assistance. They required, however, that those who used the settlements on more than an occasional basis become settlement members, and that they pay (admittedly nominal) annual membership fees. This marked an important shift in the relationship between the settlement and the people it served. The second point was that unlike charity agency "visitors," settlement workers actually lived in the neighbourhoods where they worked. The term "settlement" was quite deliberately chosen for its spatial as well as metaphorical connotations. It described a household, or colony, of educated, well-to-do young people (mostly young women) who had abandoned more comfortable surroundings for a few weeks, months, or years in order to reside in a "neglected" neighbourhood.[40] Their purpose was to try to get to know the poor on a more equal basis than was normally possible in the patron-client relationship. As one settlement proponent in the *S. Hilda's Chronicle* explained, "Unless people really live the life of the poor, actually understand and perceive their difficulties and troubles, and learn something of their philosophy, they are useless to help them."[41]

Drawing on a the familiar discourse of domesticity, settlement workers saw themselves as sympathetic interpreters of everyday life—among the poor for the well-to-do, and among the well-to-do for the poor. Through direct experience settlement workers believed they could acquire some insight into the subtleties of poverty and daily life in the "neglected districts." This search for insight, they insisted, influenced every aspect of their reform praxis. Instead of assuming that the poor were poor due to personal failings and attempting to coerce them into adopting habits of thrift, sobriety, duty, and rectitude the way charity agents did, settlers maintained that the goal of the movement's proponents was to build bridges between rich and poor. One way to do this, they argued, was to demonstrate the importance and extent of the contributions, immediate and potential, of the working class to the larger society. Another way was to "give back" to labouring people the cultural heritage—the art, music, literature, theatre, and philosophy—that was rightfully theirs.[42]

A year after Cartwright presented her paper, Mary Lawson Bell and Sara Libby Carson, the founders of Evangelia House, came to speak at a University Women's Club reception. In the spring of 1902 Carson and Bell, both former YWCA organizers, had quietly established Toronto's first settlement house in a working-class neighbourhood just east of the Don River. Modelled on Toynbee Hall and Hull-House—the leading settlements of the movement—Evangelia set out to be a combined recreational centre, night school, and social agency. Its membership was mainly of British origin, at that time entirely female, and between the ages of about six and twenty.[43] The settlement's initial focus on girls and adolescent women was deliberate. As Mary Bell pointed out in 1902, "Toronto, a city of homes, has not many social attractions for the business girl or woman, outside the church social, theatre or vaudeville."[44] Bell and Carson began their venture by addressing that gap. Buoyed by early success, by the beginning of 1904 Carson and Bell decided to enlarge Evangelia's mandate beyond girls and young women to include the rest of the community, a move that entailed the expansion of the settlement's sources of financial and volunteer support. One of the first groups to which the two settlement organizers turned was the University Women's Club.

According to the minutes, UWC members listened with interest to Carson and Bell's presentation. Carson in particular was a dynamic public speaker; as Constance Laing reported in the *S. Hilda's Chronicle*,

> Different phases of this great work were dealt with in so forcible and graphic a manner that all present felt a desire to know something more of a field of labour which produces such remarkable results, and in which, by reason of her training, the college graduate should be able to give valuable assistance.[45]

Carson assured her audience that while the settlement clearly benefited its neighbourhood, settlement volunteers and staff profited as well. She especially stressed the stimulating challenges that settlement work offered: "Problems and intellects and situations" she said, "are being continually encountered which call for the exercise of all the education and power—the very best—the worker can give."[46]

Stirred by Carson's description, Edith Elwood and Jennie Pearce, a graduate of University College, made appointments to visit the settlement immediately after the talk, and within a few months Edith had resigned her teaching post to become one of Evangelia's resident workers. For Edith, settlement work provided an unprecedented opportunity to utilize fully her educational credentials, social status, and training—what Pierre Bourdieu terms "cultural capital"—along with the skills in public speaking, fundraising, and organization that she developed as a teacher, clubwoman, and school administrator.[47] Though it offered even less security and remuneration than teaching, the settlement offered in their stead access to a new and potentially significant source of power for women. For Elwood and her colleagues knew well that in the United States and Britain the number of settlements was growing rapidly and the most prominent settlement workers among them—women like Jane Addams, Alice Hamilton, and Mary Ward—were becoming increasingly influential figures in the public arena.[48] Canadian settlement workers might quite reasonably hope for a similar result. Just as importantly, women like Elwood could anticipate that through settlement work they might effect genuine social change. Movement representatives insisted that their institutions were inherently and demonstrably superior to the approaches to poor relief and social uplift utilized by missions, poor houses and private charities. One enthusiast put it this way:

> The old system of patronage is responsible for many of the greatest evils in the world, for it fosters insincerity and servility. [But] The settlement places everybody on the same true basis, as fellow-workers.... [It] is fair in applying the same rules of conduct to all alike, and in taking a man on his merits.[49]

While movement representatives sometimes fell short of that ideal in practice, settlement work nevertheless extended to women like Elwood the prospect of redefining themselves as agents of a dynamic approach to reform.

Evangelia's physical and social environment was, moreover, one that Edith and other university women would have found very familiar. Like St. Hilda's, space in Evangelia was organized—quite literally—on an ascending scale of privacy, with laundry and kitchen facilities (which doubled as domestic science classrooms) in the basement, public rooms like the library, assembly hall and gymnasium on the ground floor, dining and reception rooms, which also served as classrooms, on the second floor, and private bedrooms for the resident workers on the top floor.[50] When the settlement moved to a refurbished mansion/brewery in 1907, this private/public arrangement remained intact.

The patterns of everyday life at Evangelia also resembled those of a college residence. There was a regular routine of work, study and rest, communal meals, and servants to do the bulk of the cooking as well as the heavy cleaning. With the exception of the volunteers from the colleges and alumnae associations who, beginning in the spring of 1905, lived in the settlement for a week or two at the end of the academic year, the resident workers each had their own rooms, which they furnished and cared for themselves.[51]

Edith would also have found that she and her fellow settlement workers had a common social and educational background and similar values. Of Evangelia's first five residents, two—Elwood and Pearce—had university degrees and the other three had some form of specialized training. Like most early settlement workers in Britain and the United States, all five came from relatively privileged backgrounds, as did the Canadian women who joined them later; they were between the ages of 26 and 40, Protestant, and their commitment to social service was buttressed by their religious convictions.[52]

Indeed, from the beginning Evangelia's staff maintained that their work was spiritual as well as social and educational. In fact, though Toynbee Hall, Hull House, and other "first-tier" settlements in the United States and Britain avoided any direct allusions to religion, most settlement workers were spiritually motivated, and many were proponents of what later became known as the social gospel.[53] Like most settlements, however, Evangelia was not connected to any church, and the religion its workers endeavoured to impart was nondenominational in faith. In addition, Evangelia's worship services—for which Elwood became responsible after joining the settlement—were optional; members did not need to attend them in order to participate fully in other settlement activities.[54]

Former Evangelia members remembered Edith Elwood as having "an exceptional gift for interesting people in work that she considered important."[55] She put this knack for persuasion to work in fundraising from her earliest days as a settlement worker. It was Edith, for example, who went in 1904 to the various colleges and alumnae groups to persuade them to become "chapters" of Evangelia. Each chapter, she explained, would contribute $25 annually and would receive in exchange a seat on Evangelia's board of directors and the "privilege" of sending either two juniors to live at the settlement for a week or one junior for a fortnight. The chapter idea became very popular among Toronto's female undergraduate societies and alumnae groups; St Hilda's alumnae association, for example, expressed great pride in the fact that it was Evangelia's "Alpha" chapter.[56]

But though it drew on a strong base of volunteer support from its chapters, the settlement needed patrons with much deeper pockets in order to secure its future and allow it to grow. For this, in the end, Evangelia's residents turned to Toronto's business elite, and here Edith's connections with Trinity and Bishop Strachan School undoubtedly proved helpful. She was most likely the one, for example, who first approached Sir Edmund Osler, the wealthy financier and Trinity patron, as well as other well-to-do Anglicans including Sarah Warren, Joseph Henderson, and the families of her former Parkdale students to ask for support for Evangelia House. Impressed with Edith's educational credentials, as well as her "sound business sense," Sir Edmund soon became Evangelia's most generous benefactor. He assumed the role of president of the settlement's executive council (a position in which he remained for over a decade), and in 1905 he and three of his associates organized a subscription appeal to "one thousand gentlemen of Toronto" on Evangelia's behalf.[57] Then in 1907 he helped the settlement to buy, renovate, and equip a large building, complete with extensive grounds, at the northeast corner of Queen and River Streets. Elwood later persuaded Osler to donate a 40-acre property on Lake Simcoe to Evangelia for a summer camp.[58] While she and her co-workers still campaigned energetically among women's groups for financial and volunteer support, the sponsorship of Toronto's wealthy elite helped to elevate Evangelia into an entirely different category among non-governmental social agencies. Indeed, the importance of the occasion of Evangelia's grand opening at its Queen and River location in October 1907 was marked by the presence of a number of dignitaries, including Lieutenant-Governor Sir William Clark, Mayor Emerson Coatsworth, Robert Falconer, the recently appointed president of the University of Toronto, and the Governor-General, Earl Grey, who was guest of honour.[59]

Soon after establishing Evangelia House in its new, expanded quarters Sarah Carson resigned her post as headworker and returned to settlement work in New York, her original home. Mary Bell had already left the settlement in 1905 due to ill health. Edith Elwood then took Carson's place as Evangelia's headworker. Her work as an administrator encompassed a wide range of roles and activities, from fundraising to training and supervising staff and volunteers and attending to the minutia involved in managing a busy, multi-purpose community centre. She increased the number of resident staff to 12 and maintained a volunteer corps of over 100. Evangelia's membership also grew, from 600 to over 2500. Elwood established a dispensary at Evangelia, complete with a small infirmary, free well-baby and public health clinics, a clean milk depot, public baths and a district nursing corps. Many of these services were either new to or very rare in Toronto. She also set up a branch of the Penny Bank for those who could not qualify for an account in a regular bank. In addition, she acted as a coordinator and liaison between various church-based welfare agencies, and worked with the Social Service Commission, the Parks Department, the Toronto General Hospital, and the Public Health Department to improve the city's poor relief, public health, and recreational facilities in the Cabbagetown and Riverdale districts.[60] When Toronto began expanding its public health department in the 1910s the city gradually took over responsibility for many of Evangelia's health services, but the services themselves remained centred in the settlement, and this once again affirmed the public position that Edith and her staff had attained.

As important as these community-oriented initiatives were to the development of social services in Toronto, the real work of the settlement, as far as Elwood and her staff were concerned, went on in the settlement's social clubs. Age-graded clubs provided the organizational backbone of Evangelia's programme. Clubs for school-aged children met between four and six in the afternoon, while working teens and adult men convened in the evenings and mothers and pre-schoolers in the mornings. It was a schedule based on the assumptions that school-aged children would be in school until late afternoon, that workers would be free in the evenings, that most working-class adult women were mothers, and that mothers—especially mothers of young children—were at home during the day. Those whose lives did not fit these parameters, like newsboys or shift workers or adult women (mothers or not) employed outside the home, found it much more difficult to participate in settlement events.

Each club had its own supervisor—one of the resident workers or a university volunteer who came in for a few hours each week—its own club song and colours, and its own executive, which rotated a few times a year so that each member had a chance to be president, secretary, or treasurer and thus to practice leadership, accounting, and managerial skills. The supervisors' main job was to ensure that the weekly business meetings of the clubs under their charge were run according to strict parliamentary procedure; even five-year-olds were expected to learn how to "call the question," collect the dues, and work through an agenda.

The prominence given to clubs within the settlement movement underlines an important link between the settlements and other institutions through which women developed a sense of autonomy and independence. According to Petra Munro, women's clubs profoundly shaped women's culture and identity and played a pivotal role in the social and political development of western society in the late nineteenth and early twentieth centuries.[61] It was often through their clubs, notes Anne Firor Scott, that middle-class women first learned "how to conduct business, carry on meetings, speak in public and manage money"[62]—skills they needed in order to expand their social and cultural spheres. Since the leaders of the settlement movement saw the empowerment of the working poor as an important part of their mandate, it is scarcely surprising that they encouraged settlement members to join clubs and acquire the same skills that middle-class women had found so effective.

It is clear that in establishing clubs settlement workers were attempting to instil in their members a middle-class conception of culture and power. Yet this should not lead us to conclude that settlement members were passive participants in this exercise, or that they found the clubs, and the skills they acquired through them, to be valueless. One must remember that settlement membership was voluntary; unlike the schools, where attendance was compulsory, no one was forced to go to a settlement, and since settlements avoided, if they could dispensing charity directly, the need to secure the basic necessities of life did not compel neighbours to join either. Evangelia was, nonetheless, a very popular institution—in large part because its staff carefully monitored members' reactions to settlement initiatives and experiments, adding, altering or eliminating programs according to those responses, and in general remaining as flexible as they could to the needs and interests of the neighbourhood.

After dispensing with the formal part of the club meeting Edith and her coworkers helped club members to organize their games and snacks, and then sent them off either to the classes they had chosen or to the library for help with their homework. Most members attended settlement classes—often taught by volunteers from the university—with their fellow club-mates. The kinds of instruction clubs requested ranged from plain sewing and cooking to stenography, drawing, woodworking, nature study, and "physical culture." Like the worship services, none of these classes was compulsory; club members were not compelled to take sewing, for example, though it appears that most of the girls did, while most of the boys took woodworking. But settlement instruction did not always adhere to gender norms. Some boys' and men's clubs, for example, asked for and received permission to join the girls' cooking classes.[63]

Evangelia also established classes for young people who wanted to continue their formal education and perhaps even matriculate. Elwood herself supervised the settlement's English Department, which offered instruction in English Literature and History.[64] She made the study and performance of Shakespearean plays a particular feature of the settlement; under her supervision Evangelia became an early and avid proponent of community theatre.

In keeping with her enthusiasm for athletics, Elwood also organized Toronto's first supervised playground at Evangelia in the summer of 1905. In contrast to later play experts, however, she seems to have focused mainly on the sociality of the playground rather than the management and regulation of children's play.[65] As she noted in 1909:

> The mornings from ten to twelve were an exceedingly busy time for the little people in the neighbourhood, and many were the demands upon the helpers in charge for the building of sand forts, or the giving of high swings and "run-unders." ...Canvas hammocks swung under the trees in the garden formed an agreeable refuge for numerous infants who accompanied their older sisters and brothers to the playground.... The summer evenings were happily spent by many of our evening members in playing croquet or in enjoying the gymnastic apparatus in our well-lighted playground. At such times in especial, did we appreciate our garden tables and chairs, and many social evenings were happily concluded with ice-cream and cake under the trees.[66]

This passage suggests that Evangelia's playground supervisors were more interested in facilitating the children's play than they were in controlling or directing it—though their mere presence, of course, would have had a regulating effect. This stress on informal sociality is also reflected in the reminiscences of a former member, who recalled that the settlement "had beautiful lawns and trees and we played croquet on the lawns and had evening parties and singing, so many boys and girls who worked could come and enjoy it as well as fathers. It was well lighted and looked wonderful."[67]

Sports, however, involved a more formal disciplinary element. Along these lines, Elwood organized extramural basketball competitions as well as something called captain ball for girls, and extramural basketball, baseball, and football teams for boys, hoping, perhaps, that the contests with groups from outside the neighbourhood might help to integrate the settlement's population more closely with the larger community. She also established gymnastics classes for both children and adults. Interestingly, she encouraged adult men and women to participate in athletics, as well as children and teens. For Elwood, the overall focus of athletics was on promoting teamwork and a sense of community. It was a focus that also infused the organization of family and neighbourhood events, like weekend skating parties in winter and picnics in summer, as well as streetcar trips to Scarborough Beach, musical evenings, and general interest talks on subjects ranging from "The Oyster" to archaeological expeditions to Egypt.[68]

In a 1910 article for the *S. Hilda's Chronicle* Edith discussed the significance of these myriad activities. Drawing a parallel between the university and the settlement, she noted that the classes, entertainments, and activities in which settlement members engaged were, like those in which university students participated, ultimately aimed at revealing "latent and hitherto unknown powers and possibilities"—both to their working-class possessors and to those of the wealthier classes who were highly sceptical of the integrity, intelligence, and self-discipline of the poor.[69] For some settlement members, their "unknown powers and possibilities" seem to have led them out of the working-class altogether; for example, at least two Evangelia members became settlement workers themselves. Some of the others went into teaching, medicine, or the ministry.[70]

While Evangelia's classes provided instruction in a wide variety of skills and interests, the settlement's resident workers and volunteers were expected to model, with every word and deed, more important lessons in personal conduct, ethics, and morality. In essence, Elwood and her colleagues attempted to create what the movement's leader, Jane Addams, called an "infectious example." This endeavour extended to their style of dress and grooming as well as their behaviour. Elwood apparently took the job of role model very seriously. As one former member noted, "I remember her always dressed in a tweed skirt, plain white cotton blouse with long sleeves, stiff white 'men's' collar and narrow flowing tie with a tie pin."[71] Others remembered more her manner; she was, by these accounts "a very vital person, strong and gay."[72] Clearly, the "infectious example" that Edith hoped to set was happy, confident, and lively in manner, but practical and rather restrained in dress—perhaps in direct and deliberate contrast to the giddiness and gaudiness that, according to some jaundiced-eyed observers, characterized the behaviour and attire of too many young, working-class women.[73]

Whether or not she consciously attempted to influence what Evangelia's members wore, Elwood became a recognized authority on what they did in the workforce. In particular, she compiled the statistics on working conditions in Toronto and its surrounding districts, and was a frequent contributor to the *Labour Gazette*.[74] As convenor of the University Women's Club's social and industrial committees, and later as the Club's president, she organized a number of "investigations" of the wages, working environments, and cost of living for women employed in Toronto industries. On the basis of that research she recommended the enactment of minimum wage legislation, noting that many working women were not paid enough to cover their daily needs, and that while "the average girl wage earner is courageous and unassailable in virtue," some had been forced into prostitution, many were half starving, and all were in danger of becoming exhausted and weak. This, she darkly warned, threatened the future of Canadian citizenship, for the "working girls" of today were the mothers of tomorrow.[75] It was a powerful argument in an era in which women were defined almost entirely in terms of their reproductive role.

Elwood's concerns were not, however, limited to the plight of the "working girl." Her tenure as headworker of Evangelia saw important changes in the character of Toronto's poorest districts as the number of Eastern and Southern European immigrants settling in Toronto began to rise. Elwood and other observers began to remark upon the trend around 1909. The majority of the newcomers ended up in neighbourhoods to the west of Evangelia, especially in St. John's Ward, and between 1910 and 1912 four new settlements were organized to work with these new groups. Evangelia's neighbourhood also began to change. As Elwood told the Canadian Conference of Charities and Correction (CCCC) in 1911, the settlement's

> watchwords are cooperation and adaptation, the latter essential in meeting the conditions of a changing neighborhood, which five years ago was almost entirely English speaking, but which now presents 10 different nationalities and upon many shops, stores and churches are a variety of signs in an unknown tongue.[76]

In addition to the well-established problems of poverty, exploitation, and social isolation, Evangelia now began to wrestle, to a greater degree than it had previously, with inter-ethnic suspicion, and religious and cultural intolerance. Though the population of Evangelia's district remained mainly British, community building through neighbourhood interaction was nevertheless becoming a much more complex and challenging proposition.

In response to these new concerns, Edith began to lobby vigorously for the professionalization of social service. In 1910 she presented settlement work as a viable alternative career for university women who did not want to become teachers.[77] She had trained many workers herself—not only for her own staff, but for other social agencies in Toronto and in other Canadian cities as well.[78] Yet in the absence of a Canadian school of social work most of those who were interested in the field had to go to the United States for training, and the majority did not return home afterward. The net result was a loss for Canadian social work, and for Canadian society more generally. As Elwood explained to her reform colleagues in 1911,

> One reason for [Canada's] delay in taking up settlement work has been the lack of trained workers, for it requires to be understood that settlement

A Passion for Service

work is scientific, and the social settlement worker must either feel his way experimentally, groping in the dark amid the intricate network of city life channels, or else bring a trained intelligence to bear upon the solution of the city's problems.[79]

In response, she began to mobilize support for professional training for social workers in the women's groups and reform associations, like the Social Science Study Club and the Social Workers' Club, to which she belonged. In the fall of 1913 a delegation from these two clubs met with the University of Toronto's president, Robert Falconer, to discuss the creation of a formal, university-sponsored training program for social workers. A year later, after much wrangling, debate, and the financial intercession of Edith's friend, Sarah Warren, the University of Toronto's Department of Social Service opened its doors.[80]

The insistence of Canadian proponents of social work training that the program be housed within university walls deserves further reflection. There were, after all, a number of precedents in the United States and Britain for schools of social work that were either independent or only loosely affiliated with a college or university. One factor, no doubt, was the overall push to make the university the final arbiter of professional status in as many fields as possible. Many accepted the argument that a university credential offered proof of the intellectual breadth and depth a true professional required in order to be worthy of the title. Another factor may have been the concern to draw men to the field. As Daniel Walkowitz and others have demonstrated, professional status has been, at least until recently, strongly linked to the proportion of men to women in any given field. Elwood and other members of that first generation of Canadian university women were likely influenced, as well, by their experience of higher education and its positive effect on their ability to operate in the public sphere. But perhaps the most important factor had to do with the kind of person Elwood and her colleagues hoped to attract to social work. Employing the male pronoun to represent both men and women, according to common usage of the time, Elwood explained it this way:

> A settlement worker must be beyond all else a student of conditions, he must have a realization of what a city is, he must see beyond the bricks and mortar of its topography.... He must study the immigrant in his native land as well as in the land of his adoption, he must try to appreciate what is his inheritance of culture, of life ideals and standards, and so to arrive at the conservation of human resources.[81]

In other words, the ideal professional social worker, like the ideal academic, was a skilled researcher and dispassionate observer.

In late January of 1914 the *Telegram* reported briefly, and seemingly out of the blue, that Edith Elwood and John P. MacLaren, an Ottawa architect, were planning to marry on 11 February 1914. Edith was 38 years old and had been at Evangelia for ten years. Details of how she met her future husband, the length of the courtship, and the circumstances that led up to her decision to marry have not survived. But the society columns of Toronto newspapers covered the wedding extensively. Settlement members, social workers, and socialites alike attended the ceremony, and Sarah Warren threw a lavish reception at her home. After a brief honeymoon in New York, Elwood and her husband moved to Ottawa to begin their married life.[82]

Given the pattern of her life, it is not surprising that Edith did not allow marriage to end her public career. Though she gave birth to a son in 1917, and clearly devoted a good deal of time to her family and her church,[83] social work remained her passion. As soon as she arrived in Ottawa she joined the board of directors of the Ottawa Settlement, ultimately becoming its president. Mary Bell, Evangelia's first headworker, organized the settlement in Ottawa in 1909 with the help of Flora MacNeill, whom Bell sent to live for a year (1908) at Evangelia House in order to learn settlement methods. Edith visited the Ottawa Settlement almost daily, taking charge of one of the clubs for thirteen- to fifteen-year-old girls, organizing and supervising the settlement's summer camp from 1916 to 1918, and leading its Sunday evening worship services. In addition to her involvement in the settlement, which closed in 1920, she also took an active role as a board member of the "Home for Friendless Women."[84]

Edith also joined the Ottawa Local Council of Women in 1914, and along with two other members, Mrs. Bryce Stewart and Dr. Elizabeth Shortt, organized the Ottawa Welfare Bureau.[85] In keeping with her settlement-inspired vision of the cooperative community, Edith herself established a network of neighbourhood associations for the Bureau, dividing the city's private philanthropic agencies—churches, charities, and community organizations—into Eastern, Central and Western Neighbourhood Associations, a structure much like that of the Social Service Commission in Toronto. She undertook the leadership of the Eastern association, and was as well an active member of the Bureau's executive and several of its sub-committees. In addition, she was the Bureau's representative in the majority of its interactions with city councillors and members of the business community.[86] According to a report in the *S. Hilda's Chronicle*, under Edith's leadership the Bureau united "all the relief giving agencies of the city," operating a "social exchange" (a register of all the families receiving holiday hampers and special assistance in the summer) and a family casework agency.[87] Yet intriguingly, no mention of her was made in a 1928 article in *Social Welfare* on the history and current activities of the Ottawa Welfare Bureau;[88] the organization had by then been taken over by a group of male bureaucrats and female social workers who, like many of their colleagues elsewhere, were beginning to downplay the involvement of wealthy women volunteers in order to raise their professional status. Ironically, Elwood's role in the establishment of the Bureau was, apparently, to be dismissed or ignored by the profession that she had worked to build. Her concerns, however, had by then shifted closer to home, for just a month before *Social Welfare* published this article ill health forced Elwood to resign from the Bureau's executive. She died three years later, following a painful and lengthy illness (likely cancer).[89]

Elwood played, nevertheless, a significant part in the development of what has come to be identified as the modern welfare state. As a settlement worker Elwood worked for reform in countless venues—labour, public health, recreation, welfare, housing, and more. She made Evangelia House a creative centre for the development of many of the programs that were later subsumed into what is now termed the social safety net. As an administrator, both in Toronto and in Ottawa, she helped to establish the structures and relationships that local governmental agencies adopted as they assumed responsibility for the social programs that Elwood and her colleagues created. In the process, she became an active participant in the re-formation of the Canadian state and the redefinition of its relationship to Canadian society.

Throughout the campaign for a social work training program, and throughout her career in general, Edith Elwood relied upon the complex network of women's voluntary associations that were established in Toronto after the turn of the century. Like her counterparts working out of Hull-House, she depended both on separatism—that is, separate women's institutions, culture and consciousness—and close affiliation with male reformers and male-dominated organizations to accomplish her goals. Hull-House, argues Kathryn Kish Sklar, provided activists like Jane Addams, Florence Kelley, and Edith Abbott with "an emotional and economic substitute for traditional family life." The settlement linked them, as well, with other powerful women and women's organizations and enabled them to cooperate with male reformers and their organizations without having to submit to male control. Sklar points out that the *autonomy* of these women was the outcome of their membership in a women's *community*, which encompassed not just Hull-House but also an intricate system of women's clubs and civic associations.[90]

The same was also true for Edith Elwood; Evangelia furnished her with work she considered deeply meaningful, a supportive community of like-minded women, and access to, as well as independence within, the male-dominated arena of local politics and business. In the meantime the voluntary organizations to which Edith belonged extended her political and social influence and gave financial support and practical assistance besides.[91] Yet however effective this network helped her to be as an innovator, community leader, and reformer, once her work was subsumed into a male-dominated government bureaucracy, her work was largely forgotten.

The factors that led to this forgetting are complex. Certainly gender was crucial. While, throughout the course of her life Elwood's privileged class status provided her with opportunities available to few other women, gender roles and expectations served to limit, from an early age, many of her educational choices and occupational activities. Higher education may have been opened to women in Elwood's day, but the areas of study available to them were still restricted, as was their participation in the public sphere. Marital status was also a factor: as a married woman Elwood went from being a respected leader in the field of social service to a well-meaning volunteer, and by the late 1920s, "volunteer" had come to be synonymous with "dilettante" in professional social work circles. The professionalization of social work was itself a factor. Though it was something Elwood worked hard to bring about, by the end of the 1920s the model that many professional social workers in Canada had begun to adopt focused on individual casework and on the development of highly structured bureaucracies—quite different from the community-oriented model that Elwood and other settlement leaders advocated.

What, in the end, can Edith Elwood's life tell us about the history of women and of state formation in Canada? First, that the source of women's power has often been centered in women's organizations and coalitions. Second, that women in the early twentieth century were active participants in Canadian state formation, most often and most powerfully through their organizations and coalitions. Third, that for reformers like Elwood, reform demanded a spatial commitment that affected every aspect of their lives, at work and in leisure, in private and in public. And finally, that an examination of what women like Elwood actually did emphasizes what Shannon Jackson calls "the material acts of construction implicit in the term *reform*."[92] For Elwood, in the end, social work meant direct and daily contact, cooperation, and face-to-face conversation—a reminder, to paraphrase Jackson, of the *social* character of social reform.

Notes

[1] This historiography is huge. Some excellent examples include Alison Prentice, "Bluestockings, Feminists, or Women Workers? A Preliminary Look at Women's Early Employment at the University of Toronto," *Journal of the Canadian Historical Association* NS2 (1991): 231-61; Beverley Boutilier and Alison Prentice, *Creating Historical Memory: English-Canadian Women and the Work of History* (Vancouver: UBC Press, 1997); Judith Fingard, "College, Career and Community: Dalhousie Coeds, 1881-1921," and Diana Pedersen, " 'The Call to Service': The YWCA and Canadian College Women, 1886-1920," both in Paul Axelrod and John G. Reid, (eds.), *Youth, University and Canadian Society: Essays in the Social History of Higher Education* (Montreal: McGill-Queen's University Press, 1989); Margaret Gillett, *We Walked Very Warily: A History of Women at McGill* (Montreal: McGill-Queen's University Press, 1981); Johanna M. Selles, *Methodists and Women's Education in Ontario, 1836-1925* (Montreal: McGill-Queen's University Press, 1996); Sara Z. Burke, *Seeking the Highest Good: Gender and Social Service at the University of Toronto, 1888-1937* (Toronto: University of Toronto Press, 1996); and Mary Kinnear, "Disappointed in Discourse: Women Professors at the University of Manitoba before 1970," *Historical Studies in Education/Revue d'histoire de l'education* 4, 2 (Fall 1992): 269-87.

[2] Though after Edith married she took her husband's last name, McLaren, she was

A Passion for Service

known during her working life by her maiden name, Elwood; for the purposes of clarity, the latter is the name I shall use in referring to her in this essay.

3   Government of Canada, *Census of Canada, 1880-81* (Ottawa: Department of Agriculture, 1882-85); Andrew C. Holman, *A Sense of Their Duty: Middle-Class Formation in Victorian Ontario Towns* (Kingston and Montreal: McGill-Queen's University Press, 2000), 5.

4   "Obituary," *Huron Signal* (6 October 1875); University of Toronto (UTA) Department of Graduate Records, A73-0026/096 (63) clippings file—Edith Elwood, from the *Globe* (4 May 1921).

5   Edward Elwood and his wife, Ellen Yeats, had eleven children, of whom eight— four boys and four girls—survived into adulthood. The careers of the boys and the marriages of the girls still living in 1880 are noted in the entry on Edward L. Elwood in *The Canadian Biographical Dictionary and Portrait Gallery of Eminent and Self-Made Men: Ontario Volume* (Toronto, Chicago and New York: American Biographical Publishing Company, 1880), 59. See also Malcolm E. Campbell *et al.*, *Memories of Goderich: The Romance of the Prettiest Town in Canada* 2nd ed., (Goderich: 1979), 184-85 and Huron County Branch O.G.S. (Ontario Genealogical Society) B-21, Maitland Cemetery, Goderich, ON concession MT, Lot 4, 250, "Elwood." The family was also directly related to William Butler Yeats, the noted Irish poet; in fact, he was Edith's cousin. See "Mrs J.P. MacLaren [sic] Noted Social Worker" *Ottawa Citizen* (24 December 1931): 5.

6   See *Canadian Biographical Dictionary*, 58-59 and Holman, *A Sense of Their Duty*, especially pages 72-73 and 150-60.

7   Ethel Middleton, Edith's cousin, was another university-educated Elwood granddaughter. Indeed, Ethel was one of the first two women to take lectures at Trinity College in 1886. See Paula J.S. LaPierre, "The First Generation: The Experience of Women University Students in Central Canada," (Ph.D. diss., University of Toronto, 1993), 157. The other woman was Helen Gregory MacGill, who became the first woman to graduate from Trinity. MacGill earned a Mus. Bac. in 1886 and a B.A. in 1889. See Elsie Gregory MacGill, *My Mother the Judge: A Biography of Helen Gregory MacGill* (Toronto: 1955, repr. Toronto: PMA Books, 1955), 40-54. Ethel Middleton graduated from Trinity in 1890 and also studied for a year at Newnham College, Cambridge in 1900. See St Hilda's *Calendar* for 1893, p. 14, and "St Hilda's Notes," *Trinity University Review* 13, 3 (March 1900): 44. For an excellent discussion of elite women's private schooling, see Marjorie Theobald, *Knowing Women: Origins of Women's Education in Nineteenth-Century Australia* (Melbourne: Cambridge University Press, 1996).

8   Holman, *A Sense of Their Duty*, 111-123.

9   Government of Canada, *Census of Canada, 1880-81* (Ottawa: Department of Agriculture, 1882-85).

10 "Obituary," *Huron Signal* (6 October 1875).

11 R. D. Gidney and W.P.J. Millar, *Inventing Secondary Education: The Rise of the High School in Nineteenth-Century Ontario* (Montreal and Kingston: McGill-Queen's University Press, 1990).

12 H. M. Wright, "Opening Sketch," *This in Remembrance: A Memorial of the Life and Service of Edith Constance MacLaren* ([Ottawa]: The Dale Harris Branch of the Canadian Home Reading Union, n.d.), 3. We can conclude that the high school did well by Edith's eldest brother too, for he became a barrister and eventually a court justice in Regina, Saskatchewan. Interestingly, at seventeen Edith's sister

Mary attended the elite and academically exacting Bishop Strachan School in Toronto in 1886-87. See Bishop Strachan School Archives (BSSA), Student Register, 1886-87.
13   *The Calendar for S. Hilda's College in Toronto, 1893* (Toronto: Rowsell and Hutchison, Printers, 1893), 19-23.
14   Trinity College Archives (hereafter TCA), Box 74, Degree Book, 1852-1904. At that time still an independent church institution, the college did not affiliate with the University of Toronto until ten years later.
15   See LaPierre, "The First Generation," 58-61, 157 and MacGill, *My Mother*, 49-50.
16   Ethel Middleton boarded at the Bishop Strachan School while attending lectures at Trinity in 1886. Ethel's presence at BSS may have been the reason that Edith's sister Mary attended BSS for her final year of high school—essentially, to keep Ethel company. Helen Gregory, the other woman student at Trinity in 1886, stayed with family members living in town. It is not clear how this arrangement worked out: perhaps not well, for Ethel took a year off from her studies in 1887, returning in 1888 to become one of St. Hilda's first two residents. See BSSA, Student Register, 1886-87 and Ethel Middleton, "Life at S. Hilda's, 88-90," *S. Hilda's Chronicle* 3, 2 (Trinity term, 1903): 39-40.
17   Jo LaPierre, "The Academic Life of Canadian Coeds, 1880-1900" in Ruby Heap and Alison Prentice, (eds.), *Gender and Education in Ontario: An Historical Reader* (Toronto: Canadian Scholar's Press, 1991), 316.
18   While she was teaching at St. Hilda's Clara Brett Martin was also fighting to gain entry to law school. In 1893 she was finally successful, and in 1897, after a great deal of struggle, she became the first woman lawyer in the British Commonwealth. See Constance Backhouse, *Petticoats and Prejudice: Women and Law in Nineteenth-Century Canada* (Toronto: The Osgoode Society, 1991): 293-326.
19   Middleton, "Life at S. Hilda's," 39-40; see also LaPierre, "The First Generation," 155, 231.
20   Middleton, "Life at S. Hilda's," 40; see also LaPierre, "The First Generation," 186-88.
21   Middleton, "Life at S. Hilda's."
22   *Trinity College Year Book, 1897*, E.C.E., St. Hilda's College, "The Undergraduate View," 81-82; LaPierre, "The First Generation," 191.
23   LaPierre, "The First Generation," 231.
24   Middleton, "Life at S. Hilda's," 39.
25   Mabel Cartwright, "College Settlements," *S. Hilda's Chronicle* 3, 2 (Trinity term, 1903): 43.
26   LaPierre, "The Academic Life," 303-28.
27   "Examination Results," *Trinity University Review* 9, (June, July, August 1896): 79.
28   Ontario Archives (OA), RG 2-357-2-3, container 2, Ontario School of Pedagogy, Examination Results, 1897; "St. Hilda's College," *Trinity University Review* 9, 11 (November 1896): 118
29   See, for example, *Trinity College Year Book, 1897-98*, "St. Hilda's College," 84-87, and *1898-99*, 26.
30   BSSA, Minute Book 1896-1926, Minutes of the [Bishop Strachan School] Council, 1902-1905; Bishop Strachan School *Jubilee Record Bulletin, 1867-1927* (Toronto: [1927]), 21; Katherine N. Hooke, "Women's Teaching and Service: An Anglican Perspective in Ontario, 1867-1930," *Journal of the Church Historical*

Society 23, 2 (October 1990): 12.

31 "Graduates Column," *S. Hilda's Chronicle* 4, 1 (Lent 1904): 22-23. She certainly retained the affections of her pupils long after resigning from Parkdale, for a number of her former students, along with their mothers, later came to work for Edith as volunteers at Evangelia House. See BR, S54, History of Canadian Settlements, Notes—Book B, Miss Ethel Bunker to Miss Irene Hardy, 18 February 1963 and Adeline Wadsworth, 'Reminiscences.'

32 Margaret Foster, *The First Fifty Years: A History of the University Women's Club of Toronto, 1903-1953* (Toronto: Hunter Rose Co. Ltd., 1953), 1; University Women's Club Archives (UWCA), Minutes, Vol. 1, 24 April 1903.

33 TCA, Box 74, Degree Book, 1852-1904; *Calendar of Trinity University, Toronto for 1902-03* (Toronto: Arthurs & Co., Printers, 1902), 39, 66.

34 See, for example, "The Evolution of the Higher Education of Women," in the Anglican journal *Canadian Churchman* (28 July 1910): 479, as well as "Our Falling Birth Rate," editorial, *Canadian Churchman* (30 March 1911): 197.

35 Anne Firor Scott, *Natural Allies: Women's Associations in American History* (Urbana: University of Illinois Press, 1991).

36 See UWCA, Minutes, vols. I and II, *passim*. See also Foster, *The First Fifty Years*, 6-7.

37 UWC Archives, Minutes, vol. I, 24 April 1903; Johanna Selles-Roney, "A Canadian Girl at Cheltenham College: The Diary as a Historical Source," *Historical Studies in Education* 3, 1 (Fall 1991): 93-103. See also T.A. Reed, ed., *A History of the University of Trinity College, Toronto, 1852-1952* (Toronto: University of Toronto Press, 1952): 191.

38 Mabel Cartwright, "College Settlements," *S. Hilda's Chronicle* III, 2 (Trinity 1903): 43.

39 See Cathy L. James, "Reforming Reform: Toronto's Settlement Movement, 1900-1920," *Canadian Historical Review* 82, 1 (March 2001): 55-90. See also Kathryn Kish Sklar, *Florence Kelley and the Nation's Work* (Princeton: Yale University Press, 1995), and Jill Kerr Conway, *The First Generation of Women Graduates* (New York: Garland, 1987).

40 Settlement workers hated the term 'slum' and rarely, if ever, used it. See Shannon Jackson, *Lines of Activity*, (Ann Arbor: University of Michigan Press, 2000.

41 "Social Work," unsigned article, *S. Hilda's Chronicle* 5, 5 (Trinity 1906): 21-22.

42 Jane Addams, 'Social Settlements,' *Proceedings of the National Conference of Charities and Correction* 24 (1897): 339.

43 The institution's initial gender exclusivity was a reflection of its early link to the Dominion Council of the YWCA. Settlement workers, it should be said, referred to the people who used the settlements as members or neighbours, never as clients.

44 Mary Bell, "Settlement Work: As I Have Thought of It and Seen It, and Lived It," *Dominion Tie* II, 12 (December 1903): 333.

45 Constance B. Laing, "Graduates' Column," *S. Hilda's Chronicle*, 4, 1 (Lent 1904): 22.

46 UWCA, Minutes, vol. I, 22 January 1904.

47 See David Swartz, *Culture and Power: The Sociology of Pierre Bourdieu* (Chicago & London: University of Chicago Press, 1997), 136-37; see also Petra Munro, "Political Activism as Teaching: Jane Addams and Ida B. Wells," in Crocco *et al.*, *Pedagogies of Resistance*, 19.

48 See Robyn Muncy, *Creating a Female Dominion in American Reform, 1890-1935*

(New York: Oxford University Press, 1991 and Jane Lewis, *Women and Social Action in Victorian and Edwardian England* (Aldershot: Edward Elgar, 1991).
49. "Social Work," *S. Hilda's Chronicle*, 5, 3 (Trinity 1906): 21-22.
50. It is important to note that domestic science was not yet available in local public schools. Evangelia, therefore, was very much on the cutting edge, pedagogically speaking, and appears to have been remarkably well equipped as well. The *Chronicle* description of Evangelia's classes observed, "Here may be seen young girls seated behind small tables, each with her own bake-board, gas stove, and dish-pan." "Alumnae Notes," *S. Hilda's Chronicle* 4, 3 (Michaelmas 1904): 60-61.
51. "The Young Women's Settlement and Secretarial Training School," *Dominion Tie* 1, 3 (1902): 18. Initially, the charge for room and board at the settlement was $4 per week, but it should be noted that this was the fee during the few months when Evangelia was the prospective training school for Canadian YWCA workers, as well as a settlement. For reasons that are not entirely clear, plans for the training school quickly fell through and Evangelia became a settlement only. It is also not clear if the fee schedule changed as a result.
52. I am fairly certain that the fifth woman was Katherine Wright, a long-time member of Evangelia's resident staff. The backgrounds of these women—especially Sara Libby Carson, Mary Bell and Katherine Wright—have proven extremely difficult to trace, and my assertions regarding their relative class status are based on numerous small remarks and allusions I have been able to piece together from the recollections of co-workers and former members, from minutes and publications of the International YWCA in New York and YWCA groups in Toronto, and from newspaper reports and city directories.
53. Allan F. Davis, *Spearheads of Reform: The Social Settlements and the Progressive Movement 1890-1914* (New York: Oxford University Press, 1967), 15-16; Mina Carson, *Settlement Folk:Social Thought and the American Settlement Movement, 1885-1930* (Chicago: University of Chicago Press, 1990), chapters 1 and 2.
54. P. A. Magee, ed., "The College Girl," *Varsity* 24, 8 (1 December 1904): 131.
55. Bunker to Hardy, 18 February 1963.
56. See, for example, *S. Hilda's Chronicle*, 4, 3 (Michaelmas, 1904): 57.
57. BR, M.S. files, Evangelia House, 1905—"Dear."
58. Wright, *This in Remembrance*, 4.
59. "Earl Grey Here To-Day to Open Evangelia Home," *Toronto World*, October 16, 1907:2, "His Excellency Had a Busy Day," *Mail and Empire*, October 17, 1907: 2, UTA, A67-007/028—Evangelia Settlement, Edmund B. Osler, "Summary of Ten Months Work from 1st January to 1st November, 1913."
60. Bunker to Hardy, 18 February 1963.
61. Munro, "Political Activism as Teaching," 21.
62. Scott, *Natural Allies*, 2. See also Priscilla Murolo, *The Common Ground of Womanhood: Class, Gender, and Working Girls' Clubs, 1884-1928* (Urbana, IL: University of Illinois Press, 1997).
63. Bunker to Hardy, 18 February 1963.
64. Wright, *This in Remembrance*, 4
65. Dominick Cavallo, *Muscles and Morals: Organized Playgrounds and Urban Reform, 1880-1920* (Philadelphia: University of Pennsylvania Press, 1981).
66. Wright, *This in Remembrance*, 5.
67. BR, S54, History of the Canadian Settlements, Notes—Book B, "Evangelia," Carol Hogg, notes of interview with Golden Haliburton, 1961.

A Passion for Service

68   O. A. R., "Evangelia Settlement: Impressions of a Summer Visitor," *S. Hilda's Chronicle* 7, 15 (Michaelmas, 1913), 15-18. See also Cathy L. James, "'Not Merely for the Sake of an Evening's Entertainment:' The Educational Uses of Theatre in Toronto's Settlement Houses, 1910-1930," *History of Education Quarterly*, 38, 3 (Fall 1998): 287-311.

69   Edith Elwood, "II. Settlement Work" *S. Hilda's Chronicle* 6, 7 (Michaelmas, 1910): 16.

70   BR, S54, History of the Canadian Settlements, Notes—Book B, "Evangelia."

71   Bunker to Hardy, 18 February 1963.

72   Bunker to Hardy, 18 February 1963.

73   A. S. Bastedo, "A Visit to Evangelia House," *The Varsity* 25, 3 (19 October 1905): 43. See also Murolo, *Common Ground*, 44; Kathy Peiss, *Cheap Amusements: Working Women and Leisure in Turn-of-the-Century New York* (Philadelphia: Temple University Press, 1986), and Carolyn Strange, *Toronto's Girl Problem: The Perils and Pleasures of the City, 1880-1930* (Toronto: University of Toronto Press, 1995), 197.

74   Wright, *This in Remembrance*, 7

75   UWCA, Minutes, vol. II, February 1913, Edith C. Elwood, "Recommendation by the Industrial and Social Sections." See also the UWC minutes of 2 November 1910 and 10 May 1912.

76   Edith Elwood, "The Social Settlement," *Twelfth Canadian Conference of Charities and Correction, Report of Proceedings*, Hamilton, 22-25 September 1911 (Toronto: William Briggs, 1911): 32.

77   Edith Elwood, "II. Settlement Work" *S. Hilda's Chronicle* 6, 7 (Michaelmas, 1910): 16.

78   Wright, *This in Remembrance*, 5.

79   Elwood, "The Social Settlement," CCCC *Proceedings*, 31.

80   UTA, Falconer Papers, A67-0007/032 (483) file: Social Service 1913-14; see also Burke, *Seeking*, 84.

81   Elwood, "The Social Settlement," CCCC *Proceedings*, 31.

82   UTA, Department of Graduate Records, A73-0026/096(63), clippings file, "Miss Elwood to Wed," *Telegram* (26 January 1914); "Prominent Social Worker Married in the Cathedral," *News* (11 February 1914); see also the *Mail* (12 February 1914) and *S. Hilda's Chronicle* 7, 16(Lent 1914): 24.

83   "Mrs. J.P. MacLaren Noted Social Worker," *Ottawa Citizen* (24 December 1931): 5; "Mrs. J.P. MacLaren is Deeply Mourned," *Ottawa Citizen* (28 December 1931): 4; UTA, Department of Graduate Records, A73-0026/096(63) clippings file, Edith Elwood (MacLaren), *Globe* (4 May 1921).

84   Wright, *This in Remembrance*, 9-10.

85   Elizabeth Shortt's husband was Adam Shortt, the well-known economic historian and dominion civil servant.

86   Wright, *This in Remembrance*, 10-13.

87   M. Pickford, "News from a Graduate," *S. Hilda's Chronicle: Graduation Supplement* (1925): 25.

88   "News of Social Workers and Agencies: Ottawa" *Social Welfare* 10, 6(March 1928): 142-43.

89   UTA, Department of Graduate Records, A73-0026/096(63), clippings file, *Mail* (24 December 1931).

90   Kathryn Kish Sklar, "Hull House in the 1890s: A Community of Women

Cathy James

Reformers," in Ellen Carol DuBois and Vicki L. Ruiz, (eds.), *Unequal Sisters: A Multicultural Reader in U.S. Women's History* (New York and London: Routledge, 1990), 109-122, quotation on 110.

[91] The Club for the Study of Social Science, for example, was a women's organization, established in 1910, which numbered among its 272 members many of Toronto's most prominent philanthropists, reformers, and settlement supporters. According to its president, Adelaide Plumptre, the club was established "for the study of social science," and "for the enlightenment and formation of public opinion" regarding the pressing issues of the day, such as housing and immigration. Club members perceived their main role to be the support of Toronto's small circle of full-time, paid social workers. The Social Workers' Club, though not exclusively female, was predominantly so by virtue of the preponderance of women in social work. See Adelaide Plumptre, "President's Address," The Club for the Study of Social Science, Programme of Meetings, 1911-12, 8-9 [pamphlet]. See also Agnes C. McGregor, "The Department of Social Science, University of Toronto, 1914-1940," in *Training for Social Work in the Department of Social Science University of Toronto 1914-1940* (Toronto: University of Toronto Press, 1940), 12.

[92] Jackson, *Lines of Activity*, 8.

Gender and Class

State Formation and Schooling Reform in 1880s Toronto

HARRY SMALLER

On the eve of the 1880s, school principal Samuel McAllister addressed the Toronto Teachers' Association:

> We have all Africa and her prodigies in us ... and it is the eternal aim of all disciplines to place these under such control that bad propensities may not grow into worse habits, and that the relics of the image of our Maker left in us may see the light and make each of us a reminiscence of the lost Eden. It is very well worth considering, therefore, how this discipline can be best exercised to secure these important matters.[1]

McAllister's overall agenda seems clear enough—arguing for changes in schooling in order to help to "secure these important matters" relating to the proper socialization of young people. Although there were some children of Black ancestry in Toronto schools at this time, one could correctly assume that his reference to race was also very much a code for the wide array of working-class and racial/ethnic "minority" students who populated the inner-city schools. One could certainly argue that his thinly veiled references to the "other"—race, class, gender and religion—grounded his argument for the need for a very specific socialization process, built on the foundations of "traditional" white, Christian, middle-class, heterosexual and patriarchal values, beliefs and behaviours. Indeed, his lengthy speech continued to stress the importance of this particular set of values, and the importance of schools in promoting their reproduction among young people.

McAllister's comments serve well to introduce the overall purposes of this paper. It will begin with a brief examination of the ways in which state officials in Ontario, operating in very specific social-economic-political circumstances, worked during the 1880s to enhance very specific sets of social structures, practices and ideologies within the provincial schooling system. Secondly, it will provide an examination of the ways in which officials in Toronto implemented "reforms" which operated to re-enforce patriarchal and classed social relations of schooling. Finally, it will explore some of the ways in which women teachers in Toronto worked to mediate or resist these attempts to reinforce such patriarchal and classed social relations. Much has already been written about the changes in the demographics of teachers and changes in the nature of their work during this decade—particularly the high degree of feminization (a term which covers a broad spectrum of gendered work relations), and how these "reforms" affected particularly women teachers.[2] This paper attempts to build on, and broaden, this work—particularly in exploring the connections between the larger socio-economic-political shifts of the 1880s, and the changes in state schooling during the same era. For the most part, the data for this article have been taken from official documents of the provincial government and the Toronto Board of Education. Of course, these are not the only, or even the main source of information on which to base a thorough analysis of a school system. However, for the purposes of this particular exploration, it was important to "see" and "read" the interests, intentions, words, and actions of those in charge of schooling at the time, and to attempt to understand how these forces worked to promote the social relations of difference we have come to know in our society. While these relations expand across a number of social categories— race, sexuality, (dis)ability, religion, first language, etc, limitations of space require that this paper focus on only two important factors, those of class and gender.

This exploration is, I believe, not only important in its own historical right. In addition, I would argue that the efforts undertaken in the 1880s by the elite and by state officials to "reform" education, mirror in many ways the schooling reform activities which we ourselves have been experiencing over the past two decades, almost exactly a century later. Once again, our public schools have been (and continue to be) subjected to a powerful campaign, aimed at promoting the ideology of pressing and continuing failure, and therefore the "need" to "reform" and/or "restructure" schooling.[3] It is hoped that this exploration will be underscored by understandings of the nature and power, both of structures and of agency (as unequal as they often are), and be suitably informed by more recently-developed analytical tools related to the examination of difference, social regulation, and governmentality.

Of necessity, this paper focuses on one city in one province of Canada, and deals with quite specific events that occurred in relation to public schooling in the 1880s. There is no question that some of what happened during this time and place was unique to Toronto. However, I would argue that the political structures and processes which were developed and/or enhanced during this time, as well as both their roots and their effects, were in many cases similar, or very similar, to those which developed in other jurisdictions across the country, during relative time periods. Perhaps, in those times and places where "history" did turn in different directions, the reader may wish to speculate on (or investigate) why this might have been the case!

The Social and Economic Context of the 1880s

[The state is] the entire complex of practical and theoretical activities with which the ruling class not only justifies and maintains its dominance, but manages to win the active consent of those over whom it rules.[4]

State formation refers to the historical process by which the modern state has been constructed. This includes not only the construction of the political and administrative apparatus of government and all government-controlled agencies which constitute the "public" realm but also the formation of ideologies and collective beliefs which legitimate state power and underpin concepts of nationhood and national "character."[5]

There are a number of ways in which the 1880s in Ontario could be considered a significant, if not unique, decade. It was marked by a prolonged period of dramatic economic swings, and in fact, severe depression consumed the late 1870s and early 1880s. The inhumane effects which this had on significant sectors of the population—unemployment, poverty, hunger, homelessness, ill health, family disruption, and forced transiency—were enormous, and have already been documented in a number of ways.[6] This economic depression also directly impacted other social processes in the province, and for the first time in the history of colonial settlement in Ontario, there was a significant net migration out of the rural areas of the province and into the towns and cities of the province.[7] This, of course, only magnified depression-related problems for the existing working-class residents of these larger urban centres, already inflicted with diminished job opportunities, and diminished access to housing and whatever social services might have been available. The increase also placed further pressure on many social institutions, and especially schools.[8] Increases in student enrolments normally meant increased expenditures for buildings, equipment, materials, and teachers. However, in a time of high unemployment and poverty, government revenues were down, and those in charge of public social institutions were under pressure to cut back on expenditures (understandably, given that the social strata represented by these officials was quite uninterested in further taxing themselves). School board officials restructured schools in a number of ways, largely at the expense of women teachers, in their attempts to further control public expenditures, even in a time of rising enrolment pressures.

Also clearly linked to economic depression during this decade was the manifest heightening of social tensions of class, as a result of industrialization.[9] While there were earlier signs of these changes,[10] during the 1880s the traditional sector of self-employed male artisans diminished dramatically, to be replaced by large numbers of semi and un-skilled male and female factory workers. In addition, given the increasing entrepreneurial sector, and a growing professional and managerial strata in the cities and towns of the province, the numbers of female domestic servants were also increasing significantly.[11] Clearly these were not simply quantitative changes in numbers or size, but also a transformation of industrial processes, and with it a transformation in social processes and social relations. While it was certainly the case that pre-industrialized Ontario was also highly inegalitarian in its socio-economic structures,[12] this process of dramatic class and cultural change in Toronto during the 1880s did little to improve the overall well-being and quality of life of the vast majority of the city's population. These changes also had direct bearing on social relations in the schools of the city, as we shall see.

Social unrest was ubiquitous during this decade. Labour agitation resulted in a number of protests, rallies, demonstrations, and strikes, in attempts to improve working conditions, to form unions, and to pressure the provincial government to pass labour legislation to ameliorate working conditions and legalize unions. (Among many other occupational groups, even male and female elementary school teachers in rural Ontario joined together in mid-decade in an attempt—unsuccessful, as it turned out—to form an independent province-wide union in mid-decade).[13] Equally public were the persistent tensions between ethnic and religious sectors of the population, such as the very demonstrable antagonisms which erupted during this time between the Orange Orders (associated with sectors of British Protestantism) and sectors of the Catholic population (linked to both Irish and French-speaking residents). While these tensions often arose out of the dire economic situation of the times, a number of historians have made the connection between the interests of the elite and the role played by leaders of religious and ethnic groups, in ensuring that these tensions manifested themselves along religious and ethnic lines, rather than those of class.[14] As the editors of the *Orange Sentinal* exhorted in September of 1885, anyone who expressed sympathy for Louis Riel or the native cause was "bent on precipitating a war of the races."[15]

The 1880s also marked a heightened exposition of gender tensions within the public sphere. Most visible were issues of suffrage, property ownership, and legal, health and reproductive rights, raised by groups and organizations representing mainly middle-class white women.[16] However, as a number of social and feminist historians have now shown, it was also an era when working class and "ethnic minority" women (e.g. Irish, Scottish, French) also began to increase their agitation over inequities—if only as individuals or small neighbourhood groupings. Nowhere were these agitations more apparent than in the response of working class and minority women to schooling matters of the time, and their concerns over the discriminatory ways in which their children were being treated by these institutions.[17] Understandably however, given the working class basis of these protests, and the fact that they often challenged the social reform projects implemented by government and supported by the middle class, they were seldom accorded the same "visibility" in the local media, or "official" recognition of their efforts.

These social tensions were also manifest at several levels of the state schooling system. From the schoolyard, reports abounded of student taunts and attacks on each other, based on differences of gender, race, religion, and ethnicity.[18] From the "corridors of power" similar contestations pertained, as schooling officials, trustees, politicians, and church and ethnic leaders engaged in virtually ceaseless struggle over influence and control of schooling in the province. To be sure, some autonomy and control was accorded the Catholic and French language populations of the province during the mid-decades of the nineteenth century (in the interests, not only of lessening political/sectarian tensions, but also of ensuring that schooling extended to larger segments of the youth population). However, issues of religion, ethnicity, gender, and language were to continue to plague the schooling system for the rest of the nineteenth century (not to mention the ensuing hundred years).[19]

There is no question that these economic conditions, and the resultant social disruptions, impacted directly on the governing elite's belief that increased attention to the production of the "proper subject" was paramount. Their efforts to change policies and practices relating to schools, classrooms, teachers, and students across the province during this decade becomes the subject of the next section of this chapter.

Transformations in the Provincial Governance of Schooling During the 1880s

> The nineteenth-century education system ... helped construct the very subjectivities of citizenship, justifying the ways of the state to the people and the duties of the people to the state. It sought to create each person as a universal subject but it did so differentially according to class and gender. It formed the responsible citizen, the diligent worker, the willing taxpayer, the reliable juror, the conscientious parent, the dutiful wife, the patriotic soldier, and the dependable or deferential voter.[20]

Egerton Ryerson, the "father" of the Ontario state schooling system, occupied the office of Superintendent of Education continuously from 1844 to 1876, for virtually the entire time under the aegis of a government dominated by the Conservative party and its predecessors linked closely to the British colonial masters. By the time of Ryerson's retirement in 1876 however, the Liberal party had installed itself in government, and with his departure they moved quickly to eliminate his position of Superintendent of Education—a structure they saw as a much too independent of party control. In its place, the role of Minister of Education was established—a significant change in the governance of schooling, allowing provincial education matters to be drawn much more directly into the management sphere of the cabinet, including much closer congruence with the larger political-economic agenda of government officials, whose guiding principles were frugality, efficiency, and centralization of power. To be sure, this new approach to centralization of education was undertaken within a rhetoric of continuing commitment to a politic of "local autonomy," and sometimes even with a promise of enhancing this purported independence. This phenomenon can be identified in a number of ways, ranging from short-term voting-day interests (running "politically appealing" candidates, rather than supporting more experienced/knowledgeable contestants),[21] to the appearance (at least) of being more responsive to the interests of the enfranchised strata of local communities (that minority consisting only of males with property), and particularly their pocketbooks.[22]

For the most part however, the reality was one of enhancing power at the centre.[23] Increasingly, provincial legislation, regulation, funding, and surveillance were used to promote this transformation of the schooling system, to better respond to social changes that had been effected by the changing social-economic conditions, which were resulting in an increasingly urbanized, industrialized, and proletarianized population. While these centralizing tendencies of government were wide-spread, three specific areas of reform stand out—educational funding, curriculum and pedagogy, and teacher training and certification.

Educational Finance

Given the economic climate of the times, and the official ideology of restraint, the provincial government was able to introduce significant cuts in educational expenditures during the 1880s—direct cuts in provincial expenditures, as well enforcing cuts at the local level through new provincial legislation and regulation. At the outset of the decade, for example, Education Minister Crooks was able to announce to the Legislature his success, not only in arresting the significant annual increases in overall education expenditures experienced during the previous decade, but also that he had occasioned an actual "decrease since 1875 in expenditure on capital account." However, in addition to these savings, he went on to announce further controls over local decision-making about expenditures, this time indirectly through legislated changes in structures of governance.

> I propose to place some check on School corporations in their expenditure of money on capital account, and their power of calling upon municipal corporations to furnish such sums as they might demand.... The necessary checks upon extravagance should therefore exist, and every means be employed for securing that economy with due regard to efficiency which should be found in our system.[24]

From that point on, locally-elected school boards would be responsible, and required, to control and limit the funding of school buildings, furniture and equipment—whether or not these reductions were desired by local parents, or even by school trustees themselves.

Another mechanism employed during this decade to effect savings in the provincial budget was that of "downloading" costs and responsibilities to the local level, while continuing to maintain centralized control of these prescribed activities. Although clearly a contradiction to the purported concerns of promoting economies at the local level, this downloading was astutely undertaken for those programs which provincial politicians knew were needed by local parents and trustees, and which the latter would then be required to finance from local taxes. As we shall see, most if not all of these cuts and controls on expenditures had direct and serious effects on students and their families— particularly working class families, and particularly mothers left with the responsibility for maintaining these homes.

Curriculum and Pedagogy

By 1880 there was a definite push within the cabinet to transform the curriculum and pedagogy of the classrooms across the province. Officials from the Department of Education were commissioned to visit and study school systems in the United States and Europe, and much space in the government's 1881 Annual Report was given over to their findings. Immediately following this report was a lengthy nine-page section, over the Minister's name, entitled "Suggestions and Recommendations." These recommendations ranged widely across all aspects of the provincial schooling system, but the genesis of these recommendations was clearly visible in the second paragraph of the treatise.

> If all elementary studies were taught by "reason" and not by "rote" (as under the old mode, now gradually disappearing), by competent teachers of trained experience, their practical value would, in a large measure, be secured, and at the same time the whole character of the children much improved under the influence of such teachers; for a truly national system is as much concerned in rearing up a moral as well as an intelligent population, and securing honest and fair dealing as essential qualities of every citizen, as well as mental culture.[25]

There is no question that this expressed concern for producing a "moral ... population" emanated directly from concerns about the social disruption and unrest wide-spread across the province during these turbulent economic times. Clearly, new forms of curriculum and pedagogy were seen as crucial in achieving these aims, and as we shall see, a number of new programs were introduced in municipalities. However, (then as now), finding ways of influencing these fundamental aspects of schooling was a much more complex task than simply adjusting regulations and/or funding formula. Ironically, given the worsening material conditions in the schools as a result of financial cut-backs—

increases in class size were a primary example—teachers were increasingly required to turn back to (or maintain) rote teaching methods, and basic "classroom management" techniques—rather than hoping to employ more progressive teaching methods in order to inculcate new values and habits of personal "self-regulation."[26]

Teacher Training and Certification

Among "schooling reformers" (then and now), teachers have almost always been viewed as the most important "problem" contributing to lack of success in schooling, and most in need of "improvement."[27] This was certainly the case for Ryerson, and throughout his regime he put enormous efforts into developing and "improving" structures for selecting, training, examining, certifying, employing, supervising, and inspecting teachers. However great his efforts might have been, it was clear that the provincial officials who replaced him in the late 1870s were anything but impressed with what he had been able to accomplish. Certainly, with the advent of Minister of Education Crooks and his exhortations to achieve "the complete efficiency of each teacher"[28] the stakes for control over teachers increased, and a number of major reforms were implemented.

One of the first changes effected by the new Liberal government was to abandon Ryerson's vision of provincial normal schools. Instead, local municipalities were given the opportunity to designate one or more elementary schools as "Model Schools" and enrol student teachers for three-month training programs. During each school day, they observed and assisted with teaching the children in the school, followed by after-school lectures given by the school's principal. While the introduction of over 50 of these local model schools across the province soon resulted in literally thousands of new teachers holding basic certification, the overall program resulted in very divided opinions among educators. While this change in training procedures (not to mention the cost savings) may have been lauded by central department officials, other officials pronounced them as a scourge on schooling, both in relation to the low level of training provided and certification requirements, as well as their negative effects, through over-supply, on the material conditions of virtually all teachers in the province.[29]

From the point of view of many women, however, these locally-based programs allowed them access to official training which would otherwise be much more difficult, if not impossible, to undertake. Until that point, formal teacher training programs were available only at the province's two Normal Schools, in Toronto and Ottawa. Entrance was highly competitive (male applicants, to the extent they applied, were always given priority), and the costs of travel and accommodation were prohibitive to many rural women—even assuming that their family situations were such that they could be away from the home for the extended period required. Certainly, the rolls of graduates published in the annual reports of the Department of Education each year following the implementation of these local programs suggests that many more

Gender and Class

women were able to undergo basic teacher training that had earlier been the case. Clearly however, with these new structures came new opportunities for local officials to exploit women teachers. In Toronto, School Inspector James Hughes was very explicit, in his gendered use of language, to explain to the Toronto Board the economic advantages of a city Model School.

> The young ladies in training will act in the capacity of assistants in the primary classes, and will thus to a certain extent, overcome the pressing difficulty of overcrowding. They will also do most of the necessary occasional teaching, and will thus save the Board a considerable sum each year.... It may seem at first sight that it is scarcely fair to the candidates themselves to require them to teach a year without any salary. This is not the case, however....[30]

Given this perceived diminution of the overall quality of teacher training during the 1880s, it is not surprising that state officials attempted to correct this through a massive "restructuring" of the objectives, forms, processes, and content of teacher examination and certification. At the outset of the decade, new provincial regulations were enacted, eliminating the long-standing County Boards of Examiners from all activity other than examining the "graduates" of the three-month model school programs. In their place, the Central Committee of Examiners was established, with responsibility for recreating, standardizing, and managing the examination structure for "of all classes" of teachers across the province.[31]

For the most part this new centralized system did little but intensify the arbitrary and stultified teacher examination system that Ryerson had initiated some decades previously. These tests had little to do with the art of teaching, or understanding the social, economic or political contexts in which they were required to work. Rather, teachers (including many who needed to reaffirm or upgrade their certification), were forced to spend an inordinate amount of their own time (often, according to a number of anecdotal reports, taken out of the time they otherwise would have spent on preparing for their daily teaching responsibilities), in studying massive volumes of text in order to be able to sit for lengthy examinations which required mainly, or solely, the regurgitation of a myriad of petty facts and figures.[32] This regime also did little to change the historic composition of those teachers most able to devote the time to these studies, and thus prepare themselves for advancement in the schooling system—males, without the "double burden" of work at school, and at home.[33]

Let us turn now to an examination of schooling in Toronto during the 1880s, and the ways in which schooling officials, in the midst of local social pressures, responded to the reforms imposed by the provincial government.

Schooling Reforms in Toronto in the 1880s

Given (or in spite of) the financial restrictions caused by general economic conditions, and the provincial government restraints on spending, school trustees introduced a number of pedagogical innovations during the decade, in an attempt to promote the proper socialization of young people under their authority, while, to the extent possible, also effecting financial savings. While these reforms ranged across many aspects of schooling—student discipline, dress, punctuality, and attendance, etc.—this exploration will be limited to five specific programmatic changes which had wide implications in relation to the maintenance of traditional relations of gender and class—manual training, physical education, kindergartens, special programs for "problem" students, and co-educational classrooms.

Manual Training

During the 1880s, pressures began mounting on schooling officials from prominent industrialists and employers in the city, to introduce more manual training into elementary school programs. Historically, these programs had been available only for girls—learning the traditional gendered labour of knitting, sewing, pattern-making, etc.—but by the 1880s it became increasingly apparent to schooling officials that they had to respond to the calls for manual training for boys. Judging from the historic record, however, it would appear that Toronto School Inspector James Hughes in particular, and the more "progressive" schooling officials in general, were not completely in favour of these suggestions. On the one hand, in the words of Hughes, "As most boys in attendance at our Public Schools will have to earn a livelihood by the use of their hands, it is essential to their highest success, in any department of industrial work, that their hands should have some definite training in school." However, he claimed that "various plans" to provide equivalent, gender specific, training for boys "have been tried in Toronto but, as yet, no work has been found which fulfils [sic] all the conditions of a school study so well as knitting."[34] Clearly, he was not in favour of implementing a whole new manual training program for boys, and there is no question that the costs of such a program figured prominently in this reluctance. However, he was under pressure from the "city fathers" in this regard. Accordingly, in October of 1883 a circular was issued "for Every Lady [teacher] in Highest Six Classes," directing them in the overall knitting and sewing regime for the year, and stating clearly that "*Every pupil* should do the same kind of work on the same day, as in other subjects," and that "this work should not in any way be slighted, but should receive its fair share of attention."[35]

Whatever the reasons and intents may have been for this co-educational approach to manual training, the Inspector was forced to admit, four years later, that boys were still not sewing and knitting in schools, that "girls alone have received the training. Sewing is the only work generally adopted in Public Schools." To be sure, this was a continuing problem for the Inspector. "Boys need the training as much as girls both intellectually and industrially. Girls usually get more hand training at home than boys do; it is clearly wrong to neglect the boys both at home and at school." However, it was also clear that he was not willing to expand manual training to include traditionally male pursuits. To support this position he cited what seemed, on the surface at least, to be quite non-discriminatory reasons—first, that any program adopted "should be suitable for use by boys as well as girls ... all classes of society and both sexes should share in its benefits," and secondly that any attempt to "teach special trades" is

> unfair, because it leaves the girls out of consideration; it is also unjust because it pre-disposes the pupils towards certain trades. The school has no right to do this. It should fit a boy for greater success in any department of life work, but it should in no way place limitations around him.

As equitable as these arguments appeared, it is clear that they did not represent any fundamental belief in gender equality being harboured by the chief inspector. Hughes, like most other schooling officials, was very traditional in this regard—clearly demonstrated in his support for sewing and knitting programs for girls because "The advantages, socially, financially and morally of having skilled mothers and daughters in the homes of our city, must be clear to all." In fact, one can safely conclude that his promotion of co-ed manual training programs was undertaken only for financial reasons, and not because of any inherent belief in gender equality. Knitting, as compared to industrial arts, was a cheap program to introduce, and as he himself argued, whatever program is introduced, "the material used should be inexpensive."[36]

In relation to class issues, however, it would appear that Hughes was somewhat more circumspect than many of the elite of the city, who were pressing for the adoption of trade-specific training programs for boys. He argued against the introduction of such programs, and whether or not the enormous cost of such undertakings was a basic issue, his stated arguments reflected a traditional liberal approach to issues of social class. While he was in no way advocating for change in the structures and relations of class in society, he was arguing for the advantages of a liberal education—at least at the primary school level—for all students, and against an early school streaming process.

> Manual training is admissible into our schools only as a means in general, and not of special education. The industries of this rapidly growing city are too diverse, the sentiment of equality is too strong, the ambition to rise is too general to allow of any scheme that would designate certain pupils for particular walks in life. Rather must we seek, if we use new methods, to get by means of them better results of a general nature, better trained and disciplined minds, and greater aptitudes and powers for living and doing in whatever may be the pupil's future career. Such results can be secured only by a well balanced general education.[37]

Throughout the rest of the decade, pressures continued on schooling officials to increase manual training programs, particularly for boys.[38] However, given the continuing concern for the tax dollar, schooling officials who may have been opposed in principle to the introduction of male-oriented trades training programs were able to continue citing financial reasons for lack of action in this domain.

Physical Education

At the outset of the decade, Toronto Public School Inspector James Hughes impressed upon the Board the importance of physical education for developing character. In his report for January, 1880, he stated that he "would respectfully, but strongly urge upon your Board the advisability of paying increased attention to the physical education of the pupils in our schools."[39] At the outset, however, only boys became the initial subject of these recommendations, and a "Captain Thompson," originally hired on a full-time basis as a truant officer, was soon reassigned to "regularly drill the boys in our schools, in the Third, Fourth and Fifth Book classes." That this quickly became a (gendered) success "was clearly shown in the remarkable precision and accuracy displayed by the pupils at the [first] drill competition" in July of 1881.[40]

Within the year however, Hughes' interests in subjecting girls as well to the benefits of this approach to education became apparent, when he proclaimed that

> Important as is military drill in contributing to the health of the pupils, in giving them an erect and graceful carriage, in developing prompt obedience to command, and in giving tone and spirit to the boys, it is of secondary importance when compared with an efficient system of schoolroom calisthenics [sic]. The education of mind and body should be carried on at the same time.[41]

Within two years, Hughes was clearly pleased to report that "drill and calisthenics" programs for "both boys and girls" were successful in "making the discipline of the school easy and natural, in improving the health of the pupils, and in imparting a better tone to school life."[42]

Whatever integration there may have been at the outset, however, as the decade progressed, girls and boys once again became totally segregated and differentiated. While younger girls were offered only callisthenics, and their older sisters also the possibility of "marching" exercises, boys were offered "squad drill," physical training," "rifle exercise," and "company drill, with and without arms," and the overall program shifted dramatically to congrue with the increasing civic promotion of the Empire, militarism and masculinity.[43] By 1889, the Board had approved a tender "to supply 300 wooden guns at twenty cents apiece ... for use of Drill Companies in schools requiring them."[44] The following year, even teachers (presumably both female and male) were being encouraged to participate in a series of "sixteen instruction classes in drill and physical culture." These teachers, and presumably many others, were clearly kept busy with assisting on a number of occasions during the year when "the Public School Battalions were on display" at city events, including "the celebration of the anniversary of the Battle of Queenston Heights" when "27 companies, nearly 1200 boys" were mustered for the occasion.[45] By 1890, boys were to be further immersed in the culture by plans for the "supplying of simple uniforms of blue serge for the pupils in the various drill companies in the Public Schools of Toronto for use on review day and other public occasions." In April that year, delegation of trustees was appointed to "be sent to Ottawa to interview the Honorable Minister of Militia with regard to the formation of Cadet Corps in connection with the senior classes in our advanced Public Schools."[46]

Kindergartens

The first kindergartens appeared in Toronto schools in 1883, and by the end of the decade they had expanded, not only across the city, but to other jurisdictions in the province. The provincial government's interest in these new approaches to early socialization were clearly identified through their quick action in establishing centralized training, examining and certification programs for new kindergarten teachers.[47]

Given the additional costs of this innovation to a system otherwise imbued with the rhetoric of frugality and need for fiscal cuts, it would be reasonable to wonder why such an innovation, to provide schooling for an age group not serviced to that point, would have been encouraged. However, the fact that these kindergartens were established mainly (or solely) in those areas of cities with high numbers of working class, minority and migrant families, suggests that schooling officials had a very specific clientele and agenda in mind. Certainly, Toronto's chief school inspector James Hughes was clear about what he saw as the crucial aspects of the new program, in relation to creating proper subjectivities from an early age. In looking back over the first decade of kindergartens in his jurisdiction, he concluded that

> ... perhaps the best lessons the schools have learned from the Kindergartens are those connected with the discipline and management of children—that love is the strongest stimulus and the greatest controlling force in the world; that coercive and autocratic discipline necessarily dwarfs character; that obedience should not involve subserviency; and that all discipline is evil that checks spontaneity and prevents the freest development of the spirit of individual liberty as the foundation of personal responsibility and responsive co-operation.[48]

In addition to the class and ethnic/race relations clearly apparent in the student population, teaching in these new kindergartens was clearly intended to be confined, not only solely to females, but also to the lowest wage categories possible. Schooling officials had no difficulty in extending the ideology of "maternal needs" which had already been developed to rationalize the feminization of teaching in the regular public school classroom. In addition, they were also able to exploit women kindergarten teachers even further—by offering salaries even less than those paid their elementary classroom colleagues. In fact, as Hughes was pleased to announce in his 1883 Annual Report, the first kindergarten teacher in Toronto "has been assisted by seven young ladies, who have given their services free, in order to secure a training in the principles and practice of Kindergarten work."[49] This practice was to continue through the decade, as kindergartens proved themselves highly successful in developing the "proper" socialization of children, and expanded rapidly across the working class areas of the city. As Hughes was pleased to note in his 1884 annual report, "One primary teacher reports that she 'would be willing to teach for less salary, if all her pupils had been previously trained in a Kindergarten.'"[50]

Special Programs for "Problem" Students

Not surprisingly, given the widespread poverty and social unrest of the times, particularly in the larger towns and cities, the social category of the "problem student" achieved new import within governmental discourse at both the provincial and local levels. Given the reluctance of Toronto school officials to implement manual training programs for boys in the regular schools, a number of city officials and notable citizens increasingly used the concept of "manual training" to press for separate facilities for those particular students—either as a means to deal with "problem" students, or in an attempt to provide, at public expense, more direct training for future industrial and shop workers—clearly intents which were highly gendered in nature. In 1886, for example, the City Council passed a resolution "directing the attention of the School Board to the desirability of establishing Schools for Manual Training."[51]

However, Hughes, reflecting the philosophies of the more "progressive" educators of the time in maintaining moral education at the forefront of elementary level public schooling, "strongly condemn[ed] any system of training that would subordinate intellectual development to practical utility, or encourage industrial education at the expense of true culture." Generally speaking, they continued to be successful in preventing the streaming of students, by arguing that "a manual training school need not be—should not be—a separate institution." Where necessary, it should be introduced only at the post-primary level, in the "advanced public schools, and in High Schools and Collegiate Institutes." Even there, he argued, this training should include "a more thorough study of the sciences immediately useful in connection with the leading manufacturing or agricultural interests of the district in which the school is situated," in order "to give a training in the intelligent application of mechanical principles, and in hand skill, which will fit a boy for entering any trade." In this way, they argued, it would give "young men a higher respect for

Gender and Class

6.1. *Student teachers practice teaching kindergarten at the Toronto Normal School [ca. 1898]. Courtesy of the Archives of Ontario RG 2-257, Acc. 13522 Ontario teachers' colleges historical files.*

6.2. *The Kindergarten [ca. early 1900s]. Courtesy of the Archives of Ontario RG 10-30-A-2-3.02, S15519 Public health nursing records.*

labour, by showing that the humblest work may be combined with a high degree of intelligence."[52] Whether or not this mode of rhetoric appeased other city fathers, little was done in relation to the implementation of such gendered technical programs in the primary schools of the city.

However, dealing with "problem" students became increasing challenging for schooling officials, as well as for other city officials responsible for maintaining "law and order" in these turbulent times. Given the reluctance of schooling officials to introduce manual training in the elementary schools, pressures soon shifted to the establishment of special programs, separate from regular schools and classrooms, for such children. Interestingly, although this "terrible rowdy element ... which is endangering the peace and safety of our citizens" were clearly boys, female teachers were often seen as the answer to this problem. Toronto industrialist W.C. Howland, in a letter to the Toronto Board in 1881 advocated for such a program, and stated his belief that

> To deal with this class of children it would require not only an old and experienced Teacher, and in my opinion a woman, but it must be a woman who would have the interest of such children at heart and who would be willing to sacrifice more time and attention than is usually required in the regular teacher.[53]

Given the pressures, the Board soon established a special, separately housed, school program for problematic boys—through a financial "partnership" (to use more recent parlance) with Howland. Not surprisingly, the first teacher to be assigned to this program, located at the College Avenue School, was long-time Toronto teacher Miss Hester How. Given the "sacrifice" which Miss How subsequently provided, the program soon met the expectations of its founders, and began expanding. Before the end of the decade, the chairman of the Board was advocating for three such schools to be established, "managed and conducted similarly to the College Ave. School." As he stated, "one class of accommodation that should be afforded [so that these young people could be] made good, honest and industrious citizens, adding to our wealth and prosperity instead of filling our prisons and gaols."[54] Within a month of this call, the Board agreed allow the existing program to take over the much larger Elizabeth St. School, and to add two new programs—"a class for young servants and others who can attend school for only half of each day, and another for the education of newsboys and boot-blacks, who ... should be licensed and required to attend school for a portion of each day."[55] (Miss How was to become principal of this school, and later it was named after her).

For those students who were beyond the help of the "College Street Program," city officials were also able to make use of special legislation passed in 1884, which allowed local school boards to delegate their "rights, powers and privileges" to any voluntary group operating special programs for "problem" youth. An Industrial School Board was established, under provincial government support, and a program started in Mimico (in the western suburbs of Toronto) for such students. Interestingly however, while the Toronto Board did support this endeavour to some extent (for example, it allowed one of its male teachers to be seconded to the position of head of the new program), a number of other officials remained reticent about the idea—for either philosophical or financial reasons. Over the ensuing years the Board did not offer its full participation, and a request at the end of the decade to provide a new building for the program was turned down flatly, on the claim that "the Solicitor for the Board ... states that the Board has no power to comply with the request."[56]

Co-ed Classes

Finally, it is interesting to note that even the question of allowing boys and girls in the same classroom became an issue for many trustees during this decade. Historically, while younger children were integrated, students in the senior grades were always placed in separate classes, and clearly this was the desirable mode—at least for most trustees and many parents. However, financial implications soon intervened. As the decade progressed, a Board committee found that "pupils, especially the girls remain longer at School than formerly,"[57] and with the increasing numbers of girls in these classes, the disproportionate class sizes increasingly interfered with the most "efficient" assignment of teachers. In fact, as early as 1881 School Inspector James Hughes had begun hinting at "the propriety of teaching the sexes together in the higher as well as the lower divisions,"[58] and in the following year, he reported that "the attendance in the higher classes of girls is in nearly all cases too large." As a result, he "strongly recommend[ed] that the sexes be taught together" where this would result in the more "efficient" organization of classes. "Male and female pupils are taught in the same classes in Great Britain, the United States and Canada," he explained, "and the results are most satisfactory. It is difficult to conceive how the hypothetical evil effects which suggest themselves to the minds of some, could possibly follow the seating of boys and girls in the same room." Among other advantages for these new arrangements, he argued, was that the "discipline would be improved. The effect on the characters of both boys and girls has found to be good." Besides, he assured the trustees, they would "of course occupy different playgrounds" during the recesses.[59]

By 1883, classes were combined in two schools, and Hughes was pleased to report that "the results have been perfectly satisfactory. The grading is much better than formerly, and the discipline, if it has changed at all, has been improved by the change."[60] As the decade proceeded, these mixed classes were expanded in order to allow the further increase of class sizes. However, there is no question that co-ed classes remained very contentious among city officials and school board trustees. For example, even at the end of the decade, in his inaugural address, Herbert Kent, the new chairman of the Board, suggested other ways in which classrooms could be kept filled, so that "we would be able to keep the boys and girls separate."[61]

Impact of Reform on Teachers' Work

In Toronto as well as across the province, both the financial restraints and the schooling reforms took a direct toll on teachers, students, and working-class parents alike. Interestingly, in spite of the purported interests of city fathers in drawing all young people into the proper influences of the school classroom, given their inability or unwillingness to increase expenditures, urban school boards during these times often refused to enrol all eligible students. For example, for several years during the 1880s the Toronto Board reported that at least 2,000 primary level students were not enrolled because of lack of space. These students invariably lived in working-class areas of the city, and the fact that these children were not in school must clearly have impacted on many families, and particularly mothers, attempting to eke out a living during these recession years.

There is no question however, that the largely female teaching cohort were also directly and severely affected by the Toronto trustees' interest in "keeping down the civic expenditure to the lowest point, consistent with the efficient working of our City schools."[62] These "efficiencies" were, first and foremost, spelled out in the working conditions for women teachers in the city. School classes, particularly in working-class areas, expanded dramatically. In Toronto, for example, classes in the lower grades averaged 70 to 80 students. In fact, for several years during the 1880s, to draw attention to this plight, concerned trustees drew up an official list of those classrooms in the city which had more than 100 students, although little was done about it.[63] Given that all junior classes were taught by women (a direct result of Toronto Board of Education policy—male teachers taught only the higher grades of elementary school, with average classes of less than 40 students), they alone suffered this added burden.

In addition to issues of class size, much has already been written about the highly discriminatory ways in which women teachers in Toronto (and elsewhere in Ontario) were treated, in relation to salaries, and policies and practices related to hiring, firing, and promotion.[64] However, as a direct result of the financial restraints and schooling reforms of the 1880s, there were many other ways in which the classroom work of teachers was adversely effected, and because of the disproportionate numbers of students in women teachers' classes, they were once again, disproportionately affected. The Toronto Board's sixteen-page list of "Regulations Relating to Teachers" revised and expanded during the 1880s made it clear that, in addition to the basic requirements for their own attendance, punctuality and hours of work, they were to greatly increase their attention to the social regulation of students, requirements which added heavily to their responsibilities and workload. Among other things, bureaucratic paper work for teachers increased enormously, as teachers were required to prepare "monthly reports of the attendance, punctuality, conduct and class-standing of the pupils ... [to] be sent to parents."

Teachers' responsibilities also extended much beyond just concern for the academic development of students, as they were increasingly required to attend to other aspects of their students' lives. For example, one new regulation stated that, "In addition to the daily inspection of the hands, face, boots, and clothing, the teachers shall make a more careful examination of the pupils once a week, to find out whether there are any eruptions on the hands, wrists, necks, faces or heads of the pupils." In addition, these new work obligations extended well beyond concern for students themselves, and regulations now called for "The immediate care of their respective school rooms during school hours, and be held responsible for the preservation of all furniture and apparatus thereto belonging." Nor was the classroom itself the sole space of responsibility. "Teachers shall prevent, as far as possible, the pupils from gathering on the school premises before the hours for opening the school rooms; require the pupils to leave the premises immediately after the close of school."[65]

Concomitant with these increasing controls over students, teachers themselves became subject to increasing surveillance, control, and official activities relating to their professional development. By the end of the decade, the By-laws and Regulations of the Board were very explicit about the duties of the Inspector in this regard. In addition to being required to "make monthly returns to the Board of the attendance of teachers ... the names of teachers absent, the causes of such absence, and other such matters as should be recorded," he also

> shall have the power to call meetings of the teachers of the different grades for lectures and instructions on their school work, by special masters or others, in other than school hours, and shall keep a careful record of the attendance and punctuality of the teachers and the interest they manifest in these and the regular institute meetings.[66]

Finally, there were a number of ways in which trustees also attempted to effect savings while at the same time "improving" modes of control over teachers and teaching—undertaken very much at the direct expense of women in their employ. As just one example of many such schemes, in 1887 a plan was floated to increase the powers of (male) school principals over their respective (female) teaching staff—one which, while couched in seemingly positive, supportive language, clearly displayed its underlying intents. The Inspector stated that his plan was to appoint "special assistants" to support the teaching principals in the larger Toronto schools who

> must be very frequently called away from their classes in order to attend to the general discipline and management of the Schools, [and] the advantages which would certainly result in the other classes of the Schools from the direct personal supervision of a wise and competent Head Master ... The change proposed need not entail additional outlay on the part of the Board, as with such an arrangement a male assistant would not be needed, and two female assistants could be engaged for less than the amount now paid for one male assistant.[67]

Response and Resistance to Schooling Reforms of the 1880s

The implementation of both schooling reforms and financial restraints during the 1880s clearly occasioned a plethora of responses—acceptance, compromise, resistance and/or opposition—by parents, students, teachers, local officials, taxpayers, and other residents, in Toronto and across the province. For example, parents, and particularly working-class mothers, were highly in evidence in confronting school and school board officials during this decade—over the ways in which they saw their children being negatively affected by the ways in which the increasing surveillance and controls were being imposed, and their effects.[68] However, for the purposes of this chapter, I will dwell only on some of the ways in which Toronto teachers responded to the imposition of many of the schooling reforms of the 1880s. Given the patriarchal structures which had been constructed in the Toronto school system by the 1880s, and the differential work loads and remuneration schedules based solely on gender, it is not at all surprising that virtually all of the teacher-based resistance and opposition came from women during these times.

To be sure, the nature of these responses and contestations varied considerably. In many cases, particularly in the early years of the decade, individual and small groups of women teachers confronted their direct employers (local school trustees) over what they considered to be injustices in the manner in which they were treated, or remunerated, in the workplace. In 1879, for example, a small group of women balked at a Toronto Board demand that "they muster with their classes" for a civic parade organized to welcome the Governor-General.[69] Similarly, in 1883, a number of women broke all tradition by attending a meeting of the Board trustees in order to dispute their salary situation.[70] It is certainly worthy of note that these brave women were often sanctioned, publicly and privately, for their efforts. Following their refusal to "muster" their students in 1879, for example, the *Canadian Educational Monthly* charged that their actions posed the "danger ... of encouraging a disregard of constituted authority, and of weakening the claims of school discipline in the case of those who should be the first to respect and maintain them." In addition, the journal attempted to place their actions within "proper" gendered relations, and the impropriety of "placing oneself heedlessly out of accord with one's professional brethren."[71]

However, it is precisely at the mid-point of this decade of schooling reforms and financial restraints that the women teaching in the Toronto Board joined together to form the Women Teachers' Association (WTA)—one of the first of its kind in the country. Its founding moment has been described in one account has having occurred directly following a meeting of all teachers in the city, and as a result of continued frustration over their male colleagues' disinterest in supporting their claims of inequity. In the collective words of several of the founders of WTA,

> Realizing that our point of view would receive no consideration until we united in some definite way, some of us, eight in all, lingered after the meeting and discussed ways and means. The nucleus of the first association of women teachers in Canada was formed then.[72]

Gender and Class

There is no question that from the outset this organization was effective in confronting at least some of the most blatant examples of patriarchal exploitation in its clearly determined efforts to promote the material interests of its members. For example, within a year of the organization's founding, the Board agreed to recognize the much more equitable measure of using teaching seniority as the basis for determining salary, rather than the grade level being taught. Not coincidentally, women began exercising their power by serving on the executive of the official Toronto Teachers' Association, and their lobbying efforts had resulted in a number of other successes, including the modification or outright abandonment of several of the Board's planned-for schooling reforms which would clearly have affected women teachers, and their work, adversely. For example, the attempt by the Toronto Board to restructure the role of principals in 1887 (described above) was successfully opposed by the WTA, on the basis that these officials would be even less available to assist in dealing with their classroom concerns.[73] By the end of the decade, the organization was in a position to begin discussing the renting of private facilities for their activities, and combining with the Women's Enfranchisement Association to get women elected to the school board.

Conclusion

Do changes in the larger economy of a particular community, province or nation result in changes in its state schooling system? For many, the answer is a decided yes! This was certainly the case in the 1880s in Ontario, as I have attempted to describe here. These measures included financial cut-backs and downloading of fiscal responsibility to local municipalities, increased teacher-testing and supervision, "standardization" of textbooks and other aspects of the school curriculum, and enhanced control over the ways in which teachers and the public were informed about their school system. All of these were implemented for the expressed purpose of attempting to produce, in Education Minister Crooks' words, a "truly national system ... as much concerned in rearing up a moral as well as an intelligent population."[74] To be sure, the definition of a "moral" citizen varied considerably over the years, particularly in relation to the economic "needs" of the nation at any given era.

The 1980s and 1990s have also seen significant restructuring, across many western nations. At a large scale, this economic restructuring has had a number of different aspects, including "globalizing" economies, "harmonizing" legislation and regulations, implementing "free trade" pacts, lowering taxation rates (particularly for corporations and the wealthy), reducing the role and responsibility of government for the funding of education, health care, social services, and so on.[75] As a number of observers have noted, in many cases these measures have resulted in very differential effects on people, based upon gender and class.[76]

Inherent in these recent changes has been a significant restructuring of state schooling systems—often with the same differential effects, based on the social background of students and their families. Ontario has been no exception in this regard, and, perhaps not surprisingly, many of the changes we have experienced in the past decade have mirrored closely the kinds of changes, documented in this paper, which were imposed a century ago. As one dramatic example, the contents of omnibus Bill 160 (passed in 1997, in spite of dramatic resistance by parents, teachers, and even local school trustees—including the complete closure of the provincial school system by teachers for two weeks) included several aspects very reminiscent of legislation and regulation of a century earlier—reduction in the power of local school board trustees, controls over taxation and spending by local school boards, cuts in funding at both the provincial and local levels, and increased control over teachers' work, including hours of work.

As Rebecca Coulter has noted in her article about the recent effects of neo-liberalism and globalization, whatever gains have been made in the past 30 years in relation to equalizing relations within our schooling systems, once again, "the dangers are real and immediate."[77] Boards of education are no longer required to offer Junior Kindergarten programs for three and four-year-olds, cuts that have differentially affected working-class and minority immigrant mothers and families who looked to these programs as an affordable, supportive educational environment for their children to begin formal education. Many boards have also engaged in massive layoffs of educational assistants. These workers, usually women, and often themselves from working-class backgrounds, were largely employed to assist with immigrant and working-class students—cuts that result in "double detriment" against the possibility of achieving equity within these particular families and communities. Finally, as Coulter also notes, the removal by the present neo-liberal government of all equity-related legislation and related programs has resulted in

> the discourse of equity and the understanding of discrimination as systemic ... rapidly being displaced by the more limited view of individual rights and equality of opportunity and by an uncritical call to a merit principle and standards of excellence as though these were objective criteria.[78]

Putting the state formation processes of the present day into the longer historical context, one can certainly see strong resonances with earlier times. In the case of Ontario in the 1880s and the 1990s, these moments of state restructuring, and educational change, have certainly not been positive for many students, families and communities, divided by relations of gender and class.

Notes

[1]   *The Toronto Globe*, 27 November 1879.

Gender and Class

2   See, for example, Alison Prentice, *The School Promoters* (Toronto: McLelland and Stewart 1975); Marta Danylewycz and Alison Prentice, "Teachers' Work: Changing Patterns and Perceptions in the Emerging School Systems of Nineteenth- and Early Twentieth-Century Central Canada," *Labour/Le Travail* 17 (1986); Bruce Curtis, *Building the Educational State: Canada West, 1836-1871* (London: Falmer Press, 1988); Harry Smaller, "A Room of One's Own: The Early Years of the Toronto Women Teachers' Association," in Ruby Heap and Alison Prentice, (eds.), *Gender and Education in Ontario: An Historical Reader* (Toronto: Canadian Scholars' Press, 1991).

3   Just the briefest perusal of virtually any daily newspaper can only support this premise. This is not, in any way, to suggest that I believe that our state schooling system is beyond reproach—quite the contrary. However, my interests lie much more with those students and parents of working-class and minority families, whose concerns—general and specific—would hardly be addressed by the kinds of reforms being suggested by the dominant groups in our society these days.

4   Antonio Gramsci, *Selections from the Prison Notebooks* (Q. Hoare and Nowell Smith, eds.) (New York: International Publishers, 1971): 244.

5   Andy Green, *Education and State Formation: The Rise of Education Systems in England, France and the USA.* (New York: St. Martin's Press, 1990): 77.

6   See, for example, Gregory Kealey, *Toronto Workers Respond to Industrial Capitalism, 1867-1892* (Toronto: University of Toronto Press 1980); Susan Trofimenkoff, "One Hundred and Two Muffled Voices: Canada's Industrial Women in the 1880s," in Michael Cross and Gregory Kealey, (eds.), *Canada's Age of Industry: 1849-1896* (Toronto: McClelland and Stewart, 1982); Bryan Palmer, *Working-Class Experience: Rethinking the History of Canadian Labour, 1800-1991* (Toronto: McClelland and Stewart, 1992).

7   During the eight-year period from 1876 to 1884, while the population of school-aged children living in rural areas decreased by almost 50,000, their numbers in the nine main cities of Ontario increased by 16,500 (the overall school-aged population in the province having fallen over 30,000 during this time period—an interesting statistic in itself, in relation to the social effects of economic depressions) (*Annual Report of the Minister of Education for Ontario* [hereafter *ARME*], 1890).

8   During the decade of the 1880s, Toronto almost doubled its population, from 86,415 to 144,023 (Peter Goheen, "Currents of Change in Toronto, 1850-1900," in Gilbert Stelter and Adam Artibise, (eds.), *The Canadian City: Essays in Urban and Social History* (Ottawa: Carleton University Press, 1985): 91.

9   Increasing industrialization and economic depression are not necessarily contradictory phenomena. In fact, an argument has often been made that this kind industrial "prosperity" during depressions occurs precisely because of the high levels of unemployment and the resultant low labour costs for capital. It was perhaps no coincidence that the Massey family, soon to become the world's largest manufacturer of farm machinery and equipment, moved their operations to Toronto in 1879, in the depths of a lengthy depression. See, for example D.C. Masters, *The Rise of Toronto, 1850-1890* (Toronto: University of Toronto Press, 1947) for classic arguments on both sides of this issue.

10 As early as the mid-1850s factory workers (as compared to traditional artisans and craftspeople) were beginning to emerge as a category (the Toronto Locomotive Works, for example, was established in 1852).

[11] Gregory Kealey, *Workers and Canadian History* (Montreal: McGill-Queen's Press, 1995).

[12] See, for example, Michael Katz, et al., *The Social Organization of Early Industrial Capitalism* (Cambridge: Harvard University Press, 1982).

[13] See, for example, Harry Smaller, "Teachers Union, (Neo)Liberalism and the State: The Perth County Conspiracy, Ontario 1885," *Pedagogica Historica*, 40, 1-2, (2004). Interestingly, unionization success among other workers was often cited by teachers as a reason to unionize as well.

[14] See, for example, Gregory Kealey and Bryan Palmer, *Dreaming of What Might Be: The Knights of Labor in Ontario, 1880-1900* (New York: Cambridge University Press, 1982).

[15] Masters, *Rise of Toronto*, 192.

[16] See, for example, Wendy Michenson, "Aspects of reform: Four women's organizations in nineteenth century Canada," Ph.D. thesis, York University, 1977; Linda Kealey, *A Not Unreasonable Claim: Women and Reform in Canada, 1880s-1920s* (Toronto: The Women's Press, 1979); Mariana Valverde, *The Age of Light, Soap and Water: Moral Reform in English Canada, 1885-1925* (Toronto: McClelland and Stewart, 1991).

[17] See, for example, Kari Dehli, "Women and Early Kindergartens in North America: Uses and Limitations of Post-Structuralism for Feminist History," *Curriculum Studies* 1, 1 (1993); Christopher Clubine, "Motherhood and Public Schooling in Victorian Toronto," *Ontario History* 88, 3 (1996).

[18] See, for example, Minute Book of the Toronto Board of Education, 11 June 1880; 17 April 1882; 21 March 1883.

[19] See, for example, David Welch, "Early Franco-Ontarian Schooling as a Reflection and Creator of Community Identity," *Ontario History* 85, 1 (1993); Edwin Guillett, *In the Cause of Education. Centennial History of the Ontario Educational Association, 1861-1960* (Toronto: University of Toronto Press, 1960).

[20] Green, Education and State Formation, 80.

[21] Provincial Archives of Ontario, Record Group 2-109, Mowat to Ross, 19 September 1878.

[22] Ontario Department of Education, circular entitled "Amendments in the School Law," Toronto, 14 March 1879.

[23] Indeed, in a speech to the Legislature in 1879, Education Minister Crooks was quick to laud "a system which is now found so symmetrical in its principles, and satisfactory in its practical workings" that citizens could now accept "the legitimate consequences of the principle of responsibility of their administrators to them through their chosen representatives," (*ARME* 1879: 16-17). Clearly, no further "grass-roots" intervention was needed!

[24] Ibid, 6-7.

[25] Ibid, 1881: 242.

[26] Toronto Board of Education minutes during the 1880s are replete with statistics indicating average class sizes of about 80 students, with many over 100—not to mention, innumerable instances of complaints about "excessive" corporal punishment being used on children from the earliest grades.

[27] See, for example, J. G. Althouse, *The Ontario Teacher: A Historical Account of Progress, 1800-1910* (Toronto: Ontario Teachers' Federation, 1967); W. G. Fleming, *Ontario's Educative Society, Volume 7, Educational Contributions of Associations* (Toronto: University of Toronto Press, 1972); Thomas Popkewitz,

"Professionalization in Teaching and Teacher Education: Some Notes on Its History, Ideology, and Potential," *Teaching and Teacher Education* 10, 1 (1997).

28 Ontario Department of Education, circular entitled "Amendments in the School Law," Toronto, 14 March 1879.

29 Albeit, with only "faint praise" on some occasions, even from the Department's Inspector of Model Schools, J. J. Tilley, who stated in his 1885 annual report that they "may justly claim to be considered a satisfactory and economical means of providing a fair amount of professional training" (*ARME* 1885: 79). In the words of A. J. Donly, a key-note speaker at a session of the Simcoe County Teachers' Institute in 1880, the province's model schools were but "fifty-two mills or teacher manufactories that bid fair to swamp, by their over production of an article that is now a drug on the market, the profession of teaching in this province" (*The Canadian Educational Monthly* 2, 3 (1880): 142).

30 *Annual Report of the Toronto Board of Education* (hereafter, *ARTBE*) 1880: 4.

31 *ARME* 1880: 16; 1881: 215.

32 See, for example, Guillett, *Cause of Education*; H. Smaller, "Teachers and Schools in Early Ontario," *Ontario History* 85, 4 (1993).

33 To be sure, there were other reasons why many women over the years chose not to participate in the Department of Education's elaborate hierarchy of examinations and certification, beyond obtaining a basic certificate for employment. Even if they were successful at achieving these higher certificates, there was much less (or no) chance that they would be hired for the better-paying positions within the schooling system. As it was, women's chances for remaining employed even in basic teaching positions were very much dependent upon the will of local school board trustees, and the (non)availability of males to fill these positions—particularly in rural schools.

34 *Toronto Board of Education Minutes* (hereafter *TBEMIN*) 1883, 35-6. There is little or no indication of the Toronto Board having attempted to introduce traditional industrial training programs for boys prior to this, so it is not clear on what evidence Hughes was basing these claims. To be sure, introducing programs involving the shops, tools and equipment needed to train students in traditional male craft occupations was clearly beyond the financial interests of school trustees—particularly given that they were not yet prepared to provide even the basic classroom space needed for all eligible Toronto students to enroll in school.

35 *TBEMIN* 1883, 37, emphasis in original. For the higher primary school grades, where male teachers predominated, women were employed to teach the sewing program.

36 *ARTBE* 1887, 24ff.

37 *TBEMIN* 1889 Appendix, 135.

38 See, for example, *TBEMIN* 1888 Appendix, 91ff.

39 *TBEMIN* 1880 Appendix, 8.

40 *ARTBE* 1881, 25.

41 Ibid, 25-6.

42 *ARTBE* 1883, 38.

43 For further discussion of the (re)rise of imperialism, militarism, and (British) nationalism during the 1880s, including the foundation of the Imperial Federation League in 1884, see, for example, Carl Berger, *The Sense of Power: Studies in the Ideas of Canadian Imperialism, 1867-1914* (Toronto: University of Toronto Press, 1970).

44 *TBEMIN* 1889 Appendix, 89.
45 *ARTBE* 1890, 68-9.
46 *TBEMIN* 1890 Appendix, 109.
47 *ARME* 1890, xxiv.
48 *ARTBE* 1893, 30. This first kindergarten teacher was Ada Marean, who was sent to St. Louis by the Toronto Board to study the kindergarten movement there, and then returned to start up the program in Toronto. In 1884 she married James Hughes, and given the customs of the time, gave up her paid employment with the Board.
49 *ARTBE* 1883, 25.
50 *ARTBE* 1884, 17.
51 *ARTBE* 1886, 67.
52 *ARTBE* 1886, 32-3, 36.
53 *TBEMIN* 1881 Appendix, 61.
54 *TBEMIN* 1889 Appendix, 6-7.
55 *TBEMIN* 1889 Appendix, 34.
56 *TBEMIN* 1990 Appendix, 108.
57 While there were probably many reasons for this phenomenon, the official statement at the time was that boys left school earlier because of the availability of paid work in the city (*TBEMIN* 1882 Appendix, 50).
58 *ARTBE* 1881, 14.
59 *TBEMIN* 1882 Appendix, 50.
60 *ARTBE* 1883, 17.
61 *TBEMIN* 1889 Appendix, 7.
62 *TBEMIN* 1885, 69.
63 See. for example, *TBEMIN* 1880 Appendix, 16, 81; 1881, 6.
64 See, for example, Alison Prentice, "Themes in the Early History of the Women Teachers' Association of Toronto," in Paula Bourne, ed., *Women's Paid and Unpaid Work: Historical and Contemporary Perspectives* (Toronto: New Hogtown Press, 1985); Wendy Bryans, "Virtuous Women at Half the Price: The Feminization of the Teaching Force and Early Women Teacher Organizations in Ontario" (M.A. diss., University of Toronto, 1974); Smaller, *Room of One's Own*.
65 Toronto Board of Education, *By-Laws and Regulations* (Toronto 1890): pp. 59ff.
66 Ibid, 33, 34.
67 *TBEMIN* 1887 Appendix, 8.
68 Several incidents are cited in Clubine, Motherhood and Public Schooling. To be sure, many or most of these confrontations were contained within the walls of the individual school and principal's office, with little or no documentation created, and therefore difficult to explore systematically. One well-publicized incident occurred at the eve of the decade, concerning the savage beating of a 10-year old female student by the principal of Niagara Street School, and the efforts (largely futile) of her mother to bring the principal to justice, both at the School Board and in the Police Courts (Bruce Vance, *F.S. Spence and the Issue of Corporal Punishment, 1879* (Toronto: Toronto Board of Education 1992).
69 *Canadian Educational Monthly* 1, 10 (1879): 528.
70 *Toronto Telegram*, 22 February 1883.
71 *Canadian Educational Monthly* 1, 10 (1879): 529.
72 Harriet Johnston, *et al.*, *The Story of the Women Teachers' Association of Toronto* (Toronto: Thomas Nelson and Sons, 1932): 10.

[73] Johnston, *The Story*, 23.
[74] Adam Crooks, *Speech of the Honourable Adam Crooks, Minister of Education, On Moving the Second Reading of the Bill Respecting Public, Separate and High Schools, 1879* (Toronto: Education Department, 18 February, 1979).
[75] See, for example, Tony Clarke and Maude Barlow, *MAI round 2: New Global and Internal Threats to Canadian Sovereignty* (Toronto: Stoddart, 1998).
[76] See, for example, Gaby Weiner, et al., "Who Benefits from Schooling? Equity Issues in Britain," in Alison Mackinnon, *et al.*, (eds.), *Education into the 21st Century: Dangerous Terrain for Women?* (London: Falmer Press, 1998).
[77] Rebecca Priegert Coulter, "'Us Guys in Suits are Back:' Women, Educational Work and the Market Economy in Canada," in Mackinnon, *et al.*, *Education into the 21st Century*, 115.
[78] Ibid, 112.

"All Matter Peculiar to Woman and Womanhood"[1]

The Medical Context for Women's Education in Canada in the First Half of the Twentieth Century

WENDY MITCHINSON

Most literature on women's education has focused on how gender worked to place barriers to women's educational advancement. Historians have emphasized how the ideology of separate spheres supported privileging male education but seldom have we examined specific aspects of that ideology, whether intellectual, psychological, moral/religious, or medical, in detail. I have chosen to look at medical beliefs in the first half of the twentieth century. In recent years, historians have begun to assess the influence of psychologists and mental health and hygiene experts in the elementary and secondary levels of education.[2] Nonetheless, few historians have studied the medical views themselves. Yet they provided the context for not only physicians' attitudes toward education for women at both the secondary and university levels, but also for the general public which tended to see physicians as experts on the female body. In the early decades of the century, physicians themselves directly participated in the debate over education of girls and young women. When supporters of women's education had apparently won the day, physicians' arguments became less apocalyptic but their belief about the physiological nature of women continued to be reflected in arguments for gender specific training.

The medical sources used for this paper are varied. They consist of the medical journals published in Canada in which local, national, and international articles existed side by side. The textbooks read by medical students, mostly written by non-Canadians, contained what their teachers believed was the authoritative knowledge necessary for any practitioner. Both popular health literature published in the major national magazines and the medical advice books that Canadians avidly read provided evidence of the privileging of medical expertise by the general public even on apparently non-medical topics such as the education of women.

During the years under review, Canadians generally attributed to science precision and objectivity. They believed that scientists understood and "knew" nature. Medicine shared in that glory. Especially significant were the inter-war years when Canadians could take national pride in the success of Frederick Banting's discovery of insulin and the international stature of child psychologist and physician William Blatz. Newspapers and national magazines contained advice columns and articles on health which made Drs. Helen MacMurchy, John McCullough, and Harold Atlee household names.[3] Advertisers appealed to the science of medicine to sell their products.[4] But how scientific was medicine? How scientific was science? In recent years, feminist historians and critics have pointed out that science, and medicine as its handmaiden, were (and are) cultural constructs as much as anything else in our society, that they reflected the society of which they were a part and by studying them historians can gain access to the values and mores of the past.[5] In turn, those mores became reconfigured within the scientific/medical paradigm and re-entered society as part of the general context which Canadians took for granted.

To understand the interface between medicine and the education of women, it is necessary to examine the medical perception of women's bodies. Understandably, physicians considered bodies from a physiological and functional perspective. With respect to women, the physiological view resulted in a comparison of the female body with the male. Most physicians were male and thus saw the male body as the norm with the result that the medical literature focused on the differences more than the similarities between men and women. The functional perspective taken by physicians meant that they believed those differences in the female body were there for a purpose and that purpose had to be realized for a woman to be healthy. For example, the reproductive system in women allowed them to bear children, that is, the body had the potential to bear children, and as a consequence, the body *should* bear children. It was what being a woman meant. If education was to prepare students for the future, then the future facing women as wives and mothers had to be kept in mind.

Childhood

The first area to explore is childhood. While physicians saw the differences between boys and girls as negligible relative to those of the post-pubescent period, they, nonetheless, acknowledged and gave meaning to them.[6] In 1913 Joseph B. DeLee, one of America's most prominent obstetricians acknowledged that at birth the two sexes were very much alike.

> [But] a close study will show small differences; the boy weighs, on the average, one-fourth of a pound more, the head is a little harder and larger, absolutely and also relatively to the body; a difference in the pelvis is also discernible: the female pelvis is larger and shallower than the male, and this is also true of the lower animals....

During the first years the characteristics of the sexes gradually become more marked, and as soon as the child walks the differentiation becomes apparent. The girl develops mentally and physically earlier than the boy, and one can sooner discover in her those traits of the female that distinguish it in later life.[7]

The quote revealed the firm belief that biology was destiny and that the differences in the social role of the sexes were determined by their respective bodies. By listing the differences, even in infants, the author endowed them with significance, although he left it to the reader to draw the conclusions about what that significance was, for example, of the larger head of the infant boy. At other times, however, he did not leave anything to chance as when he made a point of noting that the shallower pelvis of the girl baby reflected that of the "lower animals" suggesting that perhaps women were not as high on the evolutionary ladder as men. The differences existed for a reason, that is, they were functional in nature. In a similar vein a major 1928 gynaecology text stressed the pelvic differences of infants, the weight of the "long bones," and speculated on the existence of endocrine distinctions. Differences could lead to different skills which became part of gender identity. The 1943 *Encyclopedia of Child Guidance* noted that girls had superior "motor coordination and 'especially a more flexible rotation at the wrist'" which resulted in girls having better "dressing habits" even by the age of two or three.[8]

Psychological or mental differences between the sexes also existed. R. H. Cole, the author of the 1913 *Mental Diseases: A Textbook of Psychiatry for Medical Students and Practitioners* bluntly exclaimed that "idiocy is commoner in boys than in girls." When W. H. B. Stoddart in his 1919 text talked about the destructive phase beginning about age five, he had boys in mind.[9] Some lay people pushed the mental and psychological differences further. In 1923 Emily Murphy, a well-known reform and women's activist, insisted that it was "natural" and "easier" for a girl to be good whereas the opposite was true for boys.[10] By seeing girls as naturally good, Murphy could not give them credit for being so. Not all commentators, however, focused on the so-called "natural" differences. Some recognized that socialization played a major role in the development of personality.[11] But whether a person believed in nature or nurture, the differences between the sexes were significant and linked to social actions. One 1929 advertisement in *Chatelaine* understood this in depicting a boy who with the help of a medicinal aid had been able to fight off a cold, and was "Outdoors again—where boys belong."[12]

Puberty

None of the differences described were major compared to what doctors believed emerged at puberty. They and most Canadians saw puberty as the period when the two sexes became more dissimilar than similar. It was the time when girls became women and boys became men. The physical changes were the most obvious. Descriptions varied over time in their specificity and detail but often a sense of objective observation was present. Girls' bodies became more rounded and breasts developed. At times, however, physicians endowed such changes with cultural meaning. According to David Todd Gilliam, the author of a major gynaecological text, at puberty the girl "takes on the lines and curves that distinguish the mature female from the male. The increased development of bust and hips and general fullness of contour add greatly to her attractiveness, and proclaim her readiness for motherhood."[13] Several themes emerge from this quote. First was the use of the male as the basis for comparison, the norm; puberty was when the female was distinguished from the male not when the male was distinguished from the female. Second, the changes announced what a girl's social role was to be and her "readiness" for it. In this respect, the image raised was of a female animal in heat, attracting the male so that she could become pregnant. Third, Gilliam linked the physical changes to attractiveness, they were no longer neutral. Physicians in the interwar period at times focused on different aspects of puberty but they agreed with Gilliam in being very positive about the changes in pubescent girls, finding in them the basis for their attraction to women.[14] Clearly, puberty was more than experiencing certain physical changes; for many the meanings of those changes were equally significant.

Linked to the physical changes at puberty were moral and psychological changes which being less visible were more open to social construction. At puberty, young women took on the characteristics that defined a normative woman. For writers in the early decades of the century, such a woman was dignified, reserved, demure, shy of the opposite sex, modest, pure, and altruistic.[15] Some physicians worried that, because of the stresses placed on the body during puberty, young people, especially young women, might succumb to mental instability. J. A. MacKenzie, the Assistant Medical Superintendent of the Nova Scotia Hospital [for the Insane], Halifax, in 1902 quoted authorities to substantiate the idea that hysterical symptoms in pubescent girls were normative. What is fascinating about his view is that he seemed to be aware that what he perceived was to a certain extent socially constructed. He argued that given the limitations on their lives, women did not have the same outlets that men did to release nervous tension with the result that it built up and became accentuated at the appearance and occurrence of menstruation. His belief that pubescent changes occurred over four years in females compared to ten years in males only reinforced his perception that young women were under incredible stress and likely to exhibit it through mental derangement.[16] Not all MacKenzie's contemporaries agreed. J. N. Hutchison a Winnipeg physician writing in the 1902 *Canadian Journal of Medicine and Science* believed that the "psychical" effect of puberty was more devastating on boys.[17] However, his view was unusual; the consensus was that puberty was much more emotionally and mentally upsetting for girls.

Some of the attributes associated with puberty in young women at the turn of the century were still being put forward during the inter-war years and beyond. The emphasis on shyness and sensitivity continued, although some physicians suspected these characteristics were a consequence of custom and education rather than instinct.[18] They saw excessive emotionality as a female characteristic and a negative one, often viewing young women as irritable, bad-tempered, and erratic.[19] There was a sense in the medical literature that young women were experiencing too many changes with which they were not able to cope.[20] The consequences of experiencing a "bad" puberty were future problems. Indeed, physicians viewed puberty very much as a transitional phase the importance of which was in laying the groundwork for the healthy adult. If this foundation was not properly laid, then ill health in the future could result and lead to problems in bearing children and undermine woman's primary social role.[21]

Puberty and Education

Physicians throughout the first half of the twentieth century had a very specific notion of how the female body functioned. That functioning determined what women could and should do. Physicians had, in part, created a female construct and the point of education was for young women to conform to not challenge that construct. Physicians did not see themselves as educational experts but rather experts on the physiological makeup of women that meant they knew the limits of young women's physical energies better than the educators. They used the logic of science to bolster their words and cited one another as experts in a way that brooked no denial.[22]

Underlying most of the medical assessments of education for girls was the belief that the body controlled when and if education should occur. It was a privileging of body over mind, an appeal to the immutability of nature. Physicians were the experts on the body, which enabled them to offer opinions on a subject that many might not think of as medical. Central to their concern were the pressures of puberty/menstruation. The problem with the education of girls was that it coincided with a time when their bodies were undergoing tremendous changes—changes they saw as central to female development and physically and psychologically upsetting to the young woman. Education was another pressure at a time when young women needed to be relieved of pressure. It kept girls sedentary and indoors when they needed to be outdoors and more active. The former was part of the way modern "civilization" worked but unfortunately it affected the health of women so that physicians seldom saw modern women as healthy as their mothers or grandmothers had been. That being the case, education had to make adjustments.

The concerns were particularly strong in the early decades of the century. In his turn-of-the-century text, *Manual of Gynecology*, Henry T. Byford made it clear that in the first ten years of life more exercise and less study was needed. In the second crucial decade girls should have "a longer and easier course of instruction, with fewer hours of study and more hours of exercise."[23] The implication was that girls needed to work at a different pace than boys because of their bodies. The male body was the norm and education was designed with it in mind, although the repercussions of such an attitude for co-education were seldom spelled out. The proper development of the female reproduction system at puberty needed up to five years and if at the same time girls were being educated then an "antagonism between brain growth and body growth" occurred with dire consequences for both.[24] The latter had to have priority for once it broke down it was not always possible to repair it.

J. N. Hutchison feared that rather than taking into account girls' bodily developments, education, as it existed in Canada, ignored them. What was normal for girls, menstruation, made them exceptional compared to boys and required different educational responses. If the dictates of science were not enough to convince people to do something, he appealed to the notion that puberty was part of the "God-given power of reproduction." The language Hutchison used to describe a young woman and what was happening to her revealed his awe. He referred to the development of the "organs peculiar to herself, whose complexity, delicacy, sympathies and force are among the marvels of creation." If cared for they were powerful, it not, destructive. It was "an extraordinary task" that girls bore that boys did not. And that task only occurred for a few short years. For Hutchison, the development of young women's bodies demanded protection. While the development was powerful, it also engendered the urge to treat girls as delicate. Indeed he went so far as to suggest that girls be given three to four days off from school each month.[25]

Throughout the first half of the twentieth century, physicians believed that modern women were weaker than women of previous generations. In recent years, the scholarship on the body has argued that bodies are very much social constructs. This is not a new idea for many physicians in the past argued similarly with respect to women's bodies. They depicted a past in which women's bodies had functioned well. Body and social role supported one another. Modernity changed that and society now placed stresses on the body with which it was never meant to cope. The result was a body that no longer functioned as well as it did. In the early years of the century, Dr. Edward C. Hill explained that the transition to womanhood "should be as natural and uneventful as gliding from sleep into consciousness." However, the "present civilized modes of living" created problems and one aspect of the "civilized modes" was the attempt to educate girls at the same time they were entering puberty.[26] The sedentary life demanded by education was the culprit. Puberty was simply too delicate a time for energies to be directed elsewhere.[27]

Physicians did not blame women or even their bodies. "Civilized" society was at fault. Yet a truly civilized society would strengthen women. As E. C. Dudley in his 1908 gynaecology text argued, "To make the deterioration of woman, and through this the enfeeblement of the race, a price which must be paid for the higher education and civilization, would be seemingly to reverse the law of evolution and to put in its place a law of the survival of the unfittest."[28] But other than altering the educational system, Dudley and others did not see any solution. They were certainly not willing to suggest that society give up modernity or its civilized aspects, even if they did make women ill. What they seemed to want was for women to be civilized but not to engage in its trappings as much as men. They recognized the different needs of women compared to men—an equity argument—but their solution was not an equitable one. The best they could do was to appeal for the education system to take into account the differences of their students, to not assume that boys and girls at puberty could be treated in the same manner as if there were no differences between them.[29] The Minister of Health for New Brunswick, W. H. Roberts, himself a physician, picked up on these themes in recommending change to the educational system. He wanted to rearrange it to take into account the pubescent years of girls. "Man's artificial conventions," should not have priority.[30]

In the inter-war period and beyond, the focus on education lessened. By that time, the issue of women's access to higher education had been debated and the decision made to open the doors of universities, although not all faculties, to women. More emphasis was placed on physical education in the high schools offsetting some of the earlier criticisms. Physicians' interest in education had never been central to their concerns about puberty and by the 1920s was only one of many factors they felt hurt girls during those formative years. But the earlier themes still existed, even if in lesser form. In one 1930 text, the authors made a point of noting that "the mind should be trained ... but it should be trained in a way that does not interfere with the development of the body."[31] Understandably, physicians continued to privilege the body and this was reflected in non-medical venues. In an article entitled "Sex in Education" in the 1930 *Dalhousie Review*, J. A. Lindsay wrote:

> Biological considerations rise when we take into account the different rates of development of the two sexes. The female develops earlier and more rapidly than the male, and reaches her maturity at an earlier date. A girl of ten or twelve is farther on the road of life than the boy of the same age, and the young woman of seventeen or eighteen is more mature than her male contemporary, more mature, it is to be understood, physically. The bearing of these facts upon education is obscure, and has been insufficiently thought out. Nature is objective and racial, not intellectual or personal. The intellectual life is a graft upon the affective life, and later in development. As a feeling, acting animal, man is of untold antiquity; as a thinking animal, he is of yesterday. The female sex, for profound biological reasons, is nearer to nature than the male, more intimately associated with the problems of race preservation and renewal. We shall not see our way clearly in problems of sex unless we think in aeons, rather than in decades or even in centuries.[32]

Lindsay's quote echoed many of the major themes developed in the medical literature of previous years. For one he emphasized the differences between males and females more than their similarities and centred those differences in body, not in society. Even more, he argued that women were closer to body (or nature) than men because of their closer link with reproduction. Education must take those differences into consideration, not ignore them. Educators needed to take the long (racial) view rather than the short (society based) perspective. Dr. Harold Atlee agreed. He, too, argued that body had priority in any conflict between the development of body and mind. Unlike some, he recognized that this was not always fair to women and told them so. But there was little that could be done to offset that reality. He, however, did feel that society and training often accentuated the frailties of women. The focus of education should be to make them strong. "For one thing we must teach them that tears are a silly weapon in the face of conflict. That all those weaknesses we connote in the word 'womanly' must be replaced by those strengths we connote in the word 'manly.'" For Atlee what he saw as the psychological weaknesses of women were partially constructed and could be overcome. The bodily weakness could not.[33]

The connection made between puberty and education was clear. For physicians and other Canadians, puberty was a trying time and any added stress could be potentially harmful. Because of their bodily demands, young women could not engage in mental development in the same way as young men. They could not do two things well at once. If they tried, either the mind or the body would fail and for physicians bodily failure was more significant. And physicians were very specific about the problems that education caused or could lead to. Some were immediate. Some were lying-in-wait to cause future harm. Others were more general pertaining to the well-being of the race itself. But whatever the focus, the list of repercussions kept growing and, as a consequence, the scenario more apocalyptic.

At the turn of the century, R. W. Garrett in his gynaecology text made clear that the way the educational system was structured left the young girl at the end of her studies "worn out" and perhaps suffering from "constipation, anaemia, irritable hypersensitive nerves and derangement of the menstrual function." To that list others added menorrhagia, headaches, palpitations, emaciation, dysmenorrhea. Yet what did society demand—for her to marry and bear children! There was no way that any woman could or should take on the burdens of marriage and motherhood when she was not physically prepared to do so. The result could only be invalidism, uterine and ovarian disease, or nerve prostration.[34] The solution was not to delay marriage and childbearing but rather to alter the education that girls received. Women were the "mothers of the race" and so their health had to be maintained. The scenario was dire. The young woman might graduate with "plaudits" but her future was one of reproductive sterility or suffering "all the untold agonies which so often confront the physician."[35] While lay people might have been able to ignore some of the pronouncements of physicians on education, they were less likely

165

to dismiss the specificity of woman's medical problems. In that area medical expertise reigned. In 1916, R .I. Warner, Principal of Alma College, St. Thomas, Ontario, exhibited the fear engendered by physicians when he referred to a discussion he had had with a medical man who claimed that because of the problems that education led to in young women the use of opium had increased to offset their "periodic distress."[36]

More worrisome to Lapthorn Smith, Professor of Clinical Gynaecology at Bishop's University, Montreal, was the race issue. Women were marrying too late with the result that they were giving birth to fewer children. And education was to blame. Smith's utopia was a society where women married at the age of eighteen and had their first child soon after. Instead he saw women marrying at the age of 26 or even 28 because of extended education. If that was not bad enough, the children born to such "educated" women were most likely to be physically weak. If this scenario was not ominous enough, Smith argued education raised expectations in women which could only lead to dissatisfaction with marriage and eventual high divorce rates. Even worse, educated women might not even marry.[37] Smith's antagonism to women's education was palpable. It was by far the most unrestrained attack in the early decades of the century found in the medical literature. What is interesting about his diatribe was the way in which he used the issue of education to support the increasing intervention of medical practitioners. The internal examination of women was still not accepted by all in society; it allowed a "strange" man (the doctor) to view the intimate parts of a woman's body. Especially problematic was the internal exam of unmarried women. However, Smith argued that physicians had no choice. Due to the diseases of the womb which education of girls had caused, physicians had young women as patients who previously they would never have seen.[38] The breakdown in health caused by education had created new responsibilities for physicians.

In the inter-war period and after, the apocalyptic vision of education's impact was not as extreme or widespread but physicians still continued to point out that the stress and pressure of education when associated with lack of exercise, could result in health concerns such as anemia with amenorrhea.[39] An editorial in the 1932 *Canadian Medical Association Journal* gave a contrary view. It reported that the President of Dalhousie University claimed that the "health of the women students was much better than that of the men."[40] Nevertheless, the fact that the medical journal editorialized this "news" revealed how it contradicted accepted wisdom.

An Ideal Education

Given the various concerns about education, what did physicians put forward as a solution? What kind of education did they envisage? They were not against educating girls but felt education should be different and take into account the demands of their bodies and their future role in society as wives and mothers. In the early part of the century physicians specifically advised slowing down the educational process so that girls could receive more rest and exercise. As Henry T. Byford explained, it was better if a young woman completed her education at the age of 21 rather than eighteen (a suggestion which Lapthorn Smith would have found abhorrent).[41] It was unclear how Byford conceptualized such a suggestion would be integrated into the educational system as it already existed. What was noteworthy about his proposal, and indeed so many of the concerns revolving around education for women, was the focus on the high school level. It, more than university education, was problematic because it coincided with the years of puberty. Such schools had to face what physicians saw as education's central difficulties: the long hours, the sedentary existence, the lack of outdoor activity and fresh air. As well, schools promoted competitiveness which some physicians found disturbing.[42] Competitiveness was gendered male; it also created stress and stress was something pubescent girls needed to avoid.

Underlying medical arguments was the sense that education fit boys, not girls. As Lapthorn Smith made clear at puberty "boys and girls should have a different course of education."[43] And he was not alone in believing this. An article in the 1900 *Canadian Magazine* argued along similar lines as did the National Council of Women of Canada in their Annual Report.[44] Smith was explicit about what girls should be taught. "Algebra, euclid, botany, chemistry, mythology, astronomy, Greek and Latin, should be cut out, and the time devoted to dressmaking, millinery, cooking and domestic economy, including the care of the baby, the making of the home, and even the care of the husband."[45] Fredericton physician, A. B. Atherton, offered an extreme solution: take girls out of the public school for one or two years during puberty. If parents wanted their daughters to be educated then they could send them to private or boarding schools where there would not be the same focus on competition as in the public schools and where close supervision over them could occur. Realizing the class nature of such a proposal, Atherton comforted himself and his readers that poorer girls would be better off without the education during their developing years. Indeed they could occupy themselves with "domestic duties" which he felt were sorely neglected.[46] W. H. Roberts made a similar suggestion—between the ages of fourteen and sixteen the education of women should focus on *their* particular issues: the workings of their bodies, domestic science, and personal hygiene and household sanitation, all to be taught to them by a woman of high moral character. Like others who suggested such extreme notions, he was silent on how girls would return to the classroom after this academic hiatus, although his own predisposition was clear, they should only do so "if necessary."[47] Others were clearly more reasonable, simply pleading for schools to be aware of the specificity of girls' bodies and to take it and their future roles as wives and mothers into account.[48]

Similar themes continued into subsequent decades. In 1921, H. W. Hill, Dean of the Faculty of Public Health, at Western University, London, Ontario, advocated housewifery classes in the public schools from the age of twelve onwards.[49] A year later, an editorial in the *National Hygiene and Public Welfare* was more accommodating arguing that both boys and girls should be prepared for their life's duties among which it was willing to recognize women's involvement in the work force.[50] Nonetheless, the questioning of modernity continued. The authors of the 1930 textbook *Diseases of Women* questioned the "acquisitions of modern life" under which they placed "exhausting school duties" as well as "immoderate piano practice." School should train the mind but not at the expense of the body. And if the body suffered then the student (the girl) should be removed from school.[51]

In his *Dalhousie Review* article, J. A. Lindsay raised many of the issues that physicians elsewhere had outlined. He had internalized their belief in primacy of the body and its control over mind. He asked whether co-education was really possible when the differences between the sexes were so central. Yet he believed and comforted himself that nature would win out. He noted that girls did better in school than boys until puberty at which time boys surged forward and girls fell behind. But soon girls regained their lead until "between the ages of sixteen and seventeen ... a period of lassitude and dullness in the female sex [occurred]. Dame Nature is playing her profound game."[52] Nature, then, would protect girls even from the pressures of education. But it would not hurt to help nature.

Harold Atlee did not disagree with the above but what is interesting is that he did not come to the issue from the point of view of bemoaning the decline in womanly attributes as many of his colleagues and others did. Rather he took a "feminist" perspective in that he wanted to encourage women in their differences. He wanted women to think about the educational system and how it was structured. The pre-college years were almost totally under the domination of female teachers that raised questions about how young boys were being educated. The university years, however, were dominated by male teachers and male goals. How would a young woman develop her own sense of self if she was constantly bombarded by goals which men said were significant?[53]

The connection between medical rhetoric and its impact on education is not always obvious. Nonetheless, changes in education occurred that, in part, seemed to be a response to the medical concerns about the "frailty" of young women in the years surrounding puberty. By the end of the nineteenth century some form of physical culture for girls existed in many schools. Private schools especially pursued sports with Ellen Knox of Havergal College in Toronto arguing that a "sturdy, wholesome body" was necessary to maintain a strong mind.[54] In public schools, light calisthenics dominated the early years of the century but after World War I more strenuous exercise became the norm. Sports were gendered reflecting the perceived differences between the two sexes which emerged at puberty.[55] The introduction of sports occurred at the university level as well and educators deemed them even more important to offset critics who argued that university study was too demanding for women and would weaken their health. At McGill University, Ethel Mary Cartwright created and introduced a physical education programme that became a requirement for all first year women students and eventually for all women undergraduates. In the 1920s, at all levels of schooling, girls' rules emerged to ensure that in playing sport, girls and young women did not over exert themselves or develop the attributes of competitive male athletes. The seriousness with which educators took the need for healthy bodies for girls and young women was also evidenced by the training of teachers in physical education. [56]

Sport was not the only response to the desire to balance health and education. The introduction of nurses, physicians, and dentists into the schools signaled a commitment to the health of all students. The introduction and expansion of domestic science both reflected the determination that girls would understand that their future roles were as wives and mothers and be trained for those roles despite the schools' emphasis on educating boys and girls together on what some saw as a competitive basis. The Daniel McIntyre Collegiate Institute in Winnipeg introduced health instruction into its domestic science course and as Cynthia Comacchio concluded. "The mode of delivery supported the medical view that girls especially needed health training because of their special vulnerability at that age."[57] Elsewhere sex hygiene courses played the same role.

Conclusion

The response of educators revealed how entrenched the view of women's separateness was. While the separateness was admirable and offered much, it was based in a body that was not only different from men's but also limited. The latter view permeated the medical literature on women. As experts on the body, physicians "knew" what the body could or could not do. With respect to women, this led physicians to speak out on a wide range of issues including education. The medical view of sexual differences provided the context for discussions on how to educate girls and for how long; in turn, the wider view of woman's role in society influenced the way in which physicians perceived the female body. It was different from the male and the differences existed for a reason. A truly civilized society did not dismiss nature but worked with nature. Consequently, educators needed to recognize the "natural" differences between their male and female students, especially at puberty when the development of the reproductive system took place. For physicians, and they hoped for educators, that development took precedence. If it did not, physicians were more than willing to detail the dire consequences that would follow.

Research for this paper was supported by the Social Sciences and Humanities Research Council of Canada and the Hannah Institute for the History of Medicine. I thank Catherine Gidney for advice on sources.

Wendy Mitchinson

Notes

1. *The Public Health Journal* 10, 11 (November 1919): 492.
2. See Mona Gleason, *Normalizing the Ideal: Psychology, Schooling, and the Family in Postwar Canada* (Toronto: University of Toronto Press, 1999); Christabelle Sethna, *The Facts of Life: The Sex Instruction of Ontario Public School Children, 1900-1950* (Ph.D. thesis, University of Toronto, 1995); Christabelle Sethna, "The Cold War and the Sexual Chill: Freezing Girls Out of Sex Education," *Canadian Woman Studies/les cahiers de la femme* 17, 4 (Spring 1998): 57-61; Christabelle Sethna, "Men, Sex, And Education: The Ontario WCTU and Children's Sex Education, 1900-1920," *Ontario History* LXXXVIII, 3 (September 1996): 185-206; Helen Lenskyj, "Moral Physiology in Physical Education and Sport for girls in Ontario, 1890-1930," *Proceedings, 5th Canadian Symposium on the History of Sport and Physical Education* (Toronto: University of Toronto Press, 1982): 139-50; Helen Lenskyj, "Femininity First: Sport and Physical Education for Ontario Girls, 1890-1930," *Canadian Journal of History of Sport* 13, 2 (December 1982): 4-17; and Helen Lenskyj, "Training for 'True Womanhood': Physical Education for girls in Ontario Schools, 1890-1920," *Historical Studies in Education* 2, 2 (Fall 1990): 205-23.
3. See Michael Bliss, *Banting: A Biography* (Toronto: University of Toronto Press, 1992) and Jocelyn Motyer Raymond, *The Nursery World of Dr. Blatz* (Toronto: University of Toronto Press, 1991). Dr. Helen MacMurchy was the Chief of the Child Welfare Division, Dominion Health Department, 1920-1934; Dr. John McCullough was the Chief Inspector for Health for Ontario and between 1930 and 1940 he wrote an advice column "The Baby Clinic" in *Chatelaine*; and Dr. Harold Atlee was Professor of Obstetrics and Gynaecology at Dalhousie Medical College, 1923-1958.
4. See *Canadian Courier* 25, 19 (June 19, 1920): 25 and *Nova Scotia Medical Bulletin* 5, 10 (October 1926): 5.
5. See especially Ludmilla Jordanova, *Nature Displayed: Gender, Science and Medicine 1760-1820* (London: Longmans, 1999); Ruth Hubbard, Mary Sue Henifen and Barbara Fried, eds., *Biological Woman, the Convenient Myth: A Collection of Feminist Essays and a Comprehensive Bibliography* (Cambridge, Mass.: Schenkman, 1982); Ruth Hubbard, *The Politics of Women's Biology* (New Brunswick: Rutgers University Press, 1990); Mariana Benjamin, ed., *Science & Sensibility: Gender and Scientific Enquiry 1780-1945* (Oxford: Basil Blackwell Inc., 1991); Ruth Bleier, *Science and Gender: A Critique of Biology and Its Theories on Women* (New York: Pergamon Press, 1984); Donna Haraway, *Primate Visions: Gender, Race, and Nature in the World of Modern Science* (New York: Routledge, 1989); Sandra Harding, *Whose Science? Whose Knowledge: Thinking From Women's Lives* (Ithaca, N.Y.: Cornell University Press, 1991); Mary Jacobus, Evelyn Fox Keller, and Sally Shuttleworth, eds., *Body/Politics: Women and the Discoveries of Science* (New York: Routledge, 1990); Evelyn Fox Keller, *Secrets of Life, Secrets of Death: Essays on Language, Gender, and Science* (New York: Routledge, 1992); Helen Longino, *Science as Social Knowledge* (Princeton, N.J.: Princeton University Press, 1990); Brian Easlea, *Science and Sexual Oppression: Patriarchy's Confrontation with Woman and Nature* (London: Weidenfeld and Nicolson, 1981); Londa Schiebinger, *Nature's Body: Gender in the Making of Modern Science* (Boston: Beacon Press, 1993); and Barbara Laslett, Sally Gregory Kohlstedt, Helen Longino, and Evelynn Hammonds, eds.,

"Gender and Scientific Authority: Essays," reprinted from *Signs: Journal of Women in Culture and Society* (Chicago: University of Chicago Press, 1996).

6   See J. Clifton Edgar, *The Practice of Obstetrics ... for the Use of Students and Practitioners* (Philadelphia: P. Blakiston's Son & Co., 1907, 3rd ed.), 36, and Arthur Hale Curtis and John William Huffman, *A Textbook of Gynecology* (Philadelphia: W.B. Saunders, 1951, 6th ed.), 100.

7   Joseph B. DeLee, *The Principles and Practice of Obstetrics* (Philadelphia: W.B. Saunders, 1913), 1.

8   Thomas Watts Eden and Cuthbert Lockyer, *Gynaecology for Students and Practitioners* (London: J. & A. Churchill, 1928, 3rd ed.), 78 and Ralph B. Winn, ed., *Encyclopedia of Child Guidance* (New York: The Philosophical Library, 1943), 126.

9   R. H. Cole, *Mental Diseases: A Textbook of Psychiatry for Medical Students and Practitioners* (London: University of London Press, 1913), 143 and W.H.B. Stoddart, *Mind and Its Disorders: A Textbook for Students and Practitioners of Medicine* (Philadelphia: P. Blakiston's Son & Co., 1919, 3rd ed.), 70.

10 *Canadian Child* 3, 7 (January 1923): 2.

11 Howard A. Kelly, *et al.*, *Gynecology* (New York: D. Appleton, 1928), 1001.

12 *Chatelaine* 2, 11 (November 1929): 39.

13 David Todd Gilliam, *A Text-book of Practical Gynecology* (Philadelphia: F.A. Davis Company, 1907, 2nd ed.), 62; see also Francis H. A. Marshall, *The Physiology of Reproduction* (London: Longmans, Green and Company, 1922, 2nd ed.), 713 and *Canadian Practitioner and Review* 27, 11 (November 1902): 662. For historical literature on the American view of menarche see Sharon Golub, *Periods: From Menarche to Menopause* (Newbury Park, CA: Sage, 1992); Sarah Stage, *Female Complaints: Lydia Pinkham and the Business of Women's Medicine* (New York: W.W. Norton & Co., 1979); Joan Jacob Brumberg, *Body Project: An Intimate History of American Girls* (New York: Random House, 1997); Joan Jacob Brumberg, "'Something Happens to Girls'! Menarche and the Emergence of the Modern American Hygiene Imperative," *Journal of the History of Sexuality* 4, 1 (July 1993): 99-127; Janice Delaney, M. J. Lupton, and Emily Toth, *The Curse: A Cultural History of Menstruation* (New York: Mentor, 1976); Laura Klosterman Kidd, "Menstrual Technology in the United States: 1854 to 1921," (Ph.D. thesis, Iowa State University, 1994); and Louise Lander, *Image of Bleeding: Menstruation as Ideology* (New York: Orlando Press, 1998).

14 See Harry Sturgeon Crossen and Robert James Crossen, *Diseases of Women* (St. Louis: The C. V. Mosby Company, 1930, 7th ed.), 828, and Percy E. Ryberg, *Health, Sex and Birth Control* (Toronto: The Anchor Press, 1942), 77.

15 See Gilliam, *A Text-book of Practical Gynecology*, 62 and W. Blair Bell, *The Principles of Gynaecology* (London: Longmans, Green & Co., 1910), 68.

16 *Maritime Medical News* 14, 12 (December 1902): 439-40.

17 *Canadian Journal of Medicine and Surgery* 11, 1 (January 1902): 4.

18 J. Munro Kerr, *et al.*, *Combined Textbook of Obstetrics and Gynaecology for Students and Medical Practitioners* (Edinburgh: E. & S. Livinstone, 1933, 2nd ed.), 38.

19 Carl Henry Davis, ed., *Gynecology and Obstetrics*, vol. 1 (Hagerstown, Maryland: W.F. Prior Company, Inc., 1935) chapter 2, p. 2; Fred L. Adair, ed., *Obstetrics and Gynecology*, Vol. 1 (Philadelphia: Lea & Febiger, 1940), 490; Winn, ed., *Encyclopedia of Child Guidance*, 335-36; Archibald Donald Campbell and Mabel A. Shannon, *Gynaecology for Nurses* (Philadelphia: F.A. Davis Company, 1946), 25; and Marion Hilliard, *Women and Fatigue: A Woman Doctor's Answer* (Garden City,

Wendy Mitchinson

   NY: Doubleday and Company, Inc., 1960), 14.
[20] See *Maclean's* 59 (December 1, 1946): 12; Winfield Scott Hall, *Sexual Knowledge* (Philadelphia: The International Bible House, 1913), 106 and *Canadian Public Health Journal* 23, 10 (October, 1932): 482-83.
[21] See *Canadian Practitioner and Review* 27, 11 (November 1902): 662; E.C. Dudley, *The Principles and Practice of Gynecology for Students and Practitioners* (Philadelphia and New York: Lea & Febiger, 1908, 5th ed.) 22; *Dominion Medical Monthly* 23, 5 (November 1904): 323; *The Public Health Journal* 10, 11 (November 1919): 492; *The Hospital World* 22, 5 (November 1922): 187; and Carl Henry Davis, ed., *Gynecology and Obstetrics* vol. 3 (Hagerstown, Maryland: W.F. Prior Company, Inc., 1935) Chapter 9, p. 32.
[22] See Charles A.L. Reed, ed., *A Text-Book of Gynecology* (New York: D. Appleton and Co., 1901), 7; Gilliam, *A Text-Book of Practical Gynecology* (Philadelphia: F. A. Davis Co., 1907), 74; *Dominion Medical Monthly* 23, 5 (November 1904): 323; Thomas Clifford Allbutt, W. S. Playfair, and Thomas Watts Eden, eds., *A System of Gynaecology* (London: Macmillan and Co., 1906, 2nd ed.), 119-20; and Crossen and Crossen, *Diseases of Women*, 835.
[23] Henry T. Byford, *Manual of Gynecology* (Philadelphia: P. Blakiston, Son and Co., 1895), 64.
[24] R. W. Garrett, *Textbook of Medical and Surgical Gynaecology* (Kingston, 1897), 11, 60.
[25] *Canadian Journal of Medicine and Surgery* 11, 1 (January 1902): 2-3.
[26] *Canadian Practitioner and Review* 27, 11 (November 1902): 662.
[27] See Henry J. Garrigues, *Gynecology, Medical and Surgical: Outlines for Students and Practitioners* (Philadelphia: J. B. Lippincott Co., 1905), 5; and *The Canada Lancet* 39, 11 (July 1906): 1051.
[28] Dudley, *The Principles and Practice of Gynecology*, 28.
[29] See Allbutt, Playfair, and Eden, eds., *A System of Gynaecology*, 119-20 and *The Canada Lancet* 41, 2 (October 1907): 98-99.
[30] *The Public Health Journal* 10, 11 (November 1919): 492-96.
[31] Crossen and Crossen, *Diseases of Women*, 832, 834.
[32] *Dalhousie Review* 10 (July 1930): 147, 150.
[33] *Canadian Home Journal* (November 1931): 83.
[34] Garrett, *Textbook of Medical and Surgical Gynaecology*, 60,11; see also *Canadian Practitioner and Review* 27, 11 (November 1902): 662 and *The Canada Lancet* 39, 11 (July 1906): 1051.
[35] *Canadian Journal of Medicine and Surgery* 11, 1 (January 1902): 2-3; see also Allbutt, Playfair, and Eden, eds., *A System of Gynaecology*, 119-20 and Gilliam, *A Text-book of Practical Gynecology*, 74.
[36] *The Public Health Journal* 7, 6 (June 1916): 311.
[37] *Dominion Medical Monthly* 23, 5 (November 1904): 323-24, 327.
[38] *Dominion Medical Monthly* 23, 5 (November 1904): 326.
[39] Crossen and Crossen, *Diseases of Women*, 832.
[40] *Canadian Medical Association Journal* 27, 5 (November 1932): 531.
[41] Byford, *Manual of Gynecology*, 64.
[42] See Garrett, *Textbook of Medical and Surgical Gynaecology*, 60; see also *The Canada Lancet* 41, 2 (October 1907): 98-99; Gilliam, *A Text-book of Practical Gynecology*, 4 and *The Public Health Journal* 10, 11 (November 1919): 490.
[43] *Dominion Medical Monthly* 23, 5 (November 1904): 323. See also *Canadian Journal*

of *Medicine and Surgery* 11, 1 (January 1902): 2.

44 *Canadian Magazine* 15, 5 (September 1900): 473 and National Council of Women, *Report of the Annual Meeting 1900*, 86; see also *Canadian Magazine* 18, 4 (February 1902): 380.

45 *Dominion Medical Monthly* 23, 5 (November 1904): 323.

46 *The Canada Lancet* 41, 2 (October 1907): 98-99.

47 *The Public Health Journal* 10, 11 (November 1919): 492-93, 496.

48 See Gilliam, *A Text-book of Practical Gynecology*, 4; Garrigues, *Gynecology, Medical and Surgical*, 5; Byford, *Manual of Gynecology*, 64 and Edgar, *The Practice of Obstetrics*, 36.

49 *Canadian Medical Association Journal* 11, 9 (September 1921): 619; see also *Canadian Medical Association Journal* 46, 1 (January 1942): 2.

50 *National Hygiene and Public Welfare* 28, 3 (March 1922): 139.

51 Crossen and Crossen, *Disease of Women*, 834-35.

52 *Dalhousie Review* 10 (July 1930): 150, 153; see also *Dalhousie Review* 25 (April 1945): 86-87; and *Saturday Night* 62 (September 28 1946): 30.

53 *Canadian Home Journal* (November 1931): 9.

54 Knox quoted in M. Ann Hall, *The Girl and the Game: A History of Women's Sport in Canada* (Peterborough: Broadview Press, 2002), 28-9.

55 For concern about the health of adolescents see Cynthia Comacchio, "'The Rising Generation': Laying Claim to the Health of Adolescents in English Canada, 1920-70," *Canadian Bulletin of Medical History* 19, 1 (2002): 139-78.

56 Hall, *The Girl and the Game*, 31-33, 74-5. For the response of American physical educators see Martha H. Verbrugge, "Recreating the Body: Women's Physical Education and the Science of Sex Differences in America, 1900-1940," *Bulletin of the History of Medicine* 71, 2 (1997): 273-304. For an examination of the way in which American colleges and universities responded to the concern about the potential debilitating effect of education on women see Margaret A. Lowe, *Looking Good: College Women and Body Image, 1875-1930* (Baltimore: The Johns Hopkins University Press, 2003), esp. 1-4, 9-10, 14-18, 20-6, 47; Paul Atkinson, "Fitness, Feminism and Schooling," in Sara Delamont and Lorna Dufin, (eds.), *The Nineteenth-Century Woman: Her Cultural and Physical World* (London: Croom Helm, 1978), 92-133.

57 Comacchio, "'The Rising Generation,'" 146-52.

III.
Women's Public and Private Lives

Travel Lessons

Canadian Women "Across the Pond" 1865-1905

SUSAN MANN

"Call on Madame Laurier," Agnes Bell instructed her husband from afar, "tell her about the children—they are learning both French and German." Agnes was in Scotland, the children, daughters Margaret and Alice, were at school in Germany while father Robert tended to his career with the Geological Survey of Canada in Ottawa. For him, connections with the wife of the newly-elected Canadian Prime Minister, Wilfrid Laurier, might be beneficial for that career and to have womenfolk who were travelled and educated was clearly a bonus. The bonus, moreover, profited the Bell women too for they were "across the pond" on numerous occasions in the late nineteenth century "seeing and learning all the time." For them, travel was part of family strategy and the women were assiduous players.[1]

In the last decade travel and travellers have invaded scholarly territory but rarely in the fashion of Agnes Bell and her contemporaries. Some historians and many more literary scholars have succumbed to the invasion, poring over travellers' published accounts with a post-modern passion for text and trope. By and large, their travellers either stay put on the page as travel becomes a literary genre or mark newly encountered territory as travel becomes imperial imposition.[2] Both approaches obscure an earlier historical—and primarily male—notion of travel as adventure, a notion that early feminists tried valiantly to claim for women. The result was the occasional "woman into the unknown" but rarely a sense of how most women likely travelled in the late nineteenth century, their families always in tow, whether present or not. Indeed, this kind of traveller tends to be dismissed as "accidental travellers," accompanying persons or merely tourists, in contrast to the *real* traveller, the one who cut ties and lit out.[3] Only one account hints peripherally at the argument developed here, that home was well tucked into the baggage of

Susan Mann

8.1. *Schoolgirl in Germany, Margaret Bell, 1897. Courtesy Library and Archives Canada.*

8.2. *Schoolgirl in Germany, Alice Bell, 1897. Courtesy Library and Archives Canada.*

women travellers.[4] But that is precisely what the thirteen Canadian travellers of this essay reveal. Their diaries and letters, free of the exigencies of editor, publisher or even reader (in the case of the diaries), are thus different from the sources that fuel contemporary travel scholarship. And by revealing a specific and unusual pattern of travel, they tell us a different story. All the women, eleven English and two French Canadians, crossing a middle-class life span of women from children to matrons and leaving their trace in the national archives of Canada or the Archives nationales du Québec, harnessed travel to a domestic agenda. The lessons they learned while abroad confirmed their own domesticity. Their destination was to be at home and they fashioned that home, with all its Victorian accoutrements of behaviour, judgment, propriety, and morality, wherever they went.

Much like travel writing itself, diaries have taken the fancy of historians and literary scholars. For almost 20 years feminist historians have combed women's diaries in particular for social history, women's culture, women's voices. A Canadian illustration is the vast search for manuscript diaries in Nova Scotia which led to the compilation *No Place Like Home*[5] the title alone revealing the domesticity of such documents. Literary scholars have focused on the distinct form and language of the texts themselves, to contend that women's diaries as autobiography warrant all the critical attention of more traditional literary productions.[6] What is striking, for the purposes of this essay, is that in a form that stresses the ordinary, that jumbles record and feeling and event, that refuses any hierarchical structuring of significance, all the travel diaries used here (and the letters too) impose a domestic order on the writer's surroundings. Whether this is the result of the diary form itself or the writer's own agency is a moot point. What does seem clear is that where literary scholars see in diaries a blurring of the boundaries "between text and experience, art and life,"[7] these travel diaries blur the boundary between home and away. In doing so they disrupt all the conventional notions of travel.

Needless to say, the imperial context facilitated this blurring of boundaries. All the Canadians knew they were travelling from a colonial periphery to an imperial centre, whether it was the political and economic magnet of London, the cultural power of Paris or the religious draw of Rome. They all knew that travel to such places marked them as socially and culturally superior. In Europe they could enlarge and enhance their domestic interest in health and education, in clothing and manners. Hence their need and their ability to be at home in the imperial centres of their culture. Agnes Bell was the only one to state that "home" literally was "among my own people" in Scotland but the others could not have escaped contemporary English Canadian discourse about the "motherland," "home," and "the old country."[8]

So these women stepped confidently onto the elegant steamships of late nineteenth century travel. Only one, Maria Bogart, travelled on a sailing ship (1865-66); her purpose in travelling with a toddler was to impose a semblance of domestic stability on her sea-faring husband, the captain of the vessel. The others expected to find that stability, with all its hierarchy of class and comfort, in the floating Victorian households of trans-Atlantic liners. There the women were assured of elegant surroundings, polite conversation, genteel entertainments and deferential service. Should they be unaccompanied by husband or father—the Bell women as a threesome and individually (1890-91; 1896-98; 1900; 1902; 1905), Juliette Routhier (1896-97), Annie Lampman (1887-88), Jennie Curran (1894) and Cairine Mackay (1904)—the ship's captain, a perfect Victorian gentleman, oversaw their well-being. The others, young woman Ethel Davies (1899-1900), newlyweds Virginie de Saint-Ours Kierzkowska (1868-69) and Gertrude Mackintosh Fleming (1891-92), matrons Ellen Bilbrough (1899; 1900) and Frances Tupper (1890), all counted on the solicitous attention and direction of father or husband. With such familial and domestic accoutrements to their Atlantic travel, the women shared in the ideal and the reality of Britannia (a female figure!) ruling the waves. They thus minimized both distance and danger: neither warranted a word in diary or letter as the ocean became a pond. Home was never far away.

The only facet of ocean travel that disturbed them was seasickness. They all anticipated it with dread and even more so once they had experienced it. Part of the dread was its very indelicacy. For what could be more impolite or unladylike than an abrupt, green-faced, heaving, retching departure from the dinner table? Part of the dread also was the sheer ghastliness of being seasick. Virginie Kierzkowska "felt as if [she] should have died during that wretched crossing" had it not been for "the kindness, care and devotedness of [a new and] dear husband."[9] In a domestic tour de force, she thus turned the sea's assault upon her senses into a test and judgment of his moral character. The more physically stable Ethel Davies prided herself on being a "marvellous sailor;" she was not sick at all and crowed her superiority over those who were. "And some are men! think of it!"[10] Seasickness, it appeared, could upset the social order as well as the stomach.

Once in Britain or on the Continent, the women ensured that nothing else upset the social order. They travelled as homemakers abroad and peeped out at their surroundings through the parlour windows of their minds. They framed their reflections in the rectangles of writing paper, diary page or new-fangled camera. And they settled in. Gertrude Fleming snuggled into the individual compartments of a British railway carriage and then into a suite of rooms in one of London's more elegant hotels, delighting in the piano, the flowers, breakfast in her own bed and supper by the fire while husband "Bobby" explored the city on his own. As a new bride from Ottawa, her travel lesson was the transition to marriage but she resisted the lessons by maintaining the attentions of young men met aboard ship and then by falling ill, both designed, one suspects, to keep Bobby at bay.[11] Ethel Davies, a much more adventurous sort, nonetheless settled into her aunt's country home at Bloxham for a long winter's stay. There the 22-year-old from Prince Edward Island was to perfect her own domesticity. She did not know how to cook; nor had she internalized the seriousness of household activities. "Auntie" set about correcting what was a major flaw in a young woman's education. The lessons took; their importance was absorbed and recorded in her diary—"I am becoming very industrious, besides the cooking I am sewing heaps of things and practising my music very religiously"—and by the end of the winter she was allowed the play time of a trip to the Continent.[12]

The same interest in domestic confinement appears in the letters of the Bell women and of Juliette Routhier. Indeed, their letters are so full of domestic detail that more than reassurance to the relatives at home would seem to be at stake. The women were rendering their surroundings familiar by the imposition of domesticity. In the Bell case—mother and children travelling abroad so Papa could get on with his work—the many Scottish relatives who took turns hosting Agnes, Margaret, Alice and wee Donald facilitated the domesticity. But Agnes took to it with relish, monitoring the girls' behaviour and upbringing in response to Robert's concern lest they be outdoors, playing too much. The eight- and ten-year-old girls should be thinking of "music and French and German lessons ... and perhaps learn to dance better," all undertakings that could only be mastered by discipline, indoors.[13] In Juliette Routhier's case, the pleurisy-prone 24-year-old was escaping the cold of a Quebec City winter by burrowing into a small family-style hotel in San Remo. The state of her health may have determined her choice but it was the home-like atmosphere that took her fancy. At the *Pension Paradis* she had a sunny room with tea-making facilities, meals with the eleven other boarders around a large dining table, chats and reading in the comfortable salon.[14] She needed to be at home.

Once ensconced, the women pursued their own domestic agenda. They seemed eager, as women from a colony, to display their feminine *savoir-faire* on the imperial stage (a stage they enlarged to include Europe), to earn for themselves and their menfolk the nod of social acceptance. Thus, in ever-widening circles, but always mediated by family, they visited, befriended, shopped, observed, and were entertained; they pursued their education informally or formally. All the activity allowed them to harness the outside world to their household responsibilities and in that, they appear to have been remarkably successful. Travel confirmed the appropriateness of their education, their pace and their gaze.

Visiting occupied an extraordinary amount of time. These travellers all had so many relatives along their route that visiting may have been a family obligation. If so, the duty was cheerfully undertaken for visiting had a significance beyond the known rituals of calling card, conversation, and clothing. It was an activity that women on their own in a strange city could comfortably and securely engage in. On one occasion, nineteen-year-old Cairine Mackay was let off the leash of a guided tour in order to go visiting; she relished the solitary train trip out of London as much as the visit.[15] Ellen Bilbrough was able to leave her husband in London and travel alone to visit friends and relations in Scotland.[16] And no sooner did Alice Bell arrive in

Rome—travelling for the first time without another family member—than she set off to track down a family acquaintance.[17] Juliette Routhier was a bit more circumspect, practising visiting with another guest in her *pension* before feeling up to a six-week visit with friends in Marseilles and then on to all the family connections in Paris.[18] This home-bound independence of visiting served to maintain family links across time and distance. It reassured both new and old-world relatives that the Atlantic was indeed a pond and the same kind of people lived on both sides.

If the travellers' visiting thus contributed to the cohesion of an Atlantic and imperial culture, the women were also quite prepared to make personal and family use of it. As wife, daughter or new bride, their presence and behaviour spoke well of their families, their husbands, and their country. Indeed, an unspoken premise of much of their travelling was to advance the careers of their menfolk by knitting imperial ties of social standing. Agnes Bell's scientist husband (Margaret and Alice's father), Juliette Routhier's jurist father, Virginie Kierzkowska's engineer and politician husband were all part of the visiting, even, as in the Routhier and Bell case, *in absentia*. Virginie's husband shone in contrast to his Polish émigré relatives in Paris, "far superior to all I see of the others here."[19] Agnes Bell found, among her family connections in Scotland, a sympathetic reviewer for one of her husband's mining reports.[20] Daughter Margaret engaged in an intense round of visiting among friends and relatives after her debut presentation at Court in 1898; the success of that visiting may have been the reason that she, rather than her mother, accompanied Robert to London in 1900 for his induction into the Royal Society. More visiting followed. When Robert received an honourary doctorate from Cambridge two years later both father and daughter acknowledged her part in this singular recognition. So much so that he was willing to pay another trip to England for her as recompense.[21] Travel had become family currency as well as family strategy. It confirmed the power and the validity of the women's social graces. Exercising that power, these women were linking a European aristocratic social order with a developing Canadian meritocracy. The women profited from it socially; their men professionally.

The visiting also netted fine friends as these women clearly preferred people to places and relished their ability to fit in rather than stand out. New female friends appear in most of the accounts, whether acquired on board ship as in the case of Jennie Curran, at school in Germany for Margaret and Alice Bell, at ports of call for Maria Bogart, in San Remo and Rome for Juliette Routhier and Virginie Kierzkowska respectively.[22] The acquisition of friends seems to have been the criterion for a memorable trip; the lack of such friends may be part of Gertrude Fleming's travel unhappiness. So important was female friendship that Agnes Bell was prepared to hire someone to provide it. Having taken lodgings of her own in Glasgow in 1896 with the younger boy and now a baby daughter, and missing her older girls off at school in Germany, she sought company. Now that "Baby will soon be walking ... " she wrote Robert, "I could have an educated woman then for company instead of a nurse."[23]

The Canadians reinforced this domestic agenda of friends and visiting with their interest in shopping. Besides sheer fun, shopping, like visiting, allowed them an independent activity where they could exercise personal choice in secure surroundings. Consumption was of course their one economic function but the rituals of shopping, like those of visiting, confirmed the women's mastery of social codes. Selection, appearance, quality, and cost said as much about the buyer as the purchase and in the case of clothing marked the sophisticated, middle-class woman. Moreover, a wardrobe acquired in Europe added to their prestige at home. So Ethel Davies and Gertrude Fleming ogled the London shops while Margaret Bell made a special trip from Canada to acquire a trousseau and Juliette Routhier selected items for her Canadian relatives from the shops in Paris.[24] Alice Bell accounted dutifully for her expenditures in Rome in 1900, no doubt in response to on-going paternal reminders of monetary limitations and social expectations. She was not to be "extravagant" but was "to keep up appearances."[25] Travel for the Bell girls meant learning how to juggle those demands. Cairine Mackay's diary records no such parental strictures and she gleefully hit the shops on every occasion of her whirlwind guided tour. The diary in fact comes to an abrupt end in Venice, in mid-piazza, "where we did some shopping."[26]

Knowing what to buy and who to befriend and what to wear meant a constant exercise in discernment. These women travelled with a compass set to propriety. They took their bearings constantly by observing others, gauging their own success in keeping up appearances by constantly noting the presentability of others. Invariably they spotted soldiers and outlandish women, a spectacle that could range from the sublime to the absurd. Finely turned out soldiers caught the eye of Virginie Kierzkowska, Gertrude Fleming, Juliette Routhier, Alice Bell, Ethel Davies and Cairine Mackay all of whom would have seen soldiers in Canada in their colonial and ceremonial guise of parades and balls.[27] In all likelihood, the soldiers represented an irresistible combination of male and imperial power, of discipline, manners, and appearance, of officially sanctioned public duty. Woe betide a shabby or disorderly soldier; the women's admiration turned instantly to ridicule.[28] They reacted similarly to women out of step as if such creatures, like shabby soldiers, were letting down the side along the nineteenth century spectrum of separate spheres. Noisy Americans and noisy Germans were particularly obnoxious when they were women. To be faded and wizened with age was an additional effrontery.[29] An "eccentric" relative in Paris dressed poorly, had no remains of beauty and must be "queer" in daily contact, recorded Virginie Kierzkowska. Just as bad was to dress well but inappropriately: some Parisian belles in church showed off their garments more than their piety.[30] Even when anxious to emulate coquettish European style and adornment, as was Gertrude Fleming, all the Canadian travellers were exercising their domestic task of assessing appropriate appearance and behaviour.[31] Travel reinforced their sense of themselves.

So did the entertainments they chose. The theatre lent itself admirably to their domestic agenda of proper circles and confined spaces. The London and Paris stage had a trans-Atlantic reputation and the women expected to encounter the slightly risqué but they also reacted with a new-world sense of moral superiority. Virginie Kierzkowska was dismayed by the vulgar plays with "immorality ... shown off and excused" to the delight of Paris audiences.[32] Gertrude Fleming thought she was "all for the gay and unconventional" but her criteria were very narrow: the theatre was not to bore her, tax her intellectually or shock her. She and her husband walked out of Meyerbeer's opera "L'Africaine" in Nice: the naked ballet scene was the last straw.[33] The more robust Ethel Davies took in a week of "delightful" entertainments in London, with "a theatre or concert every evening" but she chastised herself with the comment "too gay for the lenten season I fear."[34] Juliette Routhier dismissed Sarah Bernhardt whom she had been longing to see because the old beauty and voice had long since faded.[35] More indulgent was Alice Bell who would happily see Bernhardt twice than have to go to the opera at all. And she avoided the "fierce" music halls on Montmartre having heard that they were "disgusting and very sacrilegious."[36] Propriety thus accompanied these women wherever they went. The theatre was the perfect setting for testing their schooling in propriety: in a limited space, at one remove from reality, the women could peep and cluck and be safe all at the same time.

All this testing of their taste and standard-setting skills suggests that travel was a form of continuing education for these women. Travel confirmed and expanded their considerable formal education; that education in turn may explain the earnestness with which they travelled. All of the women had had a Canadian initiation into the "accomplishments curriculum" common to young women of their social class throughout the English-speaking western world: history, literature, modern languages, natural science, music, and art.[37] Travel to Europe was the proving ground for that education. The women all recognized literary and historical references in their travels, spotted originals of their favourite paintings in art galleries, found the London Zoo and the Paris Aquarium both entrancing and "quite an education."[38] Where one could name Mediterranean flowers seen from a train window, another created a scrap book of known leaves and blossoms from the Roman Colosseum.[39] Ethel Davies and Margaret Bell both had considerable artistic skill and practised it in England and on the Continent.[40] All appreciated serious music; singers and pianists were among them.[41] Clearly that had all been dutiful schoolgirls and this made them easy and interested travellers.

For some, however, the purpose of their European travel was to expand their education, not just confirm it. Three of the Canadians took formal schooling or training while abroad. The success of the Bell sisters and of Annie Lampman speaks to their native talent and their Canadian education; at the same time they knew they were acquiring a substance and polish deemed superior to that at home. Annie Lampman furthered her musical education in Leipzig in the late

Travel Lessons

8.3. *"Contains organ on which Handel played when organist there." Text and drawing by Ethel Davies, late winter 1900. Reproduced from trip diary, courtesy of Margot Mann.*

8.4. *Drawing by Ethel Davies, October 1899. Reproduced from trip diary, courtesy of Margot Mann.*

1880s. She considered music "the redeeming feature of Germany," absorbed all she could and freely admitted that the singing at the Nikolai-kirke or at London's St. Paul's was "a little better than St George's" in Ottawa. Back in Canada as Mrs Frank Jenkins she counted among her music pupils the daughter of the Governor General, Lord Aberdeen.[42] As for the Bell daughters, they had a year of elementary schooling in Scotland in 1891 and then two years of senior secondary schooling in Karlsruhe, 1896-98. There, in a small boarding school catering to an English and Scottish clientele, Margaret and Alice applied themselves seriously to German, French, English, geography, history, arithmetic, physics, chemistry, music, drawing, piano, scripture, and sewing lessons. In their ten-hour days and six-day weeks, they even had time for gymnastics, cycling, walking, and skating.[43] Accomplishments indeed. As a result the two girls could move easily in the British homes of their Karlsruhe school chums and returned to Canada with the cachet of "blue stockings" which made them more admirable than "any girls in Ottawa."[44] Clearly the Bell parents were educating modern young women.

For that, touring and sightseeing were a must. Almost all the Canadians undertook a female version of the continental grand tour. If that tour in itself was a kind of "secular ritual," the stride in this case was properly female: contained, controlled and always at a leisurely pace.[45] Before she even started out, Virginie Kierzkowska quoted an admonition to herself:

Qui songe à voyager
Doit savoir écouter
D'un pas égal marcher
Dès l'aube se lever
Et soucis oublier.[46]

This careful pacing of travel may have been part of the women's training in orderliness; it may even have been occasioned by their clothing. The amount, complexity, and weight of women's apparel would have slowed anyone down while the requirements of appearance could consume hours of preparation. The pace may also have been dictated by their male relatives, even at a distance. Agnes Bell's energetic husband urged her to take things slowly while she was in Paris with the children in 1891. "Rest at home and study French and read up what is best worth seeing."[47] Nine years later he had the same lesson for daughter Margaret who was about to spend a few weeks sketching in northern France (and who had given no indication of ill health): "Now you must consider it a duty to rest as much as possible ... otherwise there will be a collapse or breakdown that will be hard to get over."[48] Presumably Cairine Mackay had already absorbed the lessons in the proper pacing of travel for she, the only one to travel in this manner, bitterly resented the speed of her guided tour. The unseemly haste left her, on occasion, "nearly dead with hunger and thirst."[49]

The women therefore undertook their touring carefully. Europe became a schoolroom through which they passed along well-known routes with sure companions. They went where others had gone before: Paris, the French and Italian riviera, Rome, Venice, Switzerland, and Germany. They named things in the language of domesticity and they turned a particular female gaze upon their surroundings. A French country road became an ironing board, "clean and smooth enough to iron a boiled shirt on;" the arcades of Turin were "comfortable;" the black and white marble interior of an Italian church resembled "oilcloth."[50] Invariably the women preferred the interiors of buildings, at home among the rich, dark, ornate, draped, and safe interior spaces of churches, palaces and galleries.[51] Even the beauty of the Riviera seemed inside-out. Sights and sounds and smells accosted their senses: flowers that would require hothouse tending in Canada, perfumes of boudoir discretion or gala display all blossoming and wafting in sun-drenched, sea-sparkling spaces. The Canadians were spellbound. "A sight worth a poet's imagination;" "le calme infini de cette campagne fleurie;" " a revelation of absolute beauty."[52] They did not quite know what to make of this public display of sensuousness.

When the new and the strange involved the unseemly and the disagreeable, ugliness rather than beauty, the women knew precisely what to do. Just as they would have done at home, they held their noses and averted their eyes. All of them reacted negatively to the dirt they encountered along their route. Cairine Mackay traversed the canals of Venice with her face screwed up to avoid the smell. Alice Bell detested the "narrow, dirty streets of Naples" and found Rome "clean and tidy" in comparison. To Ethel Davies, all of Italy was squalor.[53] And Virginie Kierzkowska was shocked and disillusioned to find parts of her Roman cultural and religious heritage in less than pristine settings.[54] The flaunting of dirt in Italy was an affront to these women's middle-class and new-world sense of themselves. Worse still were disreputable people. For Frances Tupper the mere transition from a first to a third-class train carriage where she was jostled in the heat by noisy, talkative Italians was "the most unpleasant experience I ever had."[55] For Gertrude Fleming the sighting of diseased and deformed beggars in Genoa made her "faint and ill;" she became hysterical on witnessing a suicide outside the casino in Monte Carlo.[56] Less distressed by beggars (perhaps because she was in the business of importing British waifs to Canada), Ellen Bilbrough was more dismayed by drunken Englishmen on the streets of Genoa.[57] In all the situations the women were attempting to maintain their own sense of tidiness and decorum, their normal tools of control in a domestic and social environment. Unable to impose that control during some of their travels, they may have been most upset by their own improper behaviour as they reacted so strongly, and in public, to the disagreeable. This particular travel lesson they could have done without; it was the only time they lost their equanimity in all their travels.

What social criticism they occasionally voiced matched their own domestic sense of respectable activity in proper places. "Princes and princesses strut[ting] around the streets of Karlsruhe, the same as ordinary people" struck Margaret

Bell as decidedly odd, one in particular, an "Emancipated Woman" holding "views!"[58] The Italian version of such people merited Juliette Routhier's ire for neglecting their duty as arbiters of artistic taste. No wonder the interior of the Cathedral in San Remo was so ghastly; the aristocracy and the bourgeoisie had abandoned it "entre les mains du peuple."[59] As for Carnival, "childish amusements" in the street took the Canadians aback.[60] Worse still were the gaming rooms in "*l'enfer*" of Monte Carlo or Nice where anxious, fevered faces (some "very old women and very young girls ... a most revolting sight") hung over the tables in badly ventilated rooms with too many strong perfumes.[61] Less morally repulsive were children working in lace manufactures in Venice for they were producing beautiful work for the adornment of the upper classes. Cairine Mackay did nonetheless feel a twinge of pity for the younger ones: "they have to strain their eyes for very little."[62] Mostly, however, the women stayed on their side of the frontiers of social class, those frontiers remarkably similar to their own front door.

That same frontier kept politics at bay. From the diaries and letters one would hardly know these women were travelling at a time of expansive British imperialism, much less of women's emancipation, nor that they had extensive political connections themselves.[63] It was as if politics was as out of bounds on their travels as it was at home, in pre-votes for women Canada. Still, the South African War did intrude, but only Ethel Davies was torn by it. Her female and colonial upbringing clashed as she recorded the "excitement" in London and listened to drawing-room conversations in the country. "I cannot bear to dwell on this war, it seems so barbarous and cruel in this age of civilization." At the same time she acknowledged that Canadians must "lay down their lives" just like Englishmen "for the dear old Motherland and this good cause."[64] Alice Bell and Ellen Bilbrough agreed with the latter sentiment but gave no hint of the former. Each of them celebrated the war's turn in Britain's favour in the late winter of 1900: Bilbrough purchased a frock in London to mark the occasion and Bell's heart glowed on seeing "Tommies" in their red coats on Gibraltar.[65] Even with Juliette Routhier's passing acknowledgment of socialists' ire over the vast quantities of money spent in the luxurious boutiques of Paris, one can easily imagine all the women sharing Virginie Kierzkowska's earlier revulsion at "horrid revolutionary ideas."[66] From their domestic viewpoint, confirmed by their travels, all was generally right with the world.

Perhaps for this very reason the women's travels have no precise endings. The women may have succeeded so well in harnessing travel to their domestic agenda that it becomes hard to tell when their voyage ends and their home life begins. Granted, the sources are hazy, letters and diaries simply ceasing (only Ethel Davies brought her account to a close while Virginie Kierzkowska did so after the fact) as the women faded back into the obscurity of their private lives. But that in itself hints at the voyage being absorbed into a regular pattern of living. Only two of the travellers ever expressed any longing to be home: the ailing Juliette Routhier and the elderly Frances Tupper.[67] Young

Alice Bell did dither in a charmingly protracted manner in 1900 about whether she should cut a trip short in order to be with her mother in Canada or follow her mother's instructions (and example) of being across the pond as much as possible. She then resolved the ambivalence these travellers may well have begun to feel about the location of home by doing both: joining her sister in London for a round of visiting, touring Ireland and then returning to Canada.[68] Margaret Bell acknowledged that her travelling might make her "more useful as a Cook's tourist guide than a housekeeper" but in fact she maintained both ways of being, establishing a marital home in the American west and joining a club in London. Meanwhile sister Alice picked up her schooling in Ottawa where she had left off in Europe, taking lessons in Latin, literature and history from a private teacher.[69] There is no hint among any of the homecomers of a personal or spatial adjustment, only a temporal one: the travel became an "inoubliable souvenir."[70]

These women's ability to domesticate travel reveals much about them and their world. Their pattern of travel is quite the opposite of that theorized by literary scholars who oppose home and the destination of travel.[71] For the Canadians, English and French alike, home is both their own domestic dwelling place in Canada *and* the space which their travel embraced. They moved about quite comfortably within an empire, a class, a gender—spaces in short that were home to them—and they showed little inclination to explore, much less step beyond those confines. Indeed, they did not see them as confines at all. On the contrary, domesticity and empire gave them the scope to traverse space safely, to gauge their bearings abroad, to display and augment their accomplishments, and declare them sound whether in Canada, Britain or Europe.

Although it might be tempting to see these women merely as "keepers of transplanted British society"[72] or as dependent colonials in the overlapping structures of gender, class and empire, this would deny them their active engagement with their surroundings. That engagement is particularly evident in the power of their female gaze. Reading their travel lessons through domestic eyes, these women could shrink space, turning an ocean into a pond and thereby obliterating danger. They could put nature—the ironing board road—into a cupboard and impose moral qualities on physical terrain. Their gaze could keep families close across vast distances. It could even move the family on the checkerboard of social standing, as these travellers engaged successfully in the social practices of metropolitan upper middle-class women. Their gaze could solidify values through space and time. For by their travels these women confirmed the appropriateness, the portability and ultimately the longevity of such values as respectability and appearance, reputation and social grace, education and appreciation, judgment and distance, propriety and decorum. Remarkably, for all the power of this female gaze over geography and culture, it is a power without possession. These women travel without trespassing.

Susan Mann

Notes

1. National Archives of Canada (NA), MG 29 B15 Robert Bell Papers, Vol. 6, Agnes Bell to Robert Bell, 30 October 1896, 12 June 1896; Vol. 7, Alice Bell to Robert Bell, 14 June 1900. Subsequent references to this extensive set of papers will place the volume number after the letter.
2. For example, Sarah Mills, *Discourses of Difference. An Analysis of Women's Travel Writing and Colonialism* (London: Routledge, 1991), Mary Louise Pratt, *Imperial Eyes. Travel Writing and Transculturation* (London: Routledge, 1992), James Buzard, *The Beaten Track: European Tourism and the Ways to Culture* (Oxford: Oxford University Press, 1993), Karen Lawrence, *Penelope Voyages. Women and Travel in the British Literary Tradition* (Ithaca: Cornell University Press, 1994), William Stowe, *Going Abroad: European Travel in Nineteenth Century American Culture* (Princeton, NJ: Princeton University Press, 1994), Anne McClintock, *Imperial Leather. Race, Gender and Sexuality in the Colonial Contest* (London: Routledge, 1995), Terry Caesar, *Forgiving the Boundaries: Home as Abroad in American Travel Writing* (Athens, GA: University of Georgia Press, 1995), Susan Morgan, *Place Matters. Gendered Geography in Victorian Women's Travel Books about Southeast Asia* (New Brunswick, NJ: Rutgers University Press, 1996), Mary Suzanne Schriber, *Writing Home: American Women Abroad* (Charlottesville, VA: University Press of Virginia, 1997). The only Canadian study, also focussing on published accounts and mostly those of men, is Eva-Marie Kröller, *Canadian Travellers in Europe 1851-1900* (Vancouver: University of British Columbia Press, 1987).
3. For travel as adventure, see Eric Leed, *The Mind of the Traveler. From Gilgamesh to Global Tourism* (New York: Basic Books, 1981), Marion Tinling, *Women into the Unknown: A Sourcebook on Women Explorers and Travelers* (New York: Greenwood Press, 1989), Mary Morris, ed., *Maiden Voyages. Writings of Women Travelers* (New York: David McKay, 1993), Gertrude Bell, *The Desert and the Sown* (Boston: Virago/Beacon [1907], 1987). The accidental traveller is Schriber's phrase, *Writing Home*, 13-14, 27.
4. Angela Woolacott is aware of the ambiguity of the word "home" for an Australian headed to England but she concentrates instead on the embracing of imperialism along the lengthy route. "'All this is the Empire, I Told Myself:' Australian Women's Voyages 'Home' and the Articulation of Colonial Whiteness," *American Historical Review* 102, 4 (October 1997): 1017. For all the promise of Schriber's title *Writing Home*, what is meant is the creation of the United States (home) through travellers' letters sent to their families (home) and subsequently published.
5. Margaret Conrad, Toni Laidlaw and Donna Smyth, eds., *No Place Like Home: Diaries and Letters of Nova Scotia Women 1771-1938* (Halifax: Formac Publishing, 1988).
6. For example, Helen Buss, *Mapping Our Selves: Canadian Women's Autobiography in English* (Montreal: McGill Queen's University Press, 1993); Suzanne Bunkers and Cynthia Huff, eds., *Inscribing the Daily: Critical Essays on Women's Diaries* (Amherst: University of Massachusetts Press, 1996); Leonore Hoffman and Margo Culley, eds., *Women's Personal Narratives: Essays in Criticism and Pedagogy* (New York: Modern Language Society of America, 1985); Judy Lensink, "Expanding the Boundaries of Criticism: The Diary as Female Autobiography," *Women's Studies* 14 (1987): 39-53; Betty Jane Wylie, *Reading Between the Lines:*

The Diaries of Women (Toronto: Key Porter Books, 1995).
7 Rebecca Hogan, "Engendered Autobiographies: the Diary as Feminine Form," in Shirley Neuman, (ed.), *Autobiography and Questions of Gender* (London: Frank Cass, 1991): 100.
8 Agnes Bell to Robert Bell, 31 July 1891 (Vol. 6).
9 LAC, MG 27 I E32 Alexandre-Edouard Kierzkowski Papers, Vol. 2, Virginie de Saint-Ours Kierzkowska's travel diary, 10 December 1868, recording the crossing of the English Channel.
10 LAC, MG 29 C108 (MCF M -1957) Ethel Marion Davies Papers, Ethel Davies' travel diary, 12 September 1899.
11 LAC, MG 29 C96 Gertrude Fleming Papers, Gertrude Fleming's travel diary, 27, 28 November, 1891, 4, 6, 15, 16 December 1891. Kröller quotes the Fleming diary extensively but analyzes it more from a literary and psychological perspective. *Canadian Travellers*, 63-74.
12 Davies diary, 23 October 1899, 4 April 1900.
13 Robert Bell to Alice Bell, 2 June 1890 (Vol. 7).
14 Archives nationales du Québec (ANQ), Fonds Adolphe-Basile Routhier (MCF 131.2), Juliette Routhier's travel correspondence, J. Routhier to "ma chère vieille mamette," 4 November 1896.
15 LAC, MG 27 III C6 Cairine (Mackay) Wilson Papers, Vol. 4, Cairine Mackay travel diary, 29 July 1904.
16 LAC, MG 29 C106 Ellen Agnes Bilbrough Papers, Ellen Bilbrough travel diary, 9 March 1900.
17 Alice Bell to Agnes Bell, 26 March 1900 (Vol. 10).
18 Juliette Routhier to "mamette," 26 March 1897 (continuation of a letter dated 23 March 1897); Juliette Routhier to her father, 5 April 1897, 10 May 1897; Juliette Routhier to her sister Ange, 19 April 1897.
19 Kierzkowska diary, 10 December 1868.
20 Agnes Bell to Robert Bell, 9 October [1890] (Vol. 6).
21 Margaret Bell to Robert Bell, 16 May 1898, 29 June 1898 (Vol. 8); Agnes Bell to Alice Bell, 14 April 1900 (Vol. 10); Robert Bell to Alice Bell, 22 May 1900 (Vol. 7); Margaret Bell to Robert Bell, 17 March 1902; Robert Bell to Margaret Bell, 19 March 1902 (Vol. 8).
22 LAC, MG 30 C85 J.E.G. Curran Papers, Jennie Curran travel diary, [July 1894, 12]; Margaret Bell to Robert Bell, 17 October 1897 (Vol. 8); LAC, MG 55/29 No. 80 Bogart Family Papers, Maria Bogart travel diary, 6 September 1866; Juliette Routhier to her sister Ange, 13 February 1897 (continuation of a letter dated 11 February 1897); Juliette Routhier to her father, 9 April 1897); Kierzkowska diary, 18 February 1869.
23 Agnes Bell to Robert Bell, 25 September 1896 (Vol. 6).
24 Davies diary, 28 February 1900, 19 March 1900; Fleming diary, 28 November 1891; Margaret Bell to Agnes Bell, 6 June 1902, 3 July 1902 (Vol. 11); Juliette Routhier to her father, 2 March 1897; Juliette Routhier to her sister Ange, 19 April 1897, 23 May 1897 (continuation of a letter dated 22 May 1897).
25 Alice Bell's expenditures on the Mediterranean, dated Belfast 12 August 1900 (Vol. 50); Robert Bell to Alice Bell, 19 July 1905 (Vol. 7).
26 Mackay diary, 29 August 1904.
27 Kierzkowska diary, 28 December 1868, 18 February 1869; Fleming diary, 11 January 1892; Juliette Routhier to her father, 11 November 1896; Alice Bell to

Robert Bell, 4-11 October 1896, 8 November 1896 (Vol. 7); Davies diary, 26 November 1899; Mackay diary, 6 August 1904.

28. Juliette Routhier to her father, 9 November 1896. It might be tempting to interpret the laughter that Juliette records in her letter as Sara Mills' "transgress[ing] the notion of imperial rule, making fun of some of the heroic adventure figures" but it is the sloppiness not the politics that provokes her amusement. *Discourses of Difference*, 106.
29. Mackay diary, 21 June 1904; Juliette Routhier to her father, 22 March 1897; Juliette Routhier to her sister Jeanne, 4 June 1897.
30. Kierzkowska diary, 10 December 1868.
31. Fleming diary, 28 November 1891, 20 December 1891.
32. Kierzkowska diary, [Spring 1869].
33. Fleming diary, 31 December 1891, 23 December 1891.
34. Davies diary, 4 April 1900.
35. Juliette Routhier to her sister Ange, 22-23 May 1897.
36. Alice Bell to Margaret Bell, 7 August 1900 (Vol. 11). She names, among others, Moulin Rouge. The opening scenes of Baz Luhmann's recent film "Moulin Rouge," set in 1900, offer a sense of the "fierceness."
37. Marjorie Theobald, "'The Sin of Laura:' The Meaning of Culture in the Education of Nineteenth-Century Women," *Journal of the Canadian Historical Association* 1 (New Series, Victoria 1990): 257-71.
38. Davies diary, 28 February 1900, 13 October 1899; Fleming diary, 20 December 1891.
39. Alice Bell to Margaret Bell, 30 April 1900 (Vol. 11); Kierzkowska diary, 6 January 1869 and accompanying scrap book.
40. Davies diary, 6 October 1899; Robert Bell to Alice Bell, 29 May 1900 (Vol. 7).
41. Lampman, Davies, Kierzkowska.
42. LAC, MG 30 D183, Frank and Annie Jenkins Papers, Vol. 3, Annie Lampman to Bessie, 25 September 1887; Lady Aberdeen to Annie Jenkins, 29 May 1897; notebook with accounts of music pupils.
43. Alice Bell to Robert Bell, 4-11 October 1896, 5 December 1897 (Vol. 7); Margaret Bell to Robert Bell, 8 October 1896, 18 October 1896, 28 October 1897 (Vol. 8).
44. Margaret Bell to Robert Bell, 17 October 1897 (Vol. 8); Alice Bell to Robert Bell, 3 November 1899 (Vol. 7).
45. Secular ritual is Stowe's phrase, *Going Abroad*, 19.
46. Whoever wishes to travel needs an attentive ear and an even pace, must rise with the dawn and leave cares behind. Kierzkowska diary, frontispiece, 23 October 1868.
47. Robert Bell to Agnes Bell, 19 May 1891 (Vol. 6).
48. Robert Bell to Margaret Bell, 23 July 1900 (Vol. 8).
49. Mackay diary, 13 June 1904.
50. Bilbrough diary, 22 March 1899; Kierzkowska diary, 22 December 1868; Mackay diary, 29 August 1904.
51. Davies diary, 19 April 1900, 27 April 1900; Kierzkowska diary, 28 December 1868; Agnes Bell to Robert Bell, 29 May 1891 (Vol. 6); LAC, MG 27 III D11 William Johnston Tupper Papers, Vol. 2, Lady Tupper's European Journal, 30 March 1890.
52. Kierzkowska diary, [post 19 March 1869]; Juliette Routhier to her mother, 24 March 1897 (continuation of a letter dated 23 March 1897); Fleming diary, 24

Travel Lessons

December 1891.
53   Mackay diary, 29 August 1904; Alice Bell to Agnes Bell, 26 March 1900 (Vol. 10); Davies diary, 8 May 1900.
54   Kierzkowska diary, 28 December 1868, 2 January 1869.
55   Tupper diary, 30 March 1890.
56   Fleming diary, 6 January 1892, 1 January 1892.
57   Bilbrough diary, 15 March 1899, [14] March 1899. She refers to the selection of "Barnardo's boys," 4 April 1899, 20 April 1899. See also Joy Parr, *Labouring Children: British Immigrant Apprentices to Canada* (London: Croom Helm, 1980).
58   Margaret Bell to Robert Bell, 29 November 1896 (Vol. 8).
59   Juliette Routhier to her sister Ange, 28 February 1897 (continuation of a letter dated 27 February 1897).
60   Kierzkowska diary, 7 February 1869; Juliette Routhier to her sister Ange, 27 February 1897.
61   Juliette Routhier to her father, 3 April 1897; Tupper diary, 8 March 1890.
62   Mackay diary, 29 August 1904.
63   For example, at the time of their travels, Virginie Kierzkowska's husband Alexandre-Edouard was a Liberal member of parliament; Frances Tupper's husband Charles was Canadian high commissioner to London and subsequently Conservative prime minister (1896); the Bell women's husband and father Robert was a senior public servant (Geological Survey) in the Canadian government; Gertrude Fleming's father Charles Herbert Mackintosh was a Conservative member of parliament, owner/editor of the Ottawa *Daily Citizen* and subsequently lieutenant-governor of the North West Territories (1893-98); Juliette Routhier's father Adolphe-Basile was a judge of the Quebec Superior Court; Ethel Davies' father Sir Louis Henry, former premier of Prince Edward Island (1876-79) was a cabinet minister in Laurier's first administration and subsequently a judge, then chief justice of the Canadian Supreme Court; Cairine Mackay's father Robert was a Liberal senator. As for many women of history it is easier to find biographical material about their male relatives. Of the women in this study, only Cairine Mackay has a public record: as Cairine Wilson she became the first woman to be appointed to the Canadian Senate 1930.
64   Davies diary, 16 October, 1899, 23 October 1899, 22 February 1900.
65   Bilbrough diary, 1 March 1900; Alice Bell to Robert Bell, 11 March 1900 (Vol. 7).
66   Juliette Routhier to her sister Ange, 23 May 1897 (continuation of a letter dated 22 May 1897); Kierzkowska diary, 2 January 1869.
67   Juliette Routhier to her father, 22 February 1897, 2 March 1897; Tupper diary, 5 April 1890, 20 April 1890.
68   Alice Bell to Robert Bell, 14 June 1900 (Vol. 7).
69   Margaret Bell to Robert Bell, n.d. [1900?] (Vol. 8); Margaret Bell to Agnes Bell, 3 July 1902 (Vol. 11); Alice Bell to Robert Bell, 3 November 1899 (Vol. 7). The girls' European schooling may have effectively (deliberately?) removed them from the Ottawa marriage market. A perusal of the Bell papers beyond the travelling women reveals that Margaret married wealthy New Yorker Walter Douglas in 1902 and accompanied him to Arizona where he was general manager of a mining company. Alice never did marry.
70   Juliette Routhier to her father, 10 May 1897.
71   For example, Lawrence, *Penelope Voyages*, 211, xvii-xviii; McClintock, *Imperial Leather*, 44; Caesar, *Forgiving the Boundaries*, 6, 58.

Susan Mann

[72] James Buzard's phrase about British women in India, "Victorian Women and the Implications of Empire," Review Essay, *Victorian Studies* 36, 4 (Summer 1993): 444.

"Giving Myself a Toni, Write Thesis Tonight"[1]

Negotiating Higher Education in the 1950s

ALISON MACKINNON

In recent political discourse, the 1950s has become code for all that is deemed conservative and backward looking.[2]

"Did 'the women's movement' significantly affect your concept of yourself and your role at home and outside the home?" "Where did you go with this new self?" These questions confronted former students of Radcliffe College, Cambridge, Massachusetts, when they opened the questionnaire which was to be the basis of their fortieth reunion report.[3] The question of the "new self" elicited a wide range of replies. "I began to live more comfortably in my old self" wrote one. "[I] was more frequently outrageous" wrote another. "I have been in therapy for twenty years trying to find myself" was another response, in contrast to a classmate who wrote "not a new self, just a more confident self." Another "gradually unglued her identity from being wife-mother-daughter." In response to the question "where did you go with your new self," one woman wrote, quite literally: "into some interesting beds in that exciting window of hedonism between the sexual revolution and the onset of herpes and AIDS ... I'm grateful for my lucky timing."[4]

Of course the women's movement as we know it was not part of the landscape for the young woman who attended college or university in the 1950s, or even in the first half of the 1960s. That was yet to come. But the task of constructing a self, even if it had to be remade in the following decades, was nevertheless a vital and all consuming one. In this essay I look at that self-making and remaking both in the college years and beyond, seeking to find the ways in which higher education made a difference in that process. I draw on the lives of middle-class, predominantly white women, in Australia and the United States, who benefited from tertiary education. For educated women of the

1950s were a particularly significant group. They were observers of, often complicit in, sometimes resistant to, the major changes brought about by the women's movement that followed from the late 1960s.

To many this generation represents a particular turning point, some naming themselves as "the swing bridge generation" linking the traditionalism of parents with the more liberated generation that followed. The Wellesley Record Book, which celebrated the fortieth reunion of the graduating class of 1960, claims a special reason for the importance of the classes of '59 and '60. The class of 1959 sponsored an extensive survey, "which found that '59—hence '60 as well—is the pivotal point of a shift between those whose post graduation careers put marriage and family first (at least chronologically) and those who started to establish a professional career prior to starting marriage and family."[5] That shift is one of the major transformations for educated women in our time, one still eliciting debate. The mix of subtle changes that tipped that balance still requires elucidation. The Wellesley investigators, recognizing the multiple possibilities for their alumnae, asked them whether they had chosen to move *with* or *against* the grain of the time, a very telling metaphor around which alumnae grouped their stories.

The decade of the 1950s holds an almost mythical status in social memory in both the United States and in Australia. As Australian historian Marilyn Lake points out, it has become code for all that is deemed conservative and backward looking. Yet, Lake continues, "those who would characterize the 1950s as a dreary, dull and dutiful decade miss its vital significance for gender relations."[6] Lake and others, such as the U.S. historian Beth Bailey, are part of a small group challenging this depiction of the 1950s as one of dull, complacent domesticity and suburban bliss.[7] And those years could mean very different things to different U.S. cohorts as Janet Giele claims. The 1950s meant "the 'feminine mystique' to young brides who were setting up households. To older women who were reentering the labour force because they were needed, the 1950s were the quiet beginning of women's liberation."[8] Other historians challenge the idea that "the fifties" can even be seen as a clearly bounded decade. Ann Coombs claims, "the 1950s continued in Australia well into the following decade" while for John Murphy, "the prosperous and complacent fifties had barely started in the middle of the decade, but lasted well into the following decade.[9] Jean Duruz speaks of "a plurality of fifties."[10] The term "the fifties" then clearly encapsulates a particular understanding of a social and political *zeitgeist* which eludes the actual strictures of time, in the way that some have talked of "the short twentieth century."

How can we bring the study of women graduates, whether moving with or against the grain, into a broader history of women's education and of the history of the 1950s? Writing of women educators and activists in the United States, Margaret Smith Crocco, Petra Munro, and Kathleen Weiler claim that "education provided the subjects of this book with both the tools and space to become active subjects in history."[11] Does education always provide those tools—and those spaces? Are there particular periods when the possibilities seem fewer, the spaces more constrained? Further, are there particular circumstances that drive some women to become agents of change while others are more strongly motivated to conserve? Is there a relationship between women's higher education and feminism? Barbara Miller Solomon wrote of "the uneasy connection between feminism and women's educational advancement." Solomon also identified the "basic contradiction between women's education and their probable futures."[12]

Nowhere perhaps could that connection have seemed more uneasy, could the contradictions have been so glaring, as in that decade of the '50s, overshadowed by the Cold War, McCarthyism and conservative politics, characterized by anti-progressivism and burgeoning consumerism, hardly fruitful soil from which a liberation movement might grow. The discourses of progressivism became suspect while psychosocial and psychosexual discourses gained strength. It was a time of rigid prescriptions for "normal" sexual behaviour, of the pursuit of the vaginal orgasm, of "frigid" women. The stationwagon wife, cheerful and compliant, smiled from the pages of the *Saturday Evening Post*. At the same time economic progress and the manpower [sic] needs of this relatively affluent time drew women inexorably into the workforce.

What then, if anything, did the relatively privileged group of women who emerged from higher education at this time bring to the development of feminism? Jill Ker Conway claims that "for many decades, women's colleges have been the foremost contributors of achieving women to the society."[13] Yet even those within the bastions of privilege, the women's college, could not entirely escape the prescriptions of their time. Perhaps, for some, a developing feminism might be traced to the contradictions many young women negotiated in their education as autonomous adults on the one hand—and the constraining prescriptions they faced as women in the society beyond the campus. Those very constraints and contradictions forced thoughtful young women to assess their options, often many years later.

Lesley Johnson has argued persuasively of Australia that "second wave feminism has been prodded into existence by the question of what adulthood means for women."[14] Such a question, as she points out, was also central to U.S. debates. Betty Friedan, the questioner *par excellence* of '50s values for women, asked the very same thing.[15] Johnson claims of the 1950s that a young woman's (and a young man's) central preoccupation in the developmental stage of adolescence was "that of making a self, shaping an identity for herself, whether as an autonomous self or as some form of feminine self."[16] But could the self accommodate both autonomy and femininity? Further, Johnson claims that the focus on "surfaces or images" could lead to certain "forms of playfulness around one's identity."[17] This notion of surfaces offers a perspective for examining, through life narratives, such positionings and multiple versions of self as young women reached adulthood in privileged educational settings. As Johnson does, I "[draw on] historical evidence to make problematic contemporary understandings of the past and present project of feminism."[18] I ask to what extent that "playfulness" masked a very real struggle for a new way of relating to the world.

A Period of Decline for Women?

In 1959 Mabel Newcomer's *A Century of Higher Education for American Women* demonstrated that women's relative position in the academic world was declining.[19] Perhaps then the '50s provide an ideal decade in which to test the ideas of any link between education and feminism, for seeing writ large women's higher education as containing both a radical impulse and a conservative one as Joyce Antler and Sari Knopp Biklen have claimed. Linda Eisenmann claims that many of the professional and educational advances that women had made during the war years evaporated in the 1950s in the U.S., when women's percentage as college students (30 percent in 1950) and professionals diminished.[20] The percentages were even lower in Australia. At Sydney University in 1960 women took approximately 25 percent of degrees, and throughout Australia women were 12 percent of academic staff [faculty].[21] By 1960, Eisenmann notes of the U.S., "following a dismal decade for professional women's progress, only 22 percent of all college faculty were women, and women were earning only 10 percent of all doctorates."[22]

Australian women who entered one of the six state universities in existence at the time did not have the option of a private, women's college such as Smith or Radcliffe. They might be viewed as an elite as only about one percent of seventeen-year-old females commenced university studies in 1950 (compared to two percent of males), most through the payment of fees.[23] However a significant fraction of that group was able to attend university, often the first in their families, through winning scholarships, bursaries, and studentships, the latter requiring them to work with the sponsoring organization for a period after graduation. Some studied part-time, completing a degree laboriously subject by subject. An even smaller percentage lived in women's residential colleges, mostly run by the churches. Those colleges replicated some of the experiences of the women's colleges of the U.S., although once outside their portals the students attended lectures in a coeducational environment like that of a North American state university. Yet in these different environments Australian students too frequently felt bound by the all-pervasive constraints of expectations of marriage.

This cohort of 1950s university women in English-speaking countries is particularly self-reflexive. Their reminiscences and writings have resulted in a large archive that maps the psychic and sociological contours of their lives. Reunion books, carefully compiled by a select group of Ivy League colleges and universities in the United States, are a rich source of self-reported autobiographies, sometimes providing basic information ("married Dick Jones, physician, Harvard '54, two children") at other times searingly frank and full.[24] Published and unpublished surveys provide detailed information.[25] So too does the biographical and autobiographical writing of many of that cohort.[26] While some women's voices are heard in the public arena, Sylvia Plath, Jill Ker Conway, Germaine Greer or Adrienne Rich, for example, it is less easy to draw upon a pool of informed, articulate, but less public, voices. These reunion collections are one such source—put to very good use in the late 1950s by Betty Friedan. Famously, she based *The Feminine Mystique* on a 1957 survey of the Smith College class of 1942. As the questions above show, reunion surveys invited those who were willing to speak of both failures and successes and of their thoughts on the passing of time. Looking over their lives since graduation in 1956 Radcliffe College alumnae reveal in their fortieth reunion book almost the entire gamut of change in women's lives in the second half of the twentieth century.[27] They are very much about selves in process, a process evident during the college years, but equally compelling forty years later.

Smith College, Massachusetts, also keeps an excellent collection of alumnae reunion books, revealing women's frank reflections over many decades.[28] The papers of Alice Gorton Hart provide one such source. It was not until many years after her graduation, challenged by feminism and reflecting on her early decision to marry, that Alice Gorton Hart regretted the haste, the lost opportunities. Recognizing the value of her reflections she approached the Sophia Smith Collection in the 1980s. Their reply delighted her:

> Letter from Mary-Elizabeth Murdock, director of Sophia Smith Collection and she would be pleased indeed to accept my journals. I am relieved and delighted to be part of the archive, one of the two largest in the world, she says. Knowing this may be used to help other women is exciting, a tad of immortality ... and I don't think it will dry up my honesty.[29]

It did not. Hart's honesty is compelling. Around her 51st birthday she wrote, "Starved for good conversation. Where does one find new friends, new interests? I'll be a volunteer at the museum." Tellingly she quotes Sylvia Plath: "Winter is for women." It was in this period that Hart approached the Smith Collection as a repository for her expanding collection of journals. An Australian contemporary echoes Hart's needs. "Desperately wanted companionship of intellectuals," she wrote. "Hid my knowledge, read and had a rich fantasy life."[30]

"Until Such a Time as Women Decide to Become Persons Again"

Could women educated at elite tertiary colleges and universities elude the dominant understandings of the 1950s that women's entire role was to be married and to raise children? This expectation was in complete contrast to the views of women in higher education earlier in the century. The pervasiveness of expectations of domesticity in the 1950s worried some unmarried faculty members such as Marine Leland, teacher of French at Smith College, who had very different ideals.[31] Leland was typical of an earlier generation of highly educated women, single but living within a women-centred culture.[32] Writing to a friend in 1953 Leland observed:

> As for me I am becoming Machiavellian on the subject [of marriage]. Since *married women* and mothers are in fashion just now, and [I] have resorted to stressing the legal disabilities of *married women* who cease being *persons* before the law by virtue of their marriage. My idea is to applaud the students' natural desire while stressing the need for all women—*especially the married ones*—to be on the alert in protecting the rights which previous generations gained for them and in correcting present injustices.
>
> The present frenzy for marriage is surely a result of the war as well as a result of the growing emphasis on "normalcy" and security. I noticed the advertising in the New Haven station last night. It is largely based on this Frenzy. The "N. Y. Times", for instance, advertises "Smart Young Couples read the Times", or " the clever homemaker" (she is represented in the kitchen) "reads the Times." There is no point against trying to buck this trend, but I do think that it can be used in upholding Liberal Education for Women until such a time as women decide to become persons again.

Leland's concerns that women had abandoned the "personhood," so hard fought for by her generation,[33] seem entirely warranted if we consider the preoccupations of some Smith students, expressed in contemporary letters and journals. In 1951 Lelah Dushkin wrote home admiringly of a fellow student:

> Lore Dinkelspiel, one of the seniors in the house, got married last Wednesday, an hour and a half after spring vacation began, and is now Mrs. James Cochrane. She's the second one to get married this year…. I really must hand it to Lore. She handled all the wedding preparations herself in addition to writing a 140-page thesis on "An evaluation of Industrial Sociology." Lore's the one who could do it though. Not only has she been engaged to Jimmy for the last three years, but she's a junior phi-beta, president of Dance Group, and Vice-president of the senior class.[34]

We too can but admire the organizational skills of this enterprising senior, who could no doubt have run a major corporation.

But for most students the combination of scholarship and romance was not so easily attained. The frank journal of Alice Gorton (later Hart), documents over many years her struggles to attain the desired femininity of the time: "If I can loose [sic] 15 pounds and make good grades and snare some men I may confront father at Christmas time with an accomplished perfection."[35] Sylvia Plath, also at Smith, and "on the upward rise after bouncing around a little on rock bottom" put the good grades first but also noted the need to attract a man: "I know I am capable of getting good marks: I know I am capable of attracting males. All I need to do is keep my judgment, sense of balance and philosophic

"Giving Myself a Toni, Write Thesis Tonight"

sense of humor, and I'll be fine...."[36] Being fine, as Plath's unabridged journals—and literary work—attest, was not at all easy. For many students a perfect appearance and slim figure was an essential part of desired femininity. Dieting is a major theme in Gorton's journal as it is in so many others of the time. So too is attaining "a ring by spring," the notion that graduation would be closely followed by marriage, a goal so effortlessly achieved in the extract above.

Hurl Yourself at Goals Above Your Head ...

But for some women students other goals beckoned. Sylvia Plath, also struggling with issues of identity, looked beyond the dates and insecurities of her college years, and aspired to be a "literary light." She was prepared to work for the "personhood" alluded to by Leland, and clearly envisaged the struggle necessary to reach her goal. "Can Smith help me?" she wrote.

> Yes: more than any place within my means could. How? By opening more opportunities for aim and achievement than I could reach if I went elsewhere.... Perhaps not *more* opportunities, but different sorts of opportunities.... So what remains for me now? To throw up my hands at my inevitable narrowness? No: to meet Smith now and try and let the nagging questions ride; to get good grades.... Write about your own experience.... Read widely of others experiences in thoughts and action—stretch to others even though it hurts and strains.... Hurl yourself at goals above your head and bear the lacerations that come when you slip and make a fool of yourself....[37]

Two years later Plath wrote triumphantly:

> I am lucky: I am at Smith because I wanted it and I worked for it. I am going to be a Guest Editor on Mlle [*Mademoiselle* magazine] in June because I wanted it and worked for it. I am being published in *Harper's* because I wanted it and worked for it. Luckily I could translate wish to reality by the work.[38]

Plath struggled to reconcile autonomy and femininity. Clearly some students saw the possibilities ahead and managed to resist "the frenzy to marry" the minute they left college. This did not prevent a bitter realization of what lay ahead. As Plath confided to her journal, "I dislike being a girl, because as such I must come to realize that I cannot be a man. In other words I must force my energies through the direction and force of my mate."[39]

Worried faculty such as Marine Leland, who deplored the "frenzy for marriage" were often publicly silent during these years, their spinsterhood suspect. Wellesley's Margaret Clapp was perhaps more typical. In her President's report of 1956-58 Clapp noted:

the important demands of home making continue to debar many women from advanced study. However, the greatest difficulty seems to exist not for young married women living near a university and whose husbands approve of their intellectual interests, but for young women who are not married, who naturally wish to marry, who feel that until the central question of marriage is settled they cannot take a long look ahead and so take temporary fill in jobs.

Young women should plan ahead "flexibly" of course "in order to be able to fit into their future husband's careers" and ... to develop "abilities and interests which might well be carried into marriage, set aside in the years of child care, and then renewed without undue difficulty."[40]

This acceptance of wives' secondary ambition would have been anathema to esteemed educator of women, M. Carey Thomas, who famously declared "our failures only marry," a sentiment Marine Leland might well have endorsed.[41] Clapp's sentiments seem to have been widely accepted. A strong pattern of marrying straight out of college can be discerned in the elite colleges at least. At their fortieth reunions many Radcliffe, Smith and Wellesley women were also celebrating their fortieth wedding anniversaries.

"We Are One Step Ahead of the Game by Virtue of Having Gone to Smith"

Were young women who had earned a degree "ahead of the game" in the 1950s? And, confusingly, what was the game? One Radcliffe respondent claimed, in retrospect, "I never focused" naming one of her college's failures as not helping students to define their goals, "a failure of the times."[42] While Plath might acknowledge the benefits of a Smith education, and a nameless alumna claimed "we are one step ahead of the game by virtue of having gone to Smith," the dating and marriage game seemed hard to get ahead of for many. This could well be seen as a later version of the "double conformity" ascribed by Delamont to an earlier generation.[43] A Smith education did not change Alice Gorton's script. She met her future husband George Hart in her final year and like many of her cohort married soon after graduation. This solved the vocation scenario for Alice: "George has the problem—what for vocation; but all I must do is follow him. I can do it and do it well ... Freud which I have since come to accept, if not to believe fully...."[44] It was during her final year at Smith that she wrote the journal entry which heads this essay: "Giving myself a toni, write thesis tonight." The journal entry continued: "He is for me a miracle ever renewing.... George likes my body, which is nice from the diet business, but as yet he hasn't seen the ugly bits." The required final year thesis did not appear as a higher order preoccupation than the usual concerns about achieving the desired [slender] body and hairstyle, one permanently waved with a Toni, which could be self-administered to create the "natural" look. Can any woman who lived through the '50s forget the advertisement captioned, "Which twin has the Toni?"

9.1. Alison Prentice (left) studying for finals on the lawn in the Quad at Smith, spring 1955. Courtesy of Alison Prentice.

Seeking "Seriousness and Scruple, in the Service of the Truth"

In the late 1950s at Sydney University Jill Ker (later Conway), completing an honours degree, applied for admission into the junior ranks of the Australian Department of External Affairs. This decision conflicted with her duties as daughter of a neurotic demanding mother and with her romantic attachment. She wrote in her memoir: "I was headed for a traumatic confrontation between ambition, love and duty."[45] Her words resonate with those of earlier generations who had to choose between "love and freedom."[46] However, like Plath, she was able to acknowledge her ambition, a concept difficult for earlier generations of women to name.[47] Conway ultimately chose ambition, leaving Australia to pursue a higher degree and later an illustrious career in U.S. universities and business—and coincidentally in 1975 to become the first woman President of Smith College. As it turns out she was not offered the position with External Affairs, predominantly because she was a women and it was expected she would marry. This refusal rankled, interrupting, she claimed, the smooth flow of successes and leading to the development of a strong feminist consciousness. Her rejection by the Department of External Affairs led her to

> think what it meant that I was a woman, instead of acting unreflectingly as though I were a man, *bound to live out the script of a man's life.* This one blow of fate made me identify with other women and prompted me, long before it was politically fashionable to do so, to try and understand their lives.[48]

Alison Mackinnon

Like her U.S. counterparts growing up in the '50s Jill Ker was keenly aware of the importance of appearance. In a gap between her studies at Sydney University, she worked as a medical receptionist, earning the money to attend an evening school where she learned to enhance her looks. Advised as to her hair, her diet and, with the help of glossy magazines, her clothing, she began to gain confidence: "I was painstakingly constructing an acceptable public self."[49] An Australian contemporary remembered, "we (most of us) spent hours every morning applying make-up and selecting a Becoming outfit. Girls who wore slacks were either "Fast" or "Communists."[50]

Academically ambitious, Ker learned that it was not appropriate to reveal her love of learning to men. Echoing Plath's thoughts she wrote, "I was used to concealing how well I did academically ... This was required conduct for women in Australia."[51] Yet not all women of the period agreed. "In my involvement with men I was not prepared to pretend ignorance," wrote another Australian graduate. "A degree of assurance encouraged me to rebel against the ploys and coy behaviours women were encouraged to portray."[52]

Several Australian women faced an issue that did not seem to confront their American sisters. They wanted to escape to a place where they felt their intellects might be taken seriously as in the culture of Australian universities and of Australian society generally male dominance prevailed.[53] "The Blokes [sic] ruled," as one Australian woman recalled. Jill Ker, teaching in the history department at Sydney University after completing her degree, was advised by a sympathetic female colleague: "Go somewhere where you can see things from another perspective. Whatever you do don't just stay here."[54] Germaine Greer, University of Melbourne graduate of 1959, left Australia to find the intellectual culture and recognition as an intellect that she sought. Yet Greer had enjoyed the company and intellectual support provided by a group of mainly university-educated radicals, the Sydney Libertarians, colloquially known as "The Push," who nurtured her rebellious spirit. In their presence, Greer claimed in 1974, "I had found what I did not know I was looking for: seriousness and scruple, in the service of the truth."[55] She acknowledged the value of their opinions in a 1975 talk: "for if ever, of anyone, I desired a good report, I desire it of them, my guides, philosophers and friends, the Sydney Libertarians."[56]

While escape to another country might not have been as essential for women graduating in the U.S. in the '50s, escape of another kind frequently beckoned. Much of the published literature of the period details a need to "get away" from the place of origin, a sense that "life was elsewhere." An Australian woman noted that "the great thing about living in the country was that Uni meant escape from family."[57] Another wrote concisely, "Uni was escape."[58] Escape might be from home, from the stifling protection of a women's college to a wider university community, or from "the motherly breath of the suburbs."[59] Yet escape often brought much of the same: it was not ultimately place that was the only problem or the main problem but the pervasive sense of stifling social relations. Most women who graduated from Australian and U.S. universities during the '50s and early '60s succumbed to "the motherly breath of the suburbs." It was, as Australian activist Eva Cox relates, a more difficult jumping off place than involvement in a radical group such as the Sydney Push. "The women who tried to jump off [into political action, women's liberation] from marriage and suburbia had a lot more ground to make up."⁶⁰

The intellectual radicalism of the Sydney "Push" came with another form of social rebellion, a pushing against the narrow boundaries of accepted monogamous heterosexual behaviour. These were the same people that Jill Ker Conway describes as the "small coterie of gifted faculty and students who were iconoclasts, cultural rebels, and radical critics of Australian society." Ker Conway enjoyed their ideas but found that their originality "went along with a stultifying conformity to what were considered 'advanced' sexual mores."⁶¹ She refused the pattern of brief sexual encounters, found so liberating and daring by some women, reflecting on the asymmetry of sexual relations amongst the left and the radical, an imbalance which was to lead to the insights of the women's liberation movement of the next decade. Ann Coombs speaks of the "orthodoxy of non-conformism" created and adhered to by Push members both male and female: Conway's comment on their "stultifying conformity" on sexual matters seems, in retrospect, quite apt, yet at the time their acceptance of non-marital sex appeared daring and transgressive.

Rewriting the Self

To seek intellectual development over marriage and family as Conway did was indeed to court disapproval. To rebel both intellectually and sexually, as Greer ultimately chose, was to transgress all taboos. It is difficult to remember in these [supposedly] liberated times the courage it took in the 1950s and early '60s to challenge the prevailing discourses of sexuality. There was to be no sex outside marriage, marriage was the sole source of sexual identity and expression.⁶² Heterosexuality was the norm. Careers were to be subordinated to those of husbands, or, in the case of single women, viewed as poor alternatives. And most women graduates took those strictures on board.

They may however have imagined very different lives. Alice Gorton, writing in her student days, revealed her desires in this fantasy piece. Her difficulties in a fraught real-life relationship with "Jim" can be discursively negotiated through a fictional accident, after which new possibilities open up:

> More plans about my future after accident with Jim. The disappearance, this time to a steel town. Work in a bar, love, violent of a real man (Streetcar named Desire type) of course after I got thin. Loss of baby. Then his passion, which I resist until his mom (my landlady) talks to me. Then the burning desire, which I actually physically painfully experienced just now. Thus violent terrible self obliterating ecstasy. Brutal yet unbelievably tender. Perfect wild animal happiness for two years. I continue to write successful salable stories. We live in steel town. The red

Alison Mackinnon

9.2. *Alison Prentice (left) and friend in Paris. They were part of a junior-year group from Smith College that studied in Geneva in 1953-54. Courtesy of Alison Prentice.*

sky, the sooted earth, sordid and real, primitive, yet wholly modern and intricate. No kids. He is killed a hero, I am completely desolate because of true love and great wanting, being wholly with him. His mother dies, I am alone, but well off financially (insurance, house, pension, authorship) I go to New York, apartment, beautiful clothes, a gorgeous desirable sensual satisfied wise and loving woman. Job on New Yorker, honored, respected, a literary light. I become a discreet, highly sought-after and desired prostitute also. Greatly loving in the Biblical sense too, with no begats, luckily. I can go on as soon as the light goes off, which it must. What a great life that would be.

Gorton's fantasy resonates with the dominant sexual prescriptions and cultural preoccupations of the early 1950s.[63] From popular culture comes the working class hero (we can visualize Marlon Brando, James Dean, perhaps a character from a novel by D.H. Lawrence?), the steel town, violent but pulsing with life, rather like the "brutal but unbelievably tender" love making. The Freud-inspired expectations of romantic and yet passionate sexual love, an expectation which lead to disappointment for so many of this generation, the "wild animal happiness," "self-obliterating ecstasy," speak the language of popular culture and a particular form of psychoanalytic understanding. So too the conflation of pain with ecstasy echoes the language of Helene Deutsch and her followers.[64] Deutsch's book *The Psychology of Women*, a classic by the 1950s, theorized the healthy woman as "passive" and "masochistic," experiencing "an act of violence" as an "act of pleasure."[65]

But Gorton's fantasy departs from the expected script in significant ways. Curiously, this man, like "Jim," is conveniently killed off, and in the [unlikely] absence of any children, and the presence, unaccountably, of money, our heroine heads for New York, literary fame, total independence, and sexual autonomy, all with a rather smug sense of transgression. Such a persona, a single, literary "light"—also a high-class call girl—speaks more of an earlier era or of cosmopolitan Paris. It also contains echoes of independence—that "pathology" described by the American popularizers of Deutsch's work, Lundberg and Farnham, who "linked feminism and frigidity as related forms of social disorder."[66] The idea of a sexually fulfilled creative woman, choosing her men at will, was unimaginable in the dominant scripts of the 1950s, a time when, as Plath noted wryly, "A psychiatrist is the God of our age."[67] Perhaps more than most student texts of the time Gorton's short piece presents the desires and contradictions, the "playfulness around identity" of a young 1950s woman student.

However, Alice Gorton Hart succumbed to the "motherly breath of the suburbs" like so many of her cohort. She found herself with considerable ground to make up when in the 1970s as a mother of two sons she discovered the women's movement. In its liberating embrace she found that many of the same old ghosts of 20 years earlier still haunted her: "I'm going to one workshop at the USU [Utah State University] women's conference tomorrow—Body Image for Overweight Women." "Body image. Yes—I really care for myself," Alice wrote later,

> (must check blood pressure). Now I care about drawing and tennis, poetry and my friends ... Told George I've been a mother for 27 years and a wife for almost 30 and I'm sick of being both. I want to be companion, friend, playmate....[68]

Hart's journal traced her reading and her dawning feminist consciousness. She was reading *Touchstones*:

> something about a woman must pay her *debt* as a woman to husband, home and family before she does anything for her self "submission of will" the whole thing is so revealing of *me*. I swallowed all that crap too. Tillie Olsen's *Silences*.... But the NOW [National Organization of Women] meeting is training to lead a consciousness raising group and that could really change the quality of my life a lot.[69] If George can't or won't give me what I need, I find it elsewhere....

Alice Gorton Hart's post-college career was characteristic of her cohort, although the degree of reflexive writing was not. Her experience was certainly more typical than that the path breakers Sylvia Plath, Jill Ker Conway or Germaine Greer. Hart eventually returned to graduate work, gaining an MA in English from Utah State University in 1970. She taught part-time in the English department for many years, and was a technical writer for many academic publications as well as a sensitive poet, artist, and writer. She never gained a permanent position at the university and became increasingly disenchanted with being a part-time casual employee.

> I see the injustice even more strongly—the office is practically impossible—keep thinking of writing to Reed and then not doing it—I was in a bitter rage this morning over the injustice of it all—the last minute hiring, the key humiliation, the exclusion and separation—but then I thought it was good to stand alone and independent, went to the office and did a bang-on job on a Cummins paper preparation and then had a rather exciting class— ... I am so much more *in* to teaching this year than ever before.[70]

Mother, wife, part-time university or school teacher, museum guide, artist and writer—these were some of the varied roles that many '50s graduates filled. Some managed to translate a part-time interest or a hard won higher degree into a career, becoming respected artists, or university teachers. Many played significant voluntary roles in a range of philanthropic, religious, and welfare organizations. Few found full-time marriage and motherhood totally absorbing for more than a few years. Speaking of 1950s marriages in Australia, John Murphy claims that although marriages may have appeared traditional they also emphasized "true fulfillment" and "expression." How could the elements of the traditional and the expressive be reconciled? Did they "point to limits of domesticity" as Murphy asks?[71] For women who had been trained in the highest institutions to use their intellects that need for expression and fulfillment would become increasingly urgent in the decades to come, bursting forth in women's consciousness-raising groups, in feminist demands for well-paid work, for intellectual work and public recognition, and in demands for more equal sharing within marriage.

How then should we view the 1950s? Did they provide the spaces and the tools for women to become active subjects in history? Were highly educated women able to fulfill the required tasks, to "make a self, shape an identity for herself, whether as an autonomous self or as some form of feminine self?"[72] Yes, it was possible, as several stories here attest, but it was not easy. For female identities were in flux, the "selves" to be created made up of several, often conflicting strands and positionings. As the period itself may be seen as one of both political conservatism and increasing economic abundance, of more opportunities and more constraints, contradictory forces pulled educated women into the workplace yet urged them to find fulfillment in domestic life. "People forget how hard it was," wrote one Australian. "The put downs we just accepted—the advice to do shorthand and typing, the remarks by personnel officers 'why do you want this job. You should be married.'" Another responding to my Australian questionnaire wrote:

> somehow the questionnaire has not captured the struggle that it was. It was hard. When I look at women of my generation who tried to be the super women of the '70s we have all lost out somewhere; for some their relationships suffered, for me and for many others it has been our health; for some it has been the job itself. Professional life has come at a high price.[73]

Should we then reject the way in which the '50s have become "code for all that is deemed conservative and backward looking?" Should we instead characterize the fifties as the time when significant numbers of women first fully engaged in the changing and confusing struggle to be both intellectual beings and feminine selves? Their struggles around identity can be seen to have produced two of the elements of the 1960s women's liberation movement, firstly the writers who wrote key texts of that movement, such as Germaine Greer, Adrienne Rich, and Sylvia Plath, and secondly a group of women such as Alice Gorton Hart, ready and willing to respond to their call.[74]

Notes

[1] Quote from journal of Alice Gorton Hart, Sophia Smith Collection, Smith College. I am grateful to the Sophia Smith Collection for a Margaret Storrs Grierson "Travel to Collections" grant and to the University of South Australia for a period of study leave in 2000 which made this research possible. This chapter is drawn from an ongoing Australian Research Council funded study "Beyond Access: Women, Higher Education and the Quiet Revolution of the 1950s." For those mystified about a "toni," it was a self-administered permanent wave, a key to the desired wavy-haired image of the '50s.

[2] Marilyn Lake, "A Case of Male Justice," review of Paul Wilson, Don Toeble and Robyn Lincoln, "Jean Lee: The Last Woman Hanged in Australia," *The Australian's Review of Books* (12 February 1997), review 6-7.

[3] *Class of '56 40th Reunion*, 1996, compiled by year book committee, Arthur and Elizabeth Schlesinger Library on the History of Women in America, Radcliffe Archives, Radcliffe Institute, Harvard University, RG IX Series 7. I am grateful to Kathy Kraft and others at the Schlesinger Library for their help with these records.

[4] Ibid, anonymous excerpts from responses published in the *Reunion* book.

[5] Judy Huggins Balfe, Introduction, *Wellesley '60 40th Reunion, Record Book*. I am grateful to Judy Grace for bringing this issue to my attention.

[6] Lake, "A Case of male justice."

[7] Beth Bailey, *Sex in the Heartland* (Cambridge, Mass.: Harvard University Press, 1999). For a New Zealand perspective see also Melanie Nolan, "A Subversive State? Domesticity in Dispute in 1950s New Zealand," *Journal of Family History* 27, 1 (January 2002): 60-81. Nolan states "A recent revisionism now suggests that the 1950s were not as regressive or traditional as previously thought," 60.

Alison Mackinnon

[8] Janet Giele and Mary Gilfus, "Race and College Differences in Life Patterns of Educated Women, 1934–82," in Joyce Antler and Sari Knopp Biklen, (eds.), *Changing Education: Women as Radicals and Conservators* (Albany: State University of New York Press, 1990), 39.

[9] Ann Coombs, *Sex and Anarchy: The Life and Death of the Sydney Push* (Melbourne: Penguin, 1996), 178; John Murphy, *Imagining the Fifties: Private Sentiment and Political Culture in Menzies' Australia* (Sydney: University of NSW/Pluto Press, 2000), 219.

[10] Jean Duruz, "Food as Nostalgia: Eating the Fifties and Sixties," *Australian Historical Studies* 30, 113 (1999): 231–50. And David Hilliard claims that "in the religious history of Australia, the 1950s are remembered ... as a time of confidence and expansion." Hilliard, "Church, Family and Sexuality in Australia in the 1950s," in John Murphy and Judith Smart, (eds.), *The Forgotten Fifties: Aspects of Australian Society and Culture in the 1950s* (Melbourne: Melbourne University Press and Australian Historical Studies, 1997), 135.

[11] Margaret Smith Crocco, Petra Munro, and Kathleen Weiler, *Pedagogies of Resistance: Women Educator Activists 1880-1960* (New York and London: Teachers College Press, Colombia University, 1999), 2.

[12] Barbara Miller Solomon, *In the Company of Educated Women: A History of Women and Higher Education in America* (New Haven and London: Yale University Press, 1985), xvii and 28.

[13] Jill Ker Conway, Introduction to M. Elizabeth Tidball, et al., *Taking Women Seriously: Lessons and Legacies for Educating the Majority* (Phoenix Arizona: American Council on Education/Oryx Press, 1999), xxi.

[14] Lesley Johnson, *The Modern Girl: Girlhood and Growing Up* (Sydney: Allen & Unwin, 1993), vi.

[15] Ibid, 1.

[16] Ibid, 153.

[17] Ibid, 134.

[18] Ibid, 4.

[19] Mabel Newcomer, *A Century of Higher Education for American Women* (New York: Harper Brothers, 1959).

[20] Linda Eisenmann, ed., *Historical Dictionary of Women's Education in the United States* (Westport, Connecticut: Greenwood Press, 1998), xix.

[21] Madge Dawson, *Graduate and Married: A Report on a Survey of One Thousand and Seventy Married Women Graduates of the University of Sydney* (Sydney: University of Sydney, 1965).

[22] Eisenmann, 179.

[23] Simon Marginson, *Educating Australia: Government, Economy and Citizen Since 1960* (Cambridge/Melbourne: Cambridge University Press, 1997), 21. By 1964 those proportions had risen to "more than 3% and 6% respectively," ibid.

[24] They also reveal the differing resources available to various institutions. Harvard reunion books, for instance, are often professionally produced and bound in contrast to the Smith and Radcliffe College books that bear the hallmarks of a more amateur approach.

[25] For Australian graduates I have drawn on a survey of 200 women who graduated from the Universities of Adelaide and Melbourne: Report of "Graduating in the Fifties: Women Graduates Family Formation Study," Mackinnon, ARC funded study, 1994. See also Madge Dawson, *Graduate and Married*, 1965. There are

"Giving Myself a Toni, Write Thesis Tonight"

several U.S. studies of graduate cohorts. See, for instance, Kathleen Hulbert and Diane Schuster, eds., *Women's Lives Through Time: Educated Women of the Twentieth Century* (San Francisco: Jossey-Bass Publishers, 1993).

26   See for instance Karen V. Kukil, ed., *The Unabridged Journals of Sylvia Plath* (New York: Anchor Books, 2000), many biographies of Plath (e.g. Jacqueline Rose, *The Haunting of Sylvia Plath* [London: Virago, 1992]), Jill Ker Conway, *The Road from Coorain* (New York: Vintage, 1990), Jill Ker Conway, *True North* (New York: Vintage, 1995), Jill Ker Conway, *A Woman's Education* (New York: Alfred Knopt, 2001), Adrienne Rich, *Of Woman Born: Motherhood as Experience and Institution* (New York and London: W. W. Norton, 1995).

27   *Class of '56 40th Reunion*, compiled by year book committee, Arthur and Elizabeth Schlesinger Library on the History of Women in America, The Radcliffe Institute for Advanced Study, Harvard. R 2000-36 RG ix Series 7

28   Alumnae reunion books are much more widely available than those I have drawn on here (predominantly Radcliffe, Smith, and Wellesley) and provide rich material for a range of questions around graduate outcomes, subjectivity and changing attitudes.

29   Alice Gorton Hart papers, Sophia Smith Collection, Smith College, Journal July 1982-3.

30   Anonymous respondent, "Graduating in the Fifties: Women Graduates Family Formation Study."

31   Marine Leland, Correspondence A-D 42 folders, Smith College Archives, original emphasis. I am grateful to Alison Prentice for alerting me to these records.

32   Patricia Palmieri, *This Adamless Eden: The Community of Women Faculty at Wellesley* (New Haven: Yale University Press, 1995); Alison Mackinnon, *Love and Freedom: Professional Women and the Reshaping of Personal Life* (Cambridge and Melbourne: Cambridge University Press, 1997).

33   Alison Prentice, an admirer of Leland's work, points out that Leland would no doubt be referring to the Canadian "persons" case. Five women took the fact that they were not eligible to sit in the Canadian Senate to the Supreme Court of Canada and finally to the Privy Council in England. The latter decided, in 1929, that women were in fact "persons" before the law and were eligible to sit in the senate. Private communication with Alison Prentice.

34   Lelah Dushkin to Dorothy Smith Dushkin, Dorothy Smith Dushkin Papers 1906-88, Ms group 243, box 1a, folder 1, Sophia Smith Collection. Smith College.

35   Alice Gorton Hart papers, Sophia Smith Collection, Smith College, Folder 6 Jan 1952.

36   Kukil, ed., *Plath Journals*, 29.

37   Ibid, 47, original emphasis.

38   Ibid, 183, original emphasis.

39   Ibid, 54.

40   Liva Baker, *I'm Radcliffe! Fly Me! The Seven Sisters and the Failure of Women's Education* (New York and London: Macmillan, 1976), 167.

41   M. Carey Thomas was the dean and second president of Bryn Mawr women's college in the U.S.. She was devoted to strong academic standards. Solomon, *In the Company of Educated Women*, 84. For a biography, see H. L. Horowitz, *The Power and Passion of M. Carey Thomas* (New York: Alfred A. Knopf, 1994).

42   Radcliffe College, *Class of '56 40th Reunion Book*, R2000-36 RG 1X series 7.

43   Sara Delamont, "The Contradictions in Ladies Education," in Sara Delamont and

Alison Mackinnon

Lorna Duffin, eds., *The Nineteenth-Century Woman* (London: Croom Helm, 1978), 140-141.
44 Alice Gorton Hart papers, Box 3 of 6, folders 17-24, 1953-4.
45 Jill Ker Conway, *The Road from Coorain*, 1990, 187.
46 Alison Mackinnon, *Love and Freedom*.
47 Carolyn Heilbrun, *Writing a Woman's Life* (New York: Ballantine Books, 1988).
48 Jill Ker Conway, *The Road*, 193, my emphasis.
49 Ibid, 162.
50 Anonymous respondent to survey: "Graduating in the Fifties: Women Graduates Family Formation Study," Mackinnon, Australian Research Council funded study, 1994. Respondents to this survey had attended either the University of Melbourne or the University of Adelaide.
51 Jill Ker Conway, *The Road*, 178.
52 Anonymous respondent to "Graduating in the Fifties" study.
53 Many intelligent men in the literary and visual arts at the time also felt the need to leave a society generally perceived to be parochial and anti-intellectual.
54 Jill Ker Conway, *The Road*, 215.
55 Anne Coombs, *Sex and Anarchy*, 111.
56 Ibid, 304.
57 Quote from anonymous respondent to "Graduating in the Fifties study."
58 Ibid.
59 Sylvia Plath, from *The Bell Jar*, cited in Janet Malcolm, *The Silent Woman: Sylvia Plath and Ted Hughes* (Sydney: Picador, 1995), 53.
60 Coombs, *Sex and Anarchy*, 304.
61 Jill Ker Conway, *The Road*, 221.
62 Murphy, *Imagining the Fifties*, 56.
63 This journal entry comes from Alice Gorton Hart papers, Box 2 of 6, folder 6, 1952.
64 Jane Gerhard, "Revisiting the 'Myth of the Vaginal Orgasm'," *Feminist Studies* 26, 2 (2000): 449-76.
65 Gerhard, 454-455.
66 Gerhard, 459.
67 Kukil, *Plath Journals*, 151.
68 Hart Journals, SSC, July 1982-October 1983.
69 See Ruth Rosen, *The World Split Open: How the Modern Women's Movement Changed America* (New York and London: Penguin, 2000), for an overview of NOW.
70 Hart journals, 1970-72, SSC.
71 Murphy, *Imagining the Fifties*, 43; Beth Bailey, in *Sex in the Heartland*, makes a similar point.
72 Johnson, *The Modern Girl*, 153.
73 Anonymous respondent to "Graduating in the Fifties" study.
74 For an account of the experience of women graduates of the 1960s see M. Horn, *Rebels in White Gloves: Coming of Age With Hillary's Class-Wellesley '69* (New York: Times Books, 1999). For longitudinal studies of the lives of women graduates at Girton College, Cambridge, see the work of P. Thane and A. Eickson ("Distant Voices, Sad Lives," *The Guardian Education*, Sept. 3, 2002), 14-15.

The Ideology of Domesticity

Re-constructions Across Three Generations in Ontario

CECILIA REYNOLDS

How is it that individual women make meaning out of their lives in different contexts? This important feminist question was the basis of a study of three generations of Canadian women—eight family groupings of daughters, their mothers, and their maternal grandmothers. This essay draws on data from that interview study to describe how the ideology of domesticity changed over time. The data reveals patterns in the ways in which these changes impacted women in terms of the decisions they made about schooling and work.

A number of feminist scholars have written about how an ideology of domesticity (ideas about the proper public and private roles of females) has limited the choices women have made.[1] Only a few studies[2] have traced differences in such ideas across generations of women. The importance of looking at the narratives of women across generations is that we are afforded a "vital entry point for examining the interaction between the individual and society in the construction of gender."[3] This entry point helps us to improve our understanding of how it is that women can be historical actors who have the agency to shape their lives, and how they do so within limits afforded them by the historical contexts within which they find themselves in each era.[4]

The Study

In 1993, volunteers for an intergenerational interview study were sought from students enrolled in an undergraduate Women's Studies course at a medium-sized Ontario university. Participants were selected on the basis of meeting the criteria that the family grouping contain a daughter aged between 16-25 willing to participate and that her mother and grandmother be willing to be interviewed. There was also a stipulation that each of the women had lived most of their lives in Canada. This limitation was set in order to capture data on family groupings who had lived in Canada across the three generations. Another major purpose of the research was to document and understand changes in "small town" Ontario contexts and women's experiences in such settings over this time period.

In the volunteer sample of 24 women (eight families), the grandmothers had all been born in the early part of the twentieth century, the mothers had been born either during or immediately following the Second World War, and the daughters had been born in the 1960s and 1970s. As it turned out, not all the initial volunteers were "daughters," since some of the Women's Studies students were "mothers" and indeed one was from the "grandmothers" group. Most of the families in the study had lived the majority of their lifetime to date in communities close to where they grew up, a pattern not unusual for families in this part of Ontario. Some of the daughters attended the same high school where their own mothers had been students.

All agreed to individual video-recorded life history interviews that took place in their home settings and were facilitated by a previously distributed Interview Guide. The interviews were conducted by myself and my daughter, who worked as my research assistant. Together, we took turns asking questions and operating the camera. The tapes were transcribed and, afterwards, each family was asked if they would like to have copies of the tapes which members of their family had given personal permission to share. For some families, the tapes constituted a video library of the histories of the women in their family. Particularly, in the case of grandmothers, the tapes served to record historic details about their lives and to document their feelings. In many cases, the grandmothers' stories had been only partially known by daughters and granddaughters prior to participation in this study.

There was relative homogeneity amongst those interviewed in that none of them could be described as being from a visible minority group but they were varied in terms of class backgrounds, religion, ethnic heritage, and rural and urban residency patterns. For this essay, only the portion of the interviews that pertain to the women's memories and narratives about schooling and paid and unpaid work are considered.

Theoretical Framework

The theoretical framework upon which this study is based comes from a number of feminists who have helped to define ideology and what it means for women's experiences. Michelle Barrett defines ideology as "the generic term for the processes by which meaning is produced, challenged, reproduced and transformed."[5] Ideologies are sets of ideas that individuals hold about the world around them. Ideologies are frequently expressed in "discourses" or ways of talking about one's ideas of the world. Bronwyn Davies explains it this way:

> Each person actively takes up discourses [or ideologies] through which they and others speak/write the world into existence... Through those

discourses they are made speaking subjects at the same time as they are subjected to the constitutive forces of those discourses.[6]

Arlene Tigar McLaren contends that:

... girls' discourses about mothering and employment are intertwined in complex ways with understandings about, for example, femininity, masculinity, the family, the sexual division of labour, gender equality and nonparental childcare.[7]

Jane Gaskell claims that an ideology of domesticity affects people's perceptions of the possibility of change. She argues that "males and females make different long term assumptions about what a paid job will mean because of its relation to domestic labour."[8] She goes on to say that women and girls make life choices based on an assessment of the "way the world works, what opportunities are open, what paths are possible."[9] Gaby Weiner warns that "ideologically frozen understandings"[10] often serve women's interests poorly.

How do the narratives of women in this study shed light on the concept of an ideology of domesticity and its impact? Their stories are examined under two major themes: a) schooling experiences; and b) paid and unpaid work experiences. Within each theme, the author identifies patterns in their experiences that reveal dominant elements of the ideology of domesticity in each generation. Also discussed, are changes that can be observed across the generations. In this way, the essay offers a "gendered analysis of social life"[11] which provides insights with regard to ways in which some women have negotiated the messages of the culture and made meaning of their lives in historical contexts.

Schooling Experiences

We asked each participant to describe what she remembered of her elementary, secondary, and post-secondary schooling experiences. This section offers a summary of what the women in each generation recalled about their formal education.

Grandmothers

The grandmothers were born in the early part of the twentieth century, largely between 1910 and 1930. In their stories of schooling we can hear a description of the context of schooling for those decades.

They each talked about a "long walk to school." They revealed that the neighborhood school for them was a reality, but in rural settings that sometimes meant a large tract being considered as neighbourhood, with no school busses in sight. Those who had gone to rural schools talked about "one room schools" with one teacher and large classes of students of varying age; some described having attended girls-only schools run by women religious. All remembered liking school and retained positive memories of their, mostly female, teachers.

Cecilia Reynolds

Without exception, this group of women felt that most young people of their generation were expected only to go to school until the eighth grade. If anyone were to go on to secondary school, it was more likely to be a boy rather than a girl. They knew very few people who had attended secondary schools and they reported that there was an "entrance exam" which served to keep some students from going on. For them and many of their friends, the need for them to contribute to full-time work on the family farm or to the household income through paid employment after grade eight was a common reason for not continuing in school.

Only two out of the eight grandmothers interviewed reported that they attended school after grade eight and each had gone only to grade ten. One of these had attended a "business college" after completing grade ten and it was this woman who was a Women's Studies student at the time of the study. When the grandmothers talked about their daughters and granddaughters, they stated that increased opportunities for extended schooling was a crucial element which had improved women's lives over time. The following quote is typical of their comments in this regard:

> I am so proud of my girls because they have gone on in school. My granddaughter just graduated from university. I never had that chance. People in my generation said, "Don't waste your money on sending her to school. She is just going to get married, so, it will be a waste." I was a bit embarrassed all my life about having only finished grade eight.

When not in school, the grandmothers remembered doing a variety of home-based or community-based activities. They talked about ice-skating and roller skating at local rinks, playing "kick the can" or "hopscotch" on the road, going to the local movie theatre, or on "family outings."

While at school they reported being treated by teachers as much the same as the boys, but at home they recalled sharp differences between what was expected of them and their brothers. One woman put it this way: "The only good thing about being a girl in my family was that you didn't have to *kill* the chickens. You just had to pluck them, clean them and cook them."

The grandmothers revealed that the ideology of domesticity which held sway when they were youngsters dictated that girls and boys were expected to contribute unpaid labour to the farm and/or household while they going to school. They described spending long hours doing such chores as milking or washing. Only if a student or his or her parent, was particularly dedicated to making it happen, did any male or female student "go on" beyond what most of his/her peers in the community were doing.

Mothers

The mothers were born in the 1940s and 1950s and they remembered a very short walk to their neighborhood elementary school. That school was described

The Ideology of Domesticity

as being large, multi-grade and co-educational, with predominately female teachers. Unlike their mothers, these women reported that "everyone went on to high school in those days." Only a few of their friends, who "were not very bright" stopped going to school after grade eight. They did recall, however, that some students left after grade ten, as in the previous era. These, they said, were most often peers whose parents needed the money in the household or girls who wanted to get married early.

High school memories revealed a picture of busses and large newly constructed regional schools where "both the rich kids and the country kids were lumped together." The women remembered very strict male teachers and a few female teachers whom they especially liked. Most of the courses they took were compulsory. If they decided to go to grade thirteen, they had to sit for provincial exams at the end of that year. Many of the women and their peers only went to grade twelve. They reported that there were about equal numbers of the "smart" boys and girls who went on to grade thirteen. They recalled that you could get into teaching, nursing or "commercial school" without having grade thirteen and these routes were encouraged by "guidance counselors" at the high schools and by parents. It was mainly the "rich kids" who went to university. This comment is typical of what they said:

> I was smart and the teachers encouraged me to try my grade thirteen. It meant that I had to hang around at school a year longer than everyone else but I liked it. My family didn't have enough money though for me to go to university and I went to Teachers' College instead. My parents were delighted with this choice because they thought it was a waste of money for me to go to university since I was likely going to get married anyway. I guess they never imagined that I was also going to get divorced and have to raise three kids on my own.

The mothers described a number of school-based activities: school plays and choirs, playing baseball on school teams, and going to school dances. Like their own mothers, however, they also talked about home-based activities such as playing "red rover" and "hide and seek." The only community-based activity they recalled was going to movies, especially the Saturday matinee.

They had difficulty describing differential treatment of boys and girls at school but they agreed that most of the girls had done better at school in terms of grades than had most of the boys. Like their mothers, some grew up on farms while others had lived only in urban settings. As the grandmothers had, the mothers recalled sharp differences between what they and their brothers were expected to do at home. More clearly than the grandmothers, however, the mothers recognized a double standard for boys and girls within their families when they were young, something not articulated by the grandmothers. This double standard in their view meant that their brothers had more freedom than was available to them. This is the way one of the mothers described it:

My brothers got away with murder at home. I was always forced to do the dishes and help my Mom but they didn't have to do any of that. They got to drive the car before I did and to go out alone much more than I was allowed to do. I remember complaining loudly but it seemed to fall on deaf ears. My parents just couldn't see that it was unfair for the boys to get so much more freedom than my sisters or I had.

One obvious contrast with the previous generation was that, unlike their own mothers, these women reported that while in school they were asked to do very little work at home beyond doing the dishes. Almost all described having worked at paid part-time jobs while they were in high school. Some talked about making money picking strawberries at about twelve or thirteen years of age and, when they were older, most had held summer jobs such as working at one of the fruit markets in town. One woman had worked on Saturdays as the "popcorn girl" at the local theatre and another had worked evenings at Kresge's, a department store. They reported that most of this work was done for "pocket money" so that they could buy clothes or "go to the movies." But, three out of the eight recalled that once they turned sixteen, their parents asked them to pay "room and board" money into the household and this continued until the time they left home.

The mothers revealed that the ideology of domesticity that held sway while they were in school dictated that males would be the "breadwinners" in the future and that girls would get married and only "have to work" for pay for a short period of time. This was the explanation they offered for why so few parents in their generation and their communities expected their daughters to obtain more than a high school diploma and perhaps some further training in order to become a teacher, nurse or secretary.

The mothers, however, as we will see in the next section of this essay, actually experienced a different reality and all had gone back for some type of further schooling later in life. Three out of the eight were taking university courses and two were working on graduate degrees at the time of the study. The other three had taken courses at community colleges to obtain specialized skills.

Daughters

The daughters were born in the 1960s and 1970s. They recalled elementary schools that were "five minutes away." Those schools were of various types and three had gone to "Montessori" schools or to "French Immersion" schools. One had attended a single-sex girls' school and the other four large multi-grade coeducational schools. Unlike their mothers, they commented on the crowded nature of their classes and the number of times they were placed in "split-grades," which they had not liked. Also, unlike both previous generations, these women made substantially more negative comments about their teachers in both elementary and in secondary schools. This may reflect an era in which both parents and children began to more openly criticize schools and teachers than in previous times.

Like their mothers, the daughters believed that everyone went to high school, but they also commented that everyone they knew also went to university. It would seem that across the three generations the "basic credential" had risen from grade eight, to a high school diploma, to a university degree. Unlike either of the two previous generations, the daughters commented on the "run-down" nature of their high schools. This may have been because most were the same schools which had been new when their mothers attended high school. The daughters, unlike their mothers and grandmothers, told stories about how teachers and students clashed openly at their high schools. This is one example:

> There was one English teacher who everyone hated. One day when he started to yell at one of the kids in his usual way, I guess a group of us had just had enough and we looked around at each other and decided to close our books and walk out of the classroom. It was our own little protest march. He got all red in the face and was literally jumping up and down but we just kept on walking. We all thought we would get into huge trouble but he let it go and didn't even say anything to us about it in the next class. He also didn't yell at any of us in that group after that.

The daughters were quite articulate about the "advantages" they remember the boys receiving at both elementary and high school. They talked about the boys' sports teams getting all the money and recognition, as well as lots of time off to go to football games, while the girls' soccer or rowing teams had to struggle and try to prove that they were "just as good as the boys." The daughters noted that, even though most of the girls did better academically, they saw how the teachers encouraged the boys more about going to university and about heading into professions such as medicine and law. This is the way one put it:

> There sure weren't any feminist teachers at my high school. Both male and female teachers told my brother how smart he was and how he should try for a scholarship to Harvard or something but they didn't seem to even notice me. I was getting good scores on tests and things but whenever it was something subjective, he would always do better than me. I guess I was pretty competitive with him but who wouldn't be when you felt you were being ignored most of the time.

The daughters also commented that at home their brothers had later curfews and fewer restrictions. Unlike their mothers, however, they recounted open friction at home with their parents because of this. One daughter recalled:

> I used to be a door slammer when I was a teenager. I would get mad

about my brother being given the car when I had asked for it before he had. He didn't get into trouble when he came home after midnight, but I did. My parents used to say, "Boys can't get pregnant." There were definitely different standards for him than for me. Sometimes I think I made some headway on these things and my little sister certainly was given more freedom than I was ever allowed, but there were lots of bad feelings between my parents and I over things like this when I was young.

Daughters reported that neither they nor their brothers had to do any major household chores while they were students in high school or in elementary school. They recalled being expected to concentrate on their schoolwork rather than doing housework or part-time work for pay. Some spoke about doing volunteer work in hospitals as candy stripers, or being involved in Girl Guides for several years. They commented that they were always too busy with sports and music lessons to do much else.

Activities the daughters remembered were partly school-based, such as dances, but more often they were activities at home such as "skipping" or "hopscotch," or they were community-based activities such as sports teams. Almost all took private swimming, music, or dancing lessons and described a new activity—"hanging out at the mall." They talked a lot about sitting around the house listening to music, watching a lot of TV, having lots of parties (especially when their parents were away) and going to the movies, especially the drive-in theatres.

The daughters revealed that the ideology of domesticity which held sway for them was the notion that they could "be anything they wanted to be." If they just "worked hard enough," they could "have it all." As we will see in the next section of this essay, like their own mothers, they were later to learn that this ideology was harder to realize than they had expected. They reported experiencing pressures from the "high expectations" of their early years and worried about disappointing their mothers and grandmothers. The daughters believed that they would be working for pay for a large portion of their adult life, an expectation which troubled them at the time of the study, as we will learn more about in the next section.

Of the eight daughters, only the two youngest had not completed university degrees at the time of the study. The six others had entered relatively feminized paid work roles such as modelling, social work, lab technician work, and running a daycare centre. It is important to note, however, that none of the women in this group had taken up nursing or secretarial work, as had their mothers. Three hoped to obtain graduate degrees sometime in the near future.

Summary of Schooling Experiences

The memories of schooling experiences related by women in these three generations reveal certain changes in policies and practices regarding schooling in Canada over these years. For example, we can see in these stories the movement over time from one-room schoolhouses to multi-grade, co-educational classrooms, the development of the neighborhood school within easy walking distance for students, and the later rise of school bus policies We also hear increasingly critical comments about teachers.

Of interest, is the fact that an increasing length of time in school is accepted by these women as the norm. One explanation may centre around changing employer expectations; another factor might be the changing demographics of the school-age population (for example the baby boomer phenomenon). Changes in family economic circumstances across generations and/or in their social class self-designation or expectations may also offer a clue to why it is that these women talk about it being "natural" for them to have spent a longer time in school than their own mothers or grandmothers.

There is evidence in the data that these women assess their need for schooling in terms of paid and unpaid opportunities open to them. The data also suggest that these women were strongly influenced by what their peers were doing concerning schooling and paid and unpaid work. While they knew what was "normal" for males, it was the norm for females of their own generation which was most influential regarding their personal decisions.

Work Experiences

In the study we asked women to describe both the paid and unpaid work they had done while they were at school, before and after they were married, while they were raising their children and later in their lives. In this section we see that while some things changed over time, a lot remained the same across the generations.

Grandmothers

When asked to recall the first work they did, the grandmothers all talked about "babysitting." While in some cases they were paid to do this work for neighbours, in other cases they did it without pay in their own household. Somewhat ironically, many of the grandmothers also reported that, later in life, they babysat their grandchildren without pay in order to facilitate the paid work of their daughters.

While the grandmothers remembered having done many unpaid chores on the farm or in their parents' households (and later in their own households) only half of them had ever worked for pay beyond babysitting. Four reported having worked briefly in factories, offices, and shops before getting married These women all said that they did so because they married "late" (in their mid-20s or early 30s.) In most cases, this was explained by the circumstances of World War II, as weddings got delayed until the men returned from the war. Only the grandmother who had been widowed while she was in her 30s reported spending 25 years in paid employment.

Three recalled that, although they had wanted to become teachers or nurses, the circumstances of the great Depression of the 1930s had thwarted their

Cecilia Reynolds

aspirations and then World War II had further limited the choices available to them.

> I really wanted to become a nurse and I would have except that my family fell on hard times during the Depression and I had to stay home and help out on the farm. I almost volunteered as a nurse during World War II but my parents talked me out of it. I waited on the farm for my boyfriend and brothers to return safely. Many of them didn't make it. My husband did, thank God. We got married as soon as the war was over. I gave up on the nursing idea after that since there was lots of work to do raising my own children and making ends meet.

Many women in Canada took on non-traditional roles during World War II but the women studied stayed in their urban or rural communities and either continued to do unpaid work at home or on the farm, or worked for pay in offices or local stores until the war was over. None entered the Armed Forces, as some women did, nor had they worked in factories, as many other women did during this era. All ceased paid work shortly following the war when they married and started their own households.

The grandmothers expected their husbands to work for pay while they stayed home and cared for the needs of their families. Some, however, expressed resentment at this state of affairs. Here is what one grandmother said in this regard:

> My husband was a grand man and a good provider. But, there were times when I wanted to scream and escape from all the housework and the kids. Married people seldom went out in those days to a show or for dinner in a restaurant. It was just expected that women put their needs after those of the family. I remember complaining once to my own mother and she gave me a right good talking to about it. I just kept quiet after that when I felt a bit overwhelmed by it all.

Many grandmothers recollected fond memories of their time as wives and mothers. Some also talked about how in some ways working for pay had not been all that fulfilling. This is what one woman reported:

> I worked for four years in a shop before I got married and it was okay sometimes, but it got to be pretty boring after a while. I really had no authority in the place and I just had to follow orders and do what I was told. I could hardly wait to get away from that and spend my time running my own house. I loved my time when the kids were little. I baked every day and washed every day. It was hard work but I loved it.

The woman who had been widowed while her children were young did not have the choice of staying home and baking and washing each day:

> After I picked myself up off the floor following my husband's unexpected passing, I dug in and tried to be both mother and father. It wasn't easy. I had to ask my oldest daughter to take over a lot of things at home while I went out to work. I actually liked the work I did most of the time, but there were days when things were pretty tough, especially when some of the kids were sick or when I was under the weather myself. I look back and wonder sometimes about how we all made it through.

The ideology of domesticity that held sway for the grandmothers described for them an ideal role for women, that of the selfless but contented wife and mother. While some accepted this role and relished it, others, like the widow could not actualize it, and still others resisted it in their own ways, or resigned themselves to it. Some women's narratives showed that they did all of these things at different times. Here is what one grandmother stated:

> I didn't have many women friends, just mainly my family. We used to get together about every month or two and the women would all end up in the kitchen where we used to talk and talk. I loved those days because I could get out of the house. I did other things too to keep myself going. I always went for a long walk before bedtime just to be alone for a while. I read a lot and listened to the radio shows. It felt good not always to have to be "Mom."

Mothers
When asked about the work they had done, the mothers reported that while they had done some unpaid family chores, they couldn't remember having spent much time at these. They did remember having a lot of fun at their paid part-time or occasional jobs and they listed "babysitting," being a "counter girl" and a "car hop," a "fruit picker" and a "factory worker" among the things they had done while still in school or over the summers.

All worked for pay both before and after getting married, although many took some time to be at home when they were pregnant or when their children were babies. Of the eight, three were teachers, three were nurses and two worked "in business." While for some, these work roles were a fulfillment of aspirations, for others, they were what they "settled for" because dreams of being a "singer," an "archaeologist," or a "full-time mom, like my own mom" had not been possible given the circumstances which unfolded for them.

The mothers married in their 20s, which they felt had been "early" in retrospect but not too unusual within their communities. Three spent some time "on their own" and as a "single mom" without a husband as a result of marriage breakdowns of one sort or another. Two of these three remarried after some period and the other developed several relationships with "live in" male partners but had not remarried. All eight had spent at least 20 years in the paid labour force, even though they never expected this scenario when they were in school. One mother commented:

> If I had known when I was in school that I would have been working this long, I might have done things differently. It has worked out fine, I guess, and I don't regret having the kids. My marriage was a disaster, however, and I wasn't really prepared to take on the whole responsibility for my own support and that of the kids. He didn't ever pay one cent in support. It was a good thing I had my nursing training to fall back on.

The mothers used the term "double day" to describe how they managed both a home and a paid job on a full-time basis. They confided that it was only relatively recently that they had come to think about it that way or that they had considered questions about whether they had actually received "equal pay for equal work."

> We were all pretty naive about these things and it is only now that I look back that I realize how unfair a lot of it was. I worked in my classroom all day long and then came home and worked all night long. I had such high standards drilled into me re keeping both my classroom and my house "perfect." I was exhausted all the time and eventually I got pretty sick, which just made things a lot worse. I didn't think it was fair to ask the kids or my husband to help. Besides, they never did things the way I wanted them done. So, I just did it all.

Another mother recalled:

> I never thought to complain even though I knew that the men in the office were making more money than most of the women. I just thought that was the way things were. We didn't have a union or anything and I was afraid that if I made a fuss, I might lose my job. I was on my own and needed the money to put food on the table for the kids. I just took what they would give me. Since I started this Women's Studies course, it is really making me upset about all that I put up with over the years.

Going in and out of the paid workforce was another common theme for the mothers, as was the idea that, unless working for pay was a necessity (as in the cases where there had been a marriage break up), women should only work in ways that did not have adverse affects on the usual patterns of husbands and children.

> My husband gave me a pretty tough time about going back to work after our third child. He had a good job and felt that we didn't need the money. I had gone back briefly after the second baby but he didn't like the fact that

sometimes that had meant that dinner was late and the house was a big mess most of the time. Since I had been out of teaching for so long, I didn't have much of a chance of getting a highly paid role like that of a school principal. He didn't think it was worth it for me to go back to teaching. I went back anyway, but I had to try to keep everything going just as if I wasn't working full-time in order to keep the kids and him off my back about working. I just loved being at the school again and it was worth it, I think.

The ideology of domesticity which held sway for the mothers described for them an ideal role for women, that of the "supermom" who could work for pay outside the home *and* keep homebaked cookies on hand for her perfect family. While some tried their best to actualize this role, others encountered marriage break ups making it impossible. In this generation as well as in the previous generation, some of the women found their own ways of resisting this dominant image and of finding "ways of being" that worked for them. Here is what one mother stated:

I know it shocked the hell out of everyone I knew when I left my husband. I guess, on the outside everything looked perfect. Heaven knows I worked like a dog to make it look like that! I just couldn't be that way anymore and I took the kids with me on a ride which was pretty scary at times. I went back to work and back to school and am now pretty happy with who I have become. I still work like a dog, but it is on my terms, not anybody else's. Thank God, I have a network of friends and family who have really helped me along, especially my own Mom.

Daughters

When asked about the first work they remembered doing, the daughters, like their grandmothers, quickly replied, without exception, that it had been "babysitting." Like their mothers, these women did not do a lot of household chores when they were young, but they took on some part-time work (some paid and some volunteer unpaid work) while at school. The daughters described having been "candy-stripers" and "camp counselors," "salesgirls," "models," and "waitresses."

Because the age of daughters was relatively young, it is difficult to know what their experiences of paid and unpaid labour will ultimately include. At the time of the study, one was working as a physiotherapist, another as a model, two were in business roles in large corporations, one was a social worker and one was about to become a teacher. The two youngest were still in university. One was planning to open her own hairdressing business and the other thought she might continue in school to become a lawyer.

Among the daughters there was diversity concerning their expectations with regard to marriage and motherhood. Two had married early in their view (in their 20s): one had just had her first child, while the other said she and her husband were uncertain about whether they wanted to have children at all. Another daughter had an unplanned pregnancy at age 16 and decided to raise the child, with help from her own mother. She was not planning on marrying in the near future and was attending school at the time of the study, with aspirations to open her own business. Another daughter stated that she hoped to one day become a mother, but she definitely did not want to get married. The other four said they hoped one day in the future to get married and to perhaps have children, but both decisions would need to wait until they attained their personal career aspirations.

All of the daughters expressed some form of anxiety about "juggling home and work responsibilities." Many openly criticized what their own mothers had done in terms of what they described as "the double day." Some daughters felt that they wanted to be more like their grandmothers than their mothers in terms of having time with their children when they were young. One woman explained it this way:

> I always hated it when I came home from school to an empty house. If I can, I want to be able to afford to stay home and be there for my own kids. My immediate problem is finding the right kind of guy who will give me enough space to do what I want in terms of my career and who will be a good father and will also be there for our kids. I didn't have that from my own Dad.

The daughters expressed clear views about how they were planning to assert their rights in the paid workforce. They were not willing to receive less pay than male co-workers. This quote is typical of what they said:

> I have taken enough Women's Studies courses to know the law and to know my rights. I will never put up with some of the things my Mom has talked about. I want to be paid equally, have the right to maternity leaves, and be free from the threat of sexual harassment. I think it is possible to have that kind of work life in my generation.

The ideology of domesticity which held sway amongst the daughters delineated for them an ideal role for women, that of the self-assured career woman who could make choices about marriage and motherhood, as well as about participation in paid and unpaid work. It is hard to know, due to the age of the individuals in this group, the extent to which this ideal will have an impact on their life choices over the next decades. It would definitely be interesting to follow-up and try to interview some of them in later years. Since that study has not been done, we can only speculate that it might reveal that, like their mothers and grandmothers, some will have worked to fulfill this ideal, others will have resisted it, and still others will have found a compromise position which works for them at an individual level. Here is what one daughter speculated about the future:

> I know my baby is only small now and there are lots of things that could change, but my husband and I are both sharing the household work and the parenting work. We hope to keep doing that as we have more children. I intend to go back to work when our baby is about two years old and then to stop again and stay home when we have another child. If it makes sense financially, it may even be my husband who stays home with our second child for a year or so. I plan to keep active in my career and keep going to school to improve my credentials. It may be optimistic but that is what we have mapped out for our future.

Summary of Paid and Unpaid Work Experiences

The memories of paid and unpaid work related by these women reveal how circumstances changed and did not change over this time period for many Canadian women. Increasingly, middle-class women were accepted as members of the paid labour force following World War II and over time the roles open to them expanded as they took on some non-traditional careers. But, other things did not change. We see the repeated theme that taking care of children was a woman's role, almost always an unpaid role. Whether or not women chose to resist this theme and enter the paid workforce, some women (often their own mothers) took up the childcare role. We see some changes in attitudes towards marriage. The timing of marriage (early or late) showed change over time but repeatedly the decision about when to marry seems to have been based on economic possibilities for setting up a household based on paid labour activities open to men and to women.

All three generations studied expressed the view that motherhood was desirable for women. In the grandmothers' generation, women were expected to accept that pregnancy was part of their duty as women. In the mothers' generation, women had more choice about pregnancy but once they had a child they were expected to take full responsibility for that child, whether or not they had a male partner due to divorce or other circumstances. In the daughters' generation, there was more talk about the fact that not all women could or even should be mothers. Those who chose to become pregnant would need to adjust their other choices in light of parenthood. Rather than take on sole responsibility, however, the daughters talked about negotiating this with the child's father and expecting accommodations in their paid work to help them cope with dual roles as mother and career woman.

Women in the grandmothers' generation cited external factors, such as World War II and attitudes towards women in their community and in the broader society, as reasons why they did not fulfil some of their early dreams. Women in the mothers' generation tended to blame themselves or non-supportive household members for not having reached out and gained some of the new freedoms to pursue non-traditional paid labour or to control pregnancies. They complained that while they had worked the "double day" and achieved some "success," they had not been encouraged to dream big enough dreams about what might have been possible for them as women. Women in the daughters' generation wondered why, in spite of seemingly fewer external restraints and bigger dreams, it was still difficult to "have it all." Big expectations for paid labour activities and motherhood joys were still elusive goals for women.

In the first generation, the dominant image was that of the selfless wife and mother. For the second generation it was that of the Supermom and for the third generation it was that of the self-fulfilled career woman/wife/mother. The increasing emphasis on taking on multiple roles exemplifies one of the changes in an ideology of domesticity over this period. Identifying these images makes it easier to understand what a "generation gap" might mean for these women. We can also see how a "skip generation" effect can make sense as daughters strive not to replicate the errors they perceive their own mothers have made. Escape backwards to "simpler" times like those experienced by their grandmother can look appealing. As this study suggests, however, that simplicity is more fiction that fact. In each generation, difficult life decisions need to be made by women about schooling and work, marriage and motherhood. These decisions, while arguably influenced by an ideology of domesticity, are those of the individual based on her assessment of her opportunities.

Conclusions

This study drew on a sample of women who did not belong to a visible minority group in Canadian society. There is nothing in their conversations that reveals that they saw themselves as a racialized group, even though one could say that by their "whiteness" this was indeed the case. A study of similar generations of women of colour from multiple ethnic groups would add considerably to our knowledge of how schooling and work experiences across these generations may have been similar to or different from those described by the women in this current study. The conclusions listed here, however, can only draw on the ideas expressed by the women studied. Such ideas delineate how a dominant ideology of domesticity for the period affected these women. Such a dominant ideology may have affected women of colour quite differently across a number of ethnic groups and may have been strongly linked to religious beliefs or other factors within or across their cultures.

In the current study, we observe a steady escalation in the norm regarding time spent in school prior to entry into the paid labour force. While grandmothers talked about grade eight as the school leaving stage, mothers talked about high school graduation and daughters discussed university degree completion. This escalating time line for schooling had a direct effect on choices for women in each generation about marriage and motherhood and about when they might be able to take on full-time or part-time paid work. We also observe that increasingly over these three generations and for these women, each generation was able to focus more on school activities and less was expected of them in terms of combining schooling with domestic tasks in their parents' household. Decisions about when to start their own households for each of these women were strongly related to economic and not just social dictates. Such observations may have been quite different for women of visible minority groups or ethnic/race groups where there may have been greater expectations for domestic tasks in the parental household or requirements to remain in extended family households after marriage.

In this study, we also observe changing notions about gender and breadwinner status. While such changes may not have held for all Canadian women during this time period or across these three generations, for these women it was clear that to the grandmothers' generation only men were expected to be given the breadwinner role officially, even if some women actually made financial contributions of some significance to the household. This status difference was described by these grandmothers as one of the explanations for lower expectations or support for them for longer time spent in schools. For the mothers studied, a gradual shift happened and both men and women began to share breadwinner status, especially if the woman divorced and set up her own household. This shift is described by these women as part of the reason for a related shift to allow them more years of formal schooling than had been expected of the grandmothers. The daughters in the study described clear desires to be seen as breadwinners, at least for part of their adult lives, and they clearly saw advanced time in education as well spent in terms of helping them secure economic rewards.

There is a strong link between women's expressed aspirations, their schooling participation, and their decisions about when and how to take on paid and unpaid work. In the grandmothers' generation, most felt that due to strong societal pressures, exacerbated by events such as World War II, they had relatively limited chances to aspire to live a life outside of what was expected of them by their parents and their peers. In the mothers' generation, while greater freedoms in terms of combining paid labour and domestic unpaid labour were possible, the price often included the "double day" phenomenon and/or going "back to school" for extended periods while still maintaining motherhood responsibilities. Even with all of that, these women thought that only a few routes such as teaching, nursing and business were really open to most women they knew. In the daughters' generation it was too early to tell how they were going to manage to strive to attain their aspirations. Clearly, however, they felt that there were fewer limits placed upon them for schooling or for opportunities for paid labour in a variety of fields. Most troubling for them was anticipating how to incorporate marriage and motherhood into their plans.

Women in the daughters' generation revealed that they were not convinced that "staying at home" was such a bad thing. Despite their increased time in formal education, some expressed a wish to be at home with their children, even though this might mean giving over breadwinner status to their partner. Other women in this generation clearly intended to take and keep sole or joint breadwinner status. The daughters wanted to have more choices than they felt were available to their mothers and grandmothers about being a breadwinner.

A revealing aspect of the ideology of domesticity outlined by the women's reports is the persistent notion that women will marry and be mothers. While one daughter declared that it was not necessary to be married in order to have a child, the other women across the generations accepted the need for marriage in order to have a child. There were shifts, however, in expressions across the generations about the most appropriate age for the bride. This discussion of early or late marriage age seems to be related not so much to biology as to length of schooling and economic circumstances.

The memories of schooling and work of the women in the three generations reveal how a shifting ideology of domesticity was constructed within changing historical contexts. Several dominant elements of an ideology of domesticity are seen to change over the time period of this study. These include ideas about time needed for formal schooling, women's breadwinner status, desirable age at marriage, and the mandate for all women to become mothers.

These women appear to have learned from the previous generation but also to have made adjustments according to the economics and circumstances of their times. This leads to the observation that individuals construct their gendered identities through a process that involves their reading of ideologies, such as the ideology of domesticity, but also through their own sense of what is possible. In other words, while women may know the elements of the dominant ideology of domesticity for their own generation and that of other generations, they make individual choices about whether to conform to these elements or resist them. Despite shifting norms over time, each individual woman has to choose whether to go along with the dominant ideology, or whether she might act outside of it in some way. In each generation, even this small sample reveals that women have not simply followed cultural dictates but have carefully considered their options. That those options can be shown to have changed over time helps to dispel essentialist claims about women and furthers the view of women as historical actors.

While the data reveal tensions between mothers, daughters and grandmothers as each of them strive to make life decisions, the data also show how support, love and admiration is fostered in relationships between women across generations. Women within the family units studied expressed pride in each other's accomplishments and there was evidence of unconditional love and support when times were tough. While it is unlikely that any of the women studied would agree that "mother knows best," they admitted that they had valued many of the things that were taught to them by their mother and grandmother. Adrift in the circumstances of our own generation, it is important for each of us to know and understand our mothers' and grandmothers' as historical actors. This is a crucial piece of understanding who we are and what we might become.

Notes

1. Alison Prentice, "From Household to School House: The Emergence of the Teacher as Servant of the State," in Alison Prentice and Ruby Heap, (eds.), *Gender and Education in Ontario: An Historical Reader* (Toronto: Canadian Scholars Press, 1991), 25-46; Jane Gaskell, *Gender Matters from School to Work* (Toronto: OISE Press, 1992); Jane Kenway, "Non-Traditional Pathways: Are They the Way of the Future?" in Jill Blackmore and Jane Kenway, (eds.), *Gender Matters in Educational Administration and Policy* (London: Falmer Press, 1993), 81-100; Linda Briskin, "Feminist Pedagogy: Teaching and Learning Liberation," in Lorna Erwin and David MacLeannan, (eds.), *Sociology of Education in Canada* (Toronto: Copp Clark Longman Ltd., 1994), 443-470; Vivian Hajnal, "Can I Do a Good Job of Both Family and Work? Decisions Regarding Offspring," in Cecilia Reynolds and Beth Young, (eds.), *Women and Leadership in Canadian Education* (Calgary: Detselig, 1995); Arlene Tigar McLaren and Ann Vanderbijl, "Teenage Girls Making Sense of Mothering: What Has (Relational) Equality Got to Do With It?" in Sharon Abbey and Andrea O'Reilly, (eds.), *Redefining Motherhood: Changing Identities and Patterns* (Toronto: Second Story Press, 1998), 127-144; Marion Lynn and Milana Todoroff, "Women's Work and Family Lives," in Nancy Mandell, (ed.), *Feminist Issues: Race, Class and Sexuality*, second edition (Scarborough: Prentice Hall Allyn and Bacon Canada, 1998), 208-232.
2. Such as Greta Hoffman Nemiroff, ed., *Women's Changing Landscapes: Life Histories from Three Generations* (Toronto: Sumach Press, 2000).
3. The Personal Narratives Groups, eds., *Interpreting Women Lives: Feminist Theory and Personal Narratives* (Bloomington: Indiana University Press, 1989).
4. Ibid, 5.
5. Bronwyn Davies, *Shards of Glass: Children Reading and Writing Beyond Gendered Identities* (Cresskill, New Jersey: Hampton Press, 1993), 14.
6. Ibid, 13.
7. Arlene Tigar McLaren and Ann Vanderbijl, 143.
8. Jane Gaskell, 88.
9. Ibid, 90.
10. Gaby Weiner, "Ethical Practice in an Unjust World: Educational Evaluation and Social Justice," in Jill Blackmore and Jane Kenway, (eds.), *Gender Matters in Educational Administration and Policy* (London: Falmer Press, 1993), 120.
11. Barbara Marshall, *Engendering Modernity: Feminism, Theory and Social Change* (Boston: Northeastern University, 1994), 2.

Contributor Notes

Paula Bourne is Head of the Centre for Women's Studies in Education at the Ontario Institute for Studies in Education of the University of Toronto. Among her many publications, she is co-author, with Dorothy Smith, of *Gender Equity and the Professional Education of Teachers: A Critical Review* (Toronto: CWSE/OISE/UT, 2000).

Rebecca Priegert Coulter is Associate Professor in the Faculty of Education, University of Western Ontario and co-editor, with Helen Harper, of *History is Hers: Women Educators in Twentieth Century Ontario* (Calgary: Detselig, 2005). In addition to her interests in the history of Canadian education, Coulter does research on gender and education.

Inga Elgqvist-Saltzman is Professor of Educational Science, formerly affiliated with the Department of Education at Umeå University, Sweden, and since retirement linked to Teacher Training at the University of Kalmar. Her publications in the area of gender and education include contemporary as well as historical studies. A co-edited anthology (with Gunilla Bjerén), *Gender and Education in a Life-Perspective: Lessons from Scandinavia* (Brookfield, VT: Avebury, 1994), presents a life-line methodology.

Dianne M. Hallman is Associate Professor of Educational Foundations at the University of Saskatchewan. She teaches graduate and undergraduate courses on women and education and researches in the area of critical studies of the university and professions.

Cathy James teaches in the general arts and sciences programme at Seneca

College and is a visiting scholar at the Centre for Women's Studies in Education at the Ontario Institute for Studies in Education of the University of Toronto. She has written extensively on the early history of social work in Canada, and on women in higher education. She is currently completing a monograph on the history of the settlement movement in Toronto.

Anna H. Lathrop is Professor and Associate Dean in the Faculty of Applied Health Sciences, Brock University, St. Catharines, Ontario. Her research interests focus on the history of physical education and sport, the history of women in higher education, and women and sport.

Alison Mackinnon, Foundation Director of the Hawke Research Institute at the University of South Australia and Professor of History and Gender Studies, has written widely on the history of women's education, including the award winning book *Love and Freedom: Professional Women and the Reshaping of Personal Life* (Cambridge/Melbourne: Cambridge University Press, 1997). In 2002 she was the Kerstin Hesselgren Guest Professor at the University of Umeå, an appointment of the Swedish Research Council.

Susan Mann is an historian and President Emeritus, York University, Toronto, Ontario. As Susan Mann Trofimenkoff she has published in Quebec history and women's history; a transitional interest in the study of travel led her, as Susan Mann, to pursue Canada's military nurses. *Margaret Macdonald: Imperial Daughter* appeared in 2005 from McGill-Queen's University Press.

Wendy Mitchinson is Professor of History and University Research Chair at the University of Waterloo. She has written widely on the history of Canadian women. Her most recent book is *Childbirth in Canada, 1900-1950* (Toronto: University of Toronto Press, 2002).

Cecilia Reynolds is Professor and Dean of the College of Education at the University of Saskatchewan. Her recent publications include the edited books *Women and School Leadership: International Perspectives* (Albany: SUNY Press, 2002) and *Equity and Globalization in Education* (Calgary: Detselig, 2002).

Harry Smaller taught for many years in regular and alternative schools in inner-city Toronto. More recently, he has been at the Faculty of Education at York University, where he teaches courses in the history of education, and researches historical and contemporary aspects of teachers' work.

Elizabeth M. Smyth is Associate Professor, Department of Curriculum, Teaching and Learning, Ontario Institute for Studies in Education of the University of Toronto. Her most recent work is a co-edited volume with Ruby Heap and Wyn Millar, *Learning to Practice: Professional Education in Historical* *and Contemporary Perspectives* (Ottawa: University of Ottawa Press, 2005).

Marjorie Theobald is a senior research fellow in the History Department at the University of Melbourne. She has written extensively about the history of women's education including *Knowing Women: Origins of Women's Education in Nineteenth-Century Australia* (Cambridge/Melbourne: Cambridge University Press, 1996).

List of Illustrations

1.1. Portrait of Donald Dickie, date unknown, courtesy of Alberta Archives. Location file 2315-2; Reference information-Biographies-Donalda Dickie (p. 24).

2.1. Mary G. Hamilton. Courtesy of Monica Jenset (p. 48).

2.2. "Miss Hamilton and Mrs. Geddes," Camp Tanamakoon photo album. Courtesy of Monica Jenset (p. 53).

2.3. Irene Poelzer, 1999. Courtesy of Irene Poelzer (p. 55).

3.1. Florence Johnson, teacher, feminist and union organizer. Courtesy of State Library of Victoria (p. 76).

4.1. Cecilia Fryxell during the heydays of Rostad. Courtesy of the Museum of Kalmar (p. 86).

4.2. Rostad 1860 (detail) reproduced on the cover of notebooks used by students. Courtesyof the Museum of Kalmar (p. 96).

6.1. Student teachers practice teaching kindergarten at the Toronto Normal School [ca. 1898]. Courtesy of the Archives of Ontario RG 2-257, Acc. 13522 Ontario teachers' colleges historical files (p. 145).

6.2. The Kindergarten [ca. early 1900s]. Courtesy of the Archives of Ontario 10-30-A-2-3.02, S15519 Public health nursing records (p. 145).

8.1. Schoolgirl in Germany, Margaret Bell, 1897. Courtesy of Library and Archives Canada (p. 178).

8.2. Schoolgirl in Germany, Alice Bell, 1897. Courtesy of Library and Archives Canada (p. 178).

8.3. "Contains organ on which Handel played when organist there." Text and drawing by Ethel Davies, late winter 1900. Reproduced from trip diary, courtesy of Margot Mann (p. 185).

8.4. Drawing by Ethel Davies, October 1899. Reproduced from trip diary, courtesy of Margot Mann (p. 185).

9.1. Alison Prentice (left) studying for finals on the lawn in the Quad at Smith, spring 1955. Courtesy of Alison Prentice (p. 203).

9.2. Alison Prentice (left) and friend in Paris. They were part of a junior-year group from Smith College that studied in Geneva in 1953-54. Courtesy of Alison Prentice (p. 206).

MARQUIS
MEMBER OF SCABRINI GROUP
Québec, Canada
2006